Why Not Build the Mosque?

CONTEMPORARY ETHNOGRAPHY

Alma Gottlieb, *Series Editor*

A complete list of books in the series
is available from the publisher.

WHY NOT BUILD THE MOSQUE?

Islam, Political Cost, and the Practice of Democracy in Greece

Dimitris Antoniou

UNIVERSITY OF PENNSYLVANIA PRESS

PHILADELPHIA

Copyright © 2025 University of Pennsylvania Press

All rights reserved. Except for brief quotations used for purposes of review or scholarly citation, none of this book may be reproduced in any form by any means without written permission from the publisher.

Published by
University of Pennsylvania Press
Philadelphia, Pennsylvania 19104-4112
www.pennpress.org

Printed in the United States of America on acid-free paper
10 9 8 7 6 5 4 3 2 1

A Cataloging-in-Publication record is
available from the Library of Congress

Hardcover ISBN: 978-1-5128-2717-0
Paperback ISBN: 978-1-5128-2716-3
eBook ISBN: 978-1-5128-2718-7

To Anna and Tasos Antoniou

CONTENTS

Introduction. The Two Mosques: The Past in the Present	1
PART I. QUESTIONS	
Chapter 1. The Promise of the Mosque	17
Chapter 2. The Making of "Muslim" Subjects	49
Chapter 3. Islam as a Path to Democracy	69
PART II. ANSWERS	
Chapter 4. The Locals	93
Chapter 5. The (Other) Church	122
Chapter 6. Political Cost	141
Conclusion. The Productivity of the Unrealized	175
Notes	187
References	203
Index	231
Acknowledgments	235

INTRODUCTION

The Two Mosques:
The Past in the Present

t is not quite known when the ancient word *temenos*, "a piece of land dedicated to a god, a sacred precinct, a sanctuary," came to describe a mosque in Modern Greek. Locating the exact moment in time when this semantic shift took place is of course futile. Yet it is likely that the years-long debate over the making of a mosque in Athens had something to do with it. As this book unravels the story of this debate, it will be worth keeping in mind these different meanings of *temenos*, for it will soon become apparent that making a mosque in Greece is very much about ideas of refuge, hospitality, and belonging in a contemporary democracy.

On January 12, 2017, in the midst of seemingly endless news about the devastation of the Greek economy and the tragedy of refugees crossing the Aegean, the newspaper *Kathimerini* published a photograph depicting the laying of the foundations for a mosque in Votanikos, an industrial area in central Athens dominated by workshops, factories, and metal scrap recycling plants. Especially for international media, the development made for a good story. Athens, the cradle of democracy, had lacked a functioning central mosque—the only European capital without one, they said—and after several failed attempts, a mosque was finally being built.

The mosque in question was no typical structure. Built on a former military base known as "the naval bunker," it was locked behind a gate guarded by police. The few plans presented in the press made the project look even stranger. The mosque would be small, with space for only 350 worshippers, no minaret, and completely devoid of any ornamentation. Taxpayers would assume the cost of the mosque's construction, maintenance, and operation, and the mosque would be under complete state control.

2   Introduction

Having spent many years studying the failure of the previous attempt to build a central mosque in Athens, I now found myself asking why the Votanikos mosque was built while the previous one hadn't been. This question put a coda on the more fundamental question I had been asking throughout my research: what does it take for things to happen in Greece?

Answering this question requires looking beyond the end point of the story, for focusing on the eventual construction of a mosque can distort or obscure the revealing story of failure, delay, and misdirection that preceded it. In trying to understand the mosque project through a focus on the failure of a previous iteration, this book resists the urge to teleologically recast failure in light of eventual success and instead seeks to discover what we can understand about the project as a whole, and its end point as well, by examining its long delay on its own terms. So how far back should we start?

While the *temenos* of Athens, as the project was often called, has most often been examined from a contemporary and domestic lens, it has a surprisingly long past that transcends the country's borders. Since the project's introduction in 1890, state officials have discussed the initiative with a great many foreign interlocutors: Ottoman authorities, King Fuad of Egypt, Gamal Abdel Nasser, King Fahd of Saudi Arabia, committees of Arab ambassadors, representatives of the European Union and the U.S. State Department, and since 9/11 with police officials, security experts, and secret agents concerned with the proliferation of unofficial mosques in the capital city. As the state's interlocutors changed in response to the ever-shifting domestic and international environment, the mosque's proposed location, architecture, and administrative structure changed too. While in the late nineteenth century the mosque was to constitute property of the Ottoman Empire and be built in Piraeus, where there was also a Turkish cemetery, by the late 1990s it was to be controlled by Saudi Arabia and built as part of an Islamic cultural center off a new highway in the suburbs, hidden from the public eye. While in the mid-1930s the mosque was likely to form the orientalist centerpiece of an Athenian park with ornamented domes and minarets—like the Grande Mosquée in Paris—in its more recent, realized iteration it was constructed in a heavily industrialized district, as a structure free of any elements that would signify even the slightest connection to Islam, and under the strict control of government officials. How might we account for these shifts in the project's conception?

To answer this question, we can first return to the historical record, look at the genealogy of popular emotions, and note that the experience of Greeks as subjects of the Ottoman Empire gradually led to a popular tendency to identify Islam with the Turks and to view Orthodox Christianity as a key component of national identity. Moreover, the expansion of the Greek state in the twentieth century was marked by a systematic effort to create ethnic, religious, and linguistic homogeneity in the new territories that were being annexed, while at the same time governments were desperately trying to safeguard the position of the Greek diasporas and the Orthodox patriarchates in the Mediterranean. The exchange of populations in 1923 that sent most Muslims living in Greece to Turkey and Orthodox Christians in Turkey to Greece, the annihilation of centuries-old Jewish communities during the Second World War, and the subsequent systematic persecution of any ethnolinguistic minority that could identify with neighboring communist countries firmly established the idea in much of the population that Greece is inhabited by Greek-speaking Orthodox Christians. Nowadays, even the country's landscape seems to affirm narratives of linguistic and religious purity. A great many minarets were demolished, gravestones in Arabic script were repurposed as building material for new constructions, and the Ottoman past was mostly reduced to Turkish words that few understand. It is thus no surprise that for decades the establishment of a Muslim site of worship in the capital city has primarily been understood as an issue pertaining to Greece's foreign relations, to be handled by diplomats.

The first cracks in this understanding became evident in the late 1990s, when Greece was preparing to enter the eurozone and host the 2004 Olympic Games, and thousands of immigrants from South Asia and the Middle East were settling in the greater metropolitan area. At a time when European countries were still promoting multiculturalism, the construction of a central mosque in Athens was seen by state officials as an opportunity to show the world that Greece was now European in this way too. After much gossip and speculation, in June 2000 the government finally announced that an Islamic complex would be built in the city's outskirts in Kambos—the fictional term that I use in place of the Greek name that my hometown now uses instead of its older Albanian one.

My own connection to the mosque reveals something of the zeitgeist of the early 2000s. Only a few months after the government's decision to erect the *temenos* I received an invitation to participate in a conference on Islam in Europe scheduled to take place that October in Lisbon. The invitation had originally been addressed to ELIAMEP (the Hellenic Foundation for European and Foreign Policy), an Athens-based think tank where I was completing an internship, and since none of the senior researchers had expertise in

4   Introduction

the topic, it ended up falling to me, an undergraduate student of theology with a self-declared interest in Islamic studies.

The conference, which brought together scholars of religion, immigration, and international relations, was a testament to larger debates going on at the time about security, Muslim visibility, and Islam in a globalized world. It would consist of short presentations discussing the situation of Muslims across Europe and, owing to my country of origin, I was expected to speak on Islam in Greece. Yet the exact topic was left to me to decide. Would it be a good idea to talk about Greece's indigenous Muslims in Western Thrace, or would it be better to talk about Muslim immigrants elsewhere, I wondered? Even at that time, I was troubled by the fact that the study of contemporary Muslim presence in Greece was largely confined to the northern border areas and thus reproduced an official discourse that portrayed a single part of the country as "impure," that is, only partially inhabited by Greek-speaking Orthodox Christians. Hence, despite the challenges connected to the latter option (most notably the complete lack of literature), I decided to "keep things simple" and talk about the mosque.

I was following this controversy closely, not only through television news broadcasts and newspaper articles but also through local gossip and rumors. I had heard that the mosque was scheduled to be built in the very center of Kambos, that Muslims were already purchasing property in the area, and even that "warriors of jihad" were funding the project. If nothing else, I thought, I will be presenting something original, while at the same time not risking an engagement with theoretical discussions. Some years later, as a graduate student, I published an updated version of my conference presentation, and my interest in the nonexistent mosque of Kambos was formalized. Despite the article's significant flaws, because it addressed contemporary Islam in Greece beyond Western Thrace, it was often cited, and I received regular invitations to participate in workshops and conferences. In the eyes of others, I was now an expert.

In the meantime, public debate over the building of a *temenos* in Athens continued without leading to the construction of any such complex. There was a noticeable development, however. Certain individuals, who eventually became my primary interlocutors and the protagonists of this ethnography, emerged in the public realm as "community leaders," "human rights activists," and "Islamic studies experts" and would appear time and again in any discussion of the issue. Through media appointment they had become the unofficial interlocutors of the state. By 2006, when the government once again

The Two Mosques 5

announced its intention to move ahead with the project, the plans had somewhat changed. Kambos was no longer considered the ideal location. Another, more appropriate site was identified in Votanikos, where a mosque was eventually built eleven years later. At the time, it turns out, government officials had become convinced that local residents were vehemently opposed to the project. Most scholars and journalists covering the issue had also arrived at a similar conclusion. Unaware of what the future had in store, they were now certain that the mosque of Athens would remain forever notional, and soon questions that had been central to the conversation in the recent past—who gathers in underground mosques, who are their leaders and what exactly do they preach, and do they receive the support of governments that embrace radical interpretations of Islam?—were superseded by the following one: *why was the temenos never built?*

This was the main question motivating my fieldwork research. In following this line of inquiry, I had originally hoped to take the mosque debate as a vantage point for an exploration of the Muslim immigrant experience in the capital city and its intersection with state conceptions of nationhood. What could better explain the government's approach to Islam than nationalism and the fear of the Turks? Yet, as so often happens, fieldwork led me in other directions, and I eventually found myself asking the same question with a much different intention. As Greece found itself in a profound economic crisis, and questions about reform capacity, project failure, neoliberalism, and popular resistance dominated the public discourse, my investigation became an inquiry into government operation. Asking informants to consider why the project in Kambos never materialized became a means for me to engage in an anthropology of the state and examine the mechanisms that block government initiatives, how political risk and public opinion are assessed, and the impact that such assessments have on decision-making. Like other anthropologists of Greece have done (e.g., Herzfeld 1985; Malaby 2003; Rakopoulos 2014; Kozaitis 2021), I treated informants as progenitors of theory as I explore the use of emic concepts as explanatory tools. When construction on the Votanikos mosque began, the project was reframed yet again, so that I could test my informants and own explanations for the Kambos mosque's failure against the new reality and in this way address the much larger issue of what it takes for things to happen in the contemporary Greek democracy.

This gradual recalibration of my project from an ethnography of Islam into one of democratic governance took place over an unusually long period (almost twenty years). While I began collecting information and conducting interviews on the mosque during my undergraduate years, and then continued as a master's student writing a thesis on the issue, I carried out systematic fieldwork research between 2004 and 2006 and again between 2007 and 2009. The complete transformation of the political landscape during the crisis also presented me with new opportunities, as many high-profile politicians found themselves on the margins of political developments and were now accessible even to junior scholars like me; during a six-month period I was able to finally talk to government officials whom I had been trying to reach for a long time. Since then I have also often conducted follow-up interviews and visited the Ministry of Foreign Affairs' archives whenever new material became available.

In retrospect, I can identify two main challenges that shaped the research for and writing of this book. The first relates to delineating the public debate. Where does such a debate begin and end? In the early 2000s, the period on which my ethnography focuses, discussions about the mosque centered around the laws being introduced by the government, which were part of long legal genealogies created in response to an ever-shifting geopolitical environment. It soon became apparent that my research, contemporary as it was, had to incorporate a historical component. Understanding the laws, their language, and the institutional memory that informed them entailed investigating issues ranging from Greek-Ottoman relations at the turn of the twentieth century and in the aftermath of the Balkan Wars to the financial crisis of 1932, diaspora politics, and relations with the Arab world. Yet my intention has always been to provide historical context for a contemporary debate and not to engage in an exhaustive history of the state's attempt to construct a central mosque in the capital city.

The second challenge concerns sources. To study the debate's evolution from the start, I decided to focus on newspaper, television, and radio treatment of the issue as well as historical archives, rather than on social media, which emerged as an important platform for discussing current affairs much later in my fieldwork. Yet even these sources were not as accessible as I might have hoped. At the archives of the Ministry for Foreign Affairs, for example, I quickly realized that research on the mosque was considered sensitive. The same file, supposedly public, could be deemed available to one researcher but not another. Such decisions were ultimately the prerogative of the minister, tasked with deciding what research could potentially be harmful to the nation. Furthermore, accessing the archives of private broadcasting corporations often required using any connections (what Greeks call *mesa*) that I could mobilize, and even that was not always successful. The financial crisis further complicated things as important archives became unavailable when their institutions folded (as in the case of the newspaper *Eleftherotipia* and the television channel Mega), thus significantly delaying my research and painfully reminding me how fragmented and partial the historian's archive has always been.

The reader will also notice traces of my gradual rethinking of the project in the self-reflective tone of the narrative, the diversity of my fieldwork sites, and the literatures that I engage. The main narrative thread of *Why Not Build the Mosque?* traces how my quest for information about the mosque and encounters with the debate's protagonists allowed me to challenge conventional thinking about state operation and to realize that the making of a central mosque in Athens was much more than an issue of religion or nationalism alone. My encounters with informants appear as a series of episodes that present key moments of the research. They are meant to show how my informants accounted for the Kambos mosque's failure and how their accounts changed my own thinking about the project, leading me to sites of research that I couldn't have possibly imagined at the outset. While the book's first part focuses on the places where Islam is practiced and the different Muslim communities that became embroiled in the mosque debate, the second part is very much about the intersection of politics with the media, at local, national, and international levels. From masjids and the premises of Muslims associations, my fieldwork moves to Kambos's square and then on to polling companies, media corporations, and politicians' offices. In my accounts I avoid using information, including citations, that would reveal the identity of my interlocutors and fieldwork sites. Yet, whenever even the most basic ethnographic contextualization would make an informant's identity transparent, I obtained permission to use real names.

Writing about a rather heterogeneous group of informants who brought their own distinct ideas and agendas to the mosque debate and understanding their cosmologies also necessitated that I engage radically different literatures. I eventually ended up consulting sources about the Greek diaspora in Egypt, immigrant communities in Athens, Greece's minority politics, obscure Orthodox saints, and the history of Kambos, among other topics. These intellectual peregrinations touch on topics well known to anthropologists: colonialism and urban planning (e.g., Bayoumi 2000; Benjamin 2003; Çelik 1992; Mitchell 1991; Bissell 2011), performativity (e.g., Austin [1956] 1975; Bauman 1975; Herzfeld 1985; Butler 1990; Povinelli 2002), sacrifice (e.g., Hubert

8   Introduction

and Mauss 1964; Hammoudi 1993; Durkheim 1995; Borneman 2002; Asad 2007), imaginations of the state (e.g., Herzfeld 1992; Taussig 1997; Aretxaga 2005; Navaro-Yashin 2002, 2012), and participatory citizenship (e.g., Marshall 1983; Rosaldo 1994; Kymlicka 1996; Ong 1999; Holston 1999; Lazar 2013). While these themes offer important theoretical framings of the Athens mosque issue, I situate my research primarily in relation to two seemingly distinct but ultimately converging literatures—one concerning Islam in Greece and the other exploring the country's democratic governance.

For many years, responding to state concerns regarding modernization and security, the literature primarily focused on the uneasy coexistence of Ottoman legal legacies with the Greek constitution order (e.g., Kalliklis 1931; Bekiaridhis 1973; Minaidis 1990; Mekos 1991; Georgoulis 1993; Soltaridis 1997) and the Muslim communities that were exempted from the Lausanne Convention (e.g., Andreadis 1956; Zenginis 1988; Hidiroglou 1990; Oran 1991; Poulton 1991; Alexandris [1983] 1992; Tsioumis 1997; Christidis 1996; Akgönül 1999; Aarbakke 2000). From the early 2000s, however, a new strand emerged within this literature that focused on "Muslim immigration" to Greece and the debate over a central mosque in Athens (e.g., Tsitselikis 2004; Triandafyllidou and Gropas 2009; Anagnostou and Gropas 2010; Hatziprokopiou and Evergeti 2014; Sakellariou 2011; Salvanou 2014; Skoulariki 2010; Triandafyllidou and Kouki 2013). This strand was also very much in tune with popular media discourses, with which it shared taxonomies, key turns of phrase, sources, and arguments. Both unquestioningly referred to "Muslim immigrants" taking up residence in Athens—"the only European capital without a mosque." Journalistic coverage of the politics surrounding the mosque provided the analytic and methodological framework for scholarly analysis.

Furthermore, the works of this new scholarship on Islam in Greece were often deliverables for research projects supported by private foundations and national and international funding bodies. As these funding schemes emphasized the contemporary moment and operated within rigid timelines, the literature addressing the Athens mosque never employed systematic archival and ethnographic research. And yet this approach to scholarship shouldn't be viewed just as the by-product of a totalizing audit culture that prioritizes a certain kind of quantifiable, measurable, and supposedly more truthful and transparent account of the present (e.g., Power 1997; Shore and Wright 1999, 2015; Strathern 2000; Holmes 2014), even though this is an important part of the story. While research on the matter often depended on its successful correlation to particular criteria of excellence and transparency and the timely absorption of funds and presentation of findings, scholars still managed to venture ideas that transcended the rigid methodologies and conceptual frameworks dictated by the accounting technologies embedded in their projects. For the legal scholars, sociologists, and migration experts behind this literature, the mosque debate became an entry point to discuss identity, the nation, and the practice of liberal democracy, as evidenced in their emphasis on parliamentary debates, the Church's view of Islam, and the positions of human rights officials. Most important, these discussions clearly conveyed a longing for a more accommodating state that would treat the construction of a mosque as a matter of principle and rise beyond the narrow-minded calculations of political cost driving so many politicians.

This observation brings us to the second literature, on democratic governance, where amid discussions of Greece's semiperipheral position, political culture, civil society, bureaucratic clientelism, and rational choice institutionalism, one might also read that "there is no official place of worship for Muslims in Greece. While permission for the construction of a mosque in Athens was finally granted in 2006, construction has not yet begun" (Vasilopoulou and Halikiopoulou 2020:343). So how might an ethnography of a mosque in Athens enrich our understanding of democratic governance? If my contribution to the study of Islam in Greece has to do with an ethnographic and archival grounding of the mosque debate and an ensuing investigation of the politics behind positions that prominently featured in media and scholarly accounts, my intervention into the literature on democratic governance centers on an anthropological analysis of political cost (*politiko kostos*)—a concept that was often used by my informants to account for the project's failure. Despite the concept's popularity in mainstream political analysis, research on its origins, meaning, and use remains limited. In fact, the few works available on the subject mostly come from the field of accounting. Ross Watts and Jerold Zimmerman (founders of positive accounting theory, also known as political cost hypothesis), for example, define a particular category of costs that lobbying groups and trade unions might impose on a firm (e.g., asking for salaries to increase) when registering, for example, higher earnings (1978:115)—not quite what those using the term in public discourse usually mean.

It is only the much larger literature on the politics of cost-benefit analysis (e.g., Wildavsky 1966; Self 1975; Pearce 1971; Boadway 2006; Stern 2008; Nyborg 2014; Mouter 2018) that presents even an indirect examination of political cost, where the concept is primarily understood as the total societal price of a government project quantified and expressed in monetary terms (and in relation to people's willingness to pay; e.g., Van Wee 2012). As far as more focused examinations of Greek politics are concerned, in the few mentions of the concept (e.g., Diamandouros 1994; Featherstone 2005:737; Lyrintzis 2005:250; Sotiropoulos 2012:17), it is used descriptively, as something self-evident that actors refer to and scholars should disregard. Here is how the political scientist Dimitris Sotiropoulos, while acknowledging the concept's use by politicians, sidesteps analyzing it:

> A common answer to the question as to why reforms fail is that decision-makers do not proceed with reforms that they have already embarked upon because they are fearful of the political cost this involves. . . . However, a demand for explanations of reform failure cannot be justified by resorting only to considerations of decision-makers, and/or party behavior. *Considerations of political cost do not suffice in explaining the multitude and variety of reform failures.* Even if the most plausible answers to the question of why some reforms fail are that individual politicians want to avoid political costs associated with reform, that patronage prevails everywhere, and that the electoral strategies of political parties are at the heart of the problem, these three answers still do not tell the whole story. . . . Failure is apparent when, allegedly owing to fears of political cost, a proposed reform is retracted after its outline has been submitted to public deliberation. This is an instance of reform failure, rather than a cause, because we do not learn anything about what has made the reform costly. (Sotiropoulos 2012:17–18; emphasis added)

Sotiropoulos is certainly right to critique the concept's analytical potency. To say, for example, that a mosque in an Athenian suburb did not materialize because of political cost leaves much unexplained. Yet as analytically weak as this concept may seem to scholars, its centrality in informants' thinking and explanations makes it worthwhile to take it seriously and examine the work that it does do. In this respect, the old ethnographic tradition of analyzing local concepts at the micro level also provides an important strategy of "studying up" (Nader 1972) and in this case gaining insight that political science and, for that matter, anthropology rarely provide into the concepts used by high-level political actors.

The Two Mosques 11

In the first part of this book, "Questions" (Chapters 1, 2, and 3), I ask individuals who emerged in the media in the early 2000s as protagonists of the mosque debate to reflect on the reasons behind the project's failure. Their responses not only reveal the fantasies, micropolitics, and political maneuverings surrounding the building of a mosque in Athens but also point to three larger issues relating to the operation of a symbolic or actual economy: the productivity of an unrealized mosque in foreign policy, the construction of Muslim subjects in the context of funded research schemes, and the political possibilities that arise from assuming a public Muslim identity.

Chapter 1 provides the historical framework for the ensuing investigation and culminates with my meetings with a Middle East scholar who was regularly consulted by politicians and the media about the project. I begin with my quest to reconstruct a fuller history of the Athens mosque that goes beyond the usual listing of relevant legal provisions found in the literature. Along the way I present archival evidence that shows the project's constant transmutations since its inception in 1890 and its use as a means to achieve the country's ever-changing international objectives. My study of diplomatic correspondence, parliamentary proceedings, and newspaper and audiovisual archives and my meetings with former state officials recover key moments in the project's history and place it in the larger context of a symbolic gift economy and European colonial modernity. Ultimately, this diachronic and comparative investigation illustrates how productive the promise of building a mosque in the capital city has been for the state, and how limiting it can be to treat the many laws stipulating its construction as evidence of a primordial nationalist ideology at work.

In Chapter 2 I use my involvement in a research project on Christian-Muslim relations that allowed me to work closely with Samir and Hassan, key figures in the mosque debate, to examine the Muslim immigrant presence in Athens. Tasked with interviewing "Muslim subjects" and producing "deliverables," I ponder the unexpected coexistence of masjids and brothels in central Athens, present my research findings to Orthodox priests, and attend interfaith meetings that go horribly wrong. The ethnographic episodes that I present speak to the research economies that construct the figure of the Muslim immigrant first through the direct translation of ethnic identities into religious ones and then at the level of research design, fieldwork, and the final ethnographic text. At the same time, these episodes also explore the theme of the *temenos* as sanctuary. My accounts of key encounters serve to document an emergent aporia, even among Muslim community leaders, over the productivity of religion as a lens to study the making of a mosque in Athens, and I show how this debate is mostly about communicating the immigrants' struggles to secure equal access to Greek polity, society, and the nation.

Chapter 3 continues this problematization of religion by asking what it means to be perceived solely as a Muslim. Drawing on my encounters with Halil-Latif and Gökhan, members of the minority population of Western Thrace who settled in Athens, and Dora, a leftist activist, I show how this epistemic gaze powerfully structures reality, and I explore the economic, institutional, and publicity opportunities that emerge through its use. As journalists, scholars, government officials, and Church leaders look for local "Muslim" interlocutors and weigh the impact of Greek minority politics on the building of the mosque in the capital, the willing display of a purely religious identity becomes a means for those thus subjectified to reach out to a broader audience, acquire institutional power, and enter the central political scene. The chapter also registers my informants' frustration over the limited granting of democratic rights to non-Christians and their realization that the establishment of a Muslim religious infrastructure is linked to calculations of potential political fallout.

Three main explanations for the nonestablishment of a mosque in Kambos emerge in this first part of the book: the mosque was never built, first, due to local reactions; second, because the Orthodox Church opposed it; and third, because its materialization carried a high political cost. It is these answers that I then submit to historical and ethnographic investigation in the second part of the book (Chapters 4, 5, and 6), titled "Answers."

Chapter 4 unfolds in Kambos, where I examine the widespread belief that locals were overwhelmingly opposed to the building of the mosque, which they supposedly contemplated through the lens of radical Islam. In an attempt to investigate local imagination and the various reactions to the initiative, I invite relatives, friends, and coffee-shop patrons to use paper and pen to literally sketch the notional structure. I use this material as a prelude to a larger discussion on the place of Islam in Greek society and the interplay between local and national politics. In a departure from popular portrayals of Kambos as a space of Orthodox fundamentalism and resistance to the mosque, my interlocutors' sketches and stories mostly reveal a profound lack of interest in the debate and ultimately point to a superficial system of assessing local resistance, which town leaders and church and state officials nevertheless rely on in order to act on what they take as public opinion.

And what about the Church, so frequently described in this debate as a political force opposing the establishment of any non-Orthodox space of worship? In trying to identify its stance on the mosque and influence on the government's assessment of possible political damage in Chapter 5, I encounter through my meetings with Kostis, a Christian activist from Kambos, a marginal Orthodoxy in which saints' vitae and apocalyptic prophecies provide the framework for political behavior. Viewing the Church from its margins and considering its politics through the activist's narratives serves a double function in my analysis. First, this approach allows me to study how an individual—often portrayed in the media as representative of local attitudes toward the mosque—reconciles doctrinal theology and ecclesiastical traditions with political behavior through a rhetoric of martyrdom. Second, an ethnographic attentiveness to marginal voices reveals how these voices critique the Church from within and consider it equivalent to a contemporary political party, whose position on the mosque can only be understood in relation to assessments of public opinion, local reactions, and political cost.

The final chapter explores political cost, a concept that was often used by my informants and the media to account for the state's reluctance to follow through on its own legislation and build the mosque. As I trace its origins from the financialization of American political science to the introduction of a European audit culture of cost efficiency and accountability in Greece (Herzfeld 1992:114), I ask what happens if we engage the conceptual toolkit of political actors on its own terms and view their analytic frameworks as local concepts. I consequently map possibilities for an ethnographic study of the central political scene and talk to former ministers, pollsters, journalists, and marketing experts about the concept of political cost. My goal is to examine decision-making processes, government operation, and ultimately how government initiatives fail from the perspective of key actors. I show how political cost is assessed through technologies of citizenship inclusion and exclusion and the central place that it occupies in the workings of a tech-noeconomic apparatus that powerfully shapes understandings of the public and, ultimately, the practice of democracy. I find that the measurement and quantification of political cost through opinion polls and the close monitoring of the media does not provide definite answers. Rather—and this is the point—this approach to governance creates gray areas where the whims of the people can be understood and acted on in radically flexible terms.

As I explain in the conclusion, this is certainly the case with the mosque of Kambos. Political cost sheds light on the practice of democracy in Greece but cannot offer a definite account for the project's failure. The most fundamental response to the question at the heart of my ethnographic research—why the mosque in Kambos wasn't built—can only point to an array of factors examined in the following chapters. Yet, by studying the reasons offered by my interlocutors, situating their beliefs historically and ethnographically, and following the trajectories of their own analytic frameworks, it becomes possible to notice another thread, beyond the narrative one, connecting key figures, time periods, and fieldwork sites. The making of the mosque in Athens without any doubt created diplomatic leverage out of thin air; it produced its own distinct research economy dedicated to the study of the communities who were supposed to use it; significant opportunities for activists, local officials, and church figures to negotiate with the central government and attract considerable publicity; and, of course, endless news broadcasts structured around assessments of public opinion. Ultimately, its story demonstrates how productive unrealized structures can be, the significant gains that can be made by debating that which remains notional, and the logics and interests at work behind what might first appear to be an obvious case of failure.

The fact, then, that a mosque was eventually built in Votanikos provides us with a unique opportunity to measure my argument against reality, identify the precise factors that diminished a notional mosque's value during a period of prolonged crisis, and see how much the productivity of the unrealized depends on media agendas and assessments of the public and its whims. For, as we will see, in this new media era, projects that had gone unrealized for decades could turn into concrete structures, as long as no one was looking.

PART I

Questions

CHAPTER 1

The Promise of the Mosque

> The heavy walls and the hulking columns of Theseum, the
> voluminous roof, were not surprised by the voice, that
> melody. They remembered, they recognized it. They had
> heard it before. Both in the times of slavery and in the
> years of prosperity.
>
> —Alexandros Papadiamantis, *The Fallen Dervish*

Mosques as Gifts

In autumn 2004, I visited the Greek Parliament's library to retrieve information about Law 1851, which a human rights scholar had identified as the first stipulating the making of a mosque in the capital city (Tsitselikis 2004). This information featured in a short sketch of the endeavor's history, which, by enumerating previous legal provisions, suggested the state's diachronic suspicion and undermining of the religious other—an idea that was readily accepted by all subsequent scholarship. At the time, my goal was simply to learn more about the particular circumstances that led to this decision. That is to say that I couldn't have possibly imagined how my study of the historical record would render inadequate the framings that seemed to me obvious at the time and lead me to an exploration of the project's colonial past in European capitals and the Eastern Mediterranean, as well as to the surprising conclusion that often it is more useful to promise a mosque than build one.

Law 1851, passed on June 1, 1890, refers to the allotment of a plot of land in Piraeus for the establishment of a *Turkiko temenos*, a "Turkish place of worship": "We hereby allot to the Ottoman Government without charge for the purpose of construction of a Turkish *temenos* a nationally owned plot of

Figure 1. The Turkish Cemetery of Piraeus. Author's photograph.

land located in Piraeus in the city block numbered 95 of five hundred and fifty-four square meters and bordering in the east with Zosimadhon Street, in the south with Areos Street and in the north and in the west with construction sites and plots of land belonging to different private individuals" (GG 1890:511). As I was to establish with the help of Apostolos, one of the parliament's librarians, a few months earlier,[1] the Municipality of Piraeus had also ceded land to the Ottoman Empire to be used as a Turkish cemetery in the same district. As the law's preamble states: "The lack of a Turkish *temenos* in Piraeus has been felt for quite some time. However, the establishment of a Turkish cemetery is considered of more immediate importance, since *Mohammedans have been residing in this city either permanently or temporarily for some time*" (GPD 1890a:395; emphasis added). For Apostolos, this reference to Muslim presence in nineteenth-century Athens was by no means surprising, even though, as he noted, "it must have been rather limited."[2] He explained: "You see, the revolution [against the Ottomans in the early nineteenth century] was—to put it mildly—not particularly kind to local Turks, nor, of course, was the plague of 1854 [nicknamed *kseni*, "foreigner," as it was believed to have been brought by the French], which must have killed a significant number of Muslim sailors around the greater port area. This in turn resulted in the creation of the first ad hoc Muslim cemetery in the area of Perivolia, again in Piraeus."[3]

Yet, if Apostolos was indeed right that few Muslims lived in the metropolitan area by 1890, why would Greek authorities be concerned with a mosque in the first place? While Apostolos directed me to the Convention of Constantinople of 1881, which annexed Arta and Thessaly to Greece and laid out the country's obligation to treat these areas' Muslims equally to other Greek citizens,[4] I later found out that it was the Ottoman ambassador in Athens who had requested the building of a mosque (Glavinas 2013).[5] At a time of intense antagonism with Bulgaria, Christian-Muslim tensions on Crete, and efforts to modernize state and society and demonstrate Greek capacity to administer diverse populations, Prime Minister Trikoupis was pursuing a policy of appeasing the Ottoman Empire and, apparently, such requests were not to be overlooked (Kechriotis 2008; Divani 2014:101).[6]

The absence of any controversy at the time regarding the making of a mosque in Piraeus is remarkable. In leafing through the pages of the Gazette of Parliamentary Proceedings I realized that the issue was considered trivial and was hardly debated in plenary session. During the bill's discussion, only one member of parliament questioned the government's decision to offer the Piraeus plot of land pro bono. In response, Konstantinos Karapanos, the minister of economy, simply explained that the Sublime Porte had allotted land to Greek communities and that the state had every interest to "look after the Turkish populations, create "feelings of trust among them toward Greece both for [the fulfillment of] ulterior purposes and for the Greeks of Turkey" (GPD 1890b:716–717). Apparently this was enough of a justification, for MPs understood well that most Greeks at the time resided in Ottoman territories, outside the borders of the small kingdom, and they saw reciprocity as a necessary condition for the nation's survival and future expansion (GPD 1890b:775). As the politician Ioannis Koletis had famously remarked, forty-six years before Karapanos, while elaborating on the "Great Idea" of a new Greek Empire: "The Kingdom of Greece is not Greece; it is merely a part, the smallest, poorest part of Greece. The Greek is not he who inhabits the kingdom, but also he who inhabits Ioannina or Salonica or Serres or Andrianoupolis or Constantinople or Trebizond or Crete or Samos or any other region belonging to Greek history or the Greek race. . . . There are two great centres of Hellenism. Athens is the capital of the Kingdom. Constantinople is the great capital, the City, the dream and hope of all Greeks" (cited in Llewellyn-Smith 1998:2–3). Yet the mosque in Piraeus was never built. First, the money that the Sublime Porte committed to the cause was somehow lost along the way from Constantinople to Athens (Glavinas 2013). Next, in 1893, the economy collapsed, and then increasing tensions between Christians and Muslims in Crete led to an anti-Turkish frenzy and, in 1897, a full-scale war.

The issue became prominent again with the end of the Balkan Wars. In particular, the Fourth Article of the Third Protocol of the Treaty of Athens, signed between Greece and the Ottoman Empire on November 14, 1913, and ratified with Law 4213, described the government's responsibility: "The royal Greek government will construct, at its own cost, a mosque in the capital and four other mosques in the poor villages where the need would be felt" (GG 1913:816). In comparison to the demographic situation in the 1890s, such an obligation now made far more sense. As the nation's borders had expanded, they had incorporated substantial Muslim populations (over five hundred thousand living in Epirus, Macedonia, and Crete), which the government wished to keep in Greece.[7]

The Gazette of Parliamentary Debates of November 11, 1913 (three days before the treaty was signed) records an interesting exchange between two major political figures, Prime Minister Eleftherios Venizelos and Dimitris Kallergis, the former minister of foreign affairs, which shows how an issue that was only briefly discussed some twenty-three years before was now the topic of intense debate in the parliament and the press. Yet we shouldn't rush to conclusions. Kallergis and many other MPs of the opposition (such as Theotokis, Rallis, and Triandafillakos) did not consider a mosque a threat to Greece. Rather they believed that the very mention of an obligation to erect a *temenos* in the capital city in an international treaty would give the outside world the impression that the country did not tolerate religious difference. Instead, they proposed that the state secure Muslim citizens' rights by way of a law:

> *E. Venizelos:* In 1890 a law was passed at the instigation of the late [Mr.] Trikoupis, by which the Turkish state was granted a plot of land in Piraeus for the erection of a mosque with a cemetery. I believe that the State is obliged to respect this.
>
> *D. Kalergis:* It is fine to arrange this with a law, but there is a difference between a law and a treaty. A law constitutes a state's decision, which can be taken at any time and which can be changed.

EV: I would be happy if this [provision] had not been mentioned in
the treaty and could have been effected simply by an internal
law. But since we agree that it [i.e., a mosque] should have been
erected even through an internal law, you do not have the right
to declare both inside [parliament] and outside that the erection
of a mosque constitutes a defeat.

DK: You should not have undertaken the responsibility of erecting a
mosque with state funds.

EV: The difference is that this should have taken place through an
internal law and not a treaty. But had you been governor [of
Greece] would you have delayed the signing of the peace treaty?
(GPD 1913:30)

The discussion of the issue in the anti-Venizelist press was less refined.
It seems that the Greco-Turkish military confrontations in 1897 and 1912
had also changed attitudes toward the construction of mosques, especially in
the capital city. As becomes evident in the many articles that the newspapers
Skrip and *Athine* published in November 1913, the Treaty of Athens was frequently seen as a "triumph of Turkish diplomacy," and the same question was
posed time and again: if Greece had truly won the Balkan Wars, why was the
state obliged to erect mosques at its own expense?

What this question disregarded was the fact that the victories of 1912–
1913 were mainly over territories and not always over sentiments, while the
building of mosques operates largely on the latter plane. Venizelos, who saw
Greece as a potential regional power capable of incorporating Muslim populations (already from 1906 he had stated that "Greece is destined to become
one day . . . a Muslim power, like Russia and England" [Glavinas 2009:166;
Tsitselikis 2012:52]), had quite a different attitude on the issue. At a time of
intense rumors over an alliance between the Sublime Porte and Bulgaria
against Greece, the prime minister saw the inclusion of this provision as a
gift of great symbolic value to Mehmet the Fifth that would secure a much-
needed peace (Glavinas 2009:143). Still, as the diplomatic historian Stamatios
Antonopoulos noted four years after the signing of the treaty (1917:201), this
particular provision had not been implemented, since "there were no Muslims residing in the capital city" (*udhis Musulmanos ine katikos Athinon*) and
thus no immediate need for the state to construct a mosque. The failure of
the Greek military campaign in Asia Minor in 1922 put an abrupt end to the
"Great Idea" and Venizelos's aspirations to govern large Muslim populations.

Figure 2. Cartoons published in the newspapers *Skrip* (November 7, 1913, *left*) and *Athine* (November 17, 1913, *right*) mocking Venizelos's agreement to construct a mosque in Athens.

Greek authorities stopped pursuing the project. There were other, more pressing issues to address, most notably the settlement of over a million Orthodox refugees.

It was some time before I discovered that eighteen years after this exchange between Venizelos and Kallergis, the very same issue resurfaced. At first glance, the making of a mosque in Athens appears to be connected to Greece's development as a tourist destination. Following the visit of the wife of a high-ranking Egyptian to the hot springs of Ipati in 1931, the newly formed Tourist Organization realized that the building of a mosque might lure more Muslim tourists to Greece (the elderly Egyptian khanum was apparently afraid that she might die in Ipati with no mosque in close proximity). This was a time when the global impact of the American stock market's collapse in 1929 was becoming apparent in Greece and foreign currency was desperately needed. As the press at the time pointed out, seven thousand Egyptians visited the Greek capital in 1932 and left "so much money," while more of them were

The Promise of the Mosque 23

expected to come in the following years (Skiadas, n.d.). If we are to believe the journalistic accounts of this phenomenon, Egyptian tourists were very much appreciative of the fact that Greeks were not mocking them for wearing a fez and a djellaba, while the personnel of the Tourist Organization was inspired by the building of a central mosque in Paris and undertook the initiative to convince the municipality of Athens to build an equivalent structure.

Yet the state's interest in the project had another dimension. In the early 1930s, when relations with Turkey were fully restored, concerns over the long-term presence of Greeks in Egypt had intensified with the prospect of their capitulatory privileges coming soon to an end.[8] What would happen to the Greeks of Cairo, Port Said, Alexandria, and Mansoura if they now had to pay taxes and were subject to Egyptian law? Would Greece be able to accommodate even more refugees only a few years after the compulsory exchange of populations with Turkey? Given this context it becomes easy to understand the Greek expatriates' decision to assume the cost of the mosque (Skiadas, n.d.) and why the impending visit of Egypt's King Fuad to Greece emerged as the perfect opportunity for the project's materialization. As we learn from the reports that the consul in Alexandria sent to the Foreign Ministry in September 1933 (DHAGMFA/CS 1933), the king, "vain and megalomaniac" as he was, was indeed pleased with the prospect of inaugurating a statue of Muhammad Ali in a new square in Kavala (where he was born before becoming the ruler of Egypt in 1805) and then visiting the site that would host an Egyptian mosque, a cemetery, and an Egyptian School of Classical Studies (Eyiptiaki Arheoloyiki Skholi). On August 25, 1934, the government introduced Law 6244, the first article of which states: "It is allowed to the minister of agriculture and the minister of economy as representatives of the state to transfer to H.M. the King of Egypt the ownership of a plot of 3,350 square meters in Singru–Kuponion Park, as defined by the attached plan. This land will be allotted as a donation, whose acceptance will be formalized here by the representative of the Egyptian state under the condition that it will be used for the erection of a *temenos* and the foundation of an *Egyptian Institute* for holders of Egyptian government scholarships studying in Greece" (GG 1934:1645–1646, emphasis added). The explanatory report of June 20, 1934, distributed to all members of parliament clearly shows that the building of a mosque and an Egyptian institute in Athens was considered by the Greek government to be a "new token of friendship," capable of safeguarding the presence of Greeks in Egypt:

Figure 3. The wrapped statue of Muhammad Ali in Kavala awaiting its unveiling. Giorgos Vafiadhakis, 1934. Yiorgos Vafiadhakis Archive, National Bank of Greece Cultural Foundation, ELIA/MIET Photographic Archive.

For more than a century a substantial portion of the Greek diaspora has been resident in Egypt. Due to the beneficence of the Egyptian authorities and the ruling dynasty it prospers and lives in accordance with the religious traditions of the homeland. For the accommodation of these religious and communitarian needs of our diaspora there is a sufficient number of churches, educational, and charitable foundations, the premises of which were mostly built by the Greek communities due to the religious tolerance and generosity of the indigenous administration. By contrast, Egyptians and Muslims visiting Greece have no *temenos* to perform their religious duties, since the only one in Monastiraki is in a bad condition. In recognition of the above, it is the government's special wish to provide a new token of friendship to H.M. King Fuad of Egypt and a favor to Egyptians visiting Greece. Thus, we have the honor to submit to the vote of the Parliament this draft law, according to which a plot of state land for the erection of a *temenos* is donated to H.M. as a representative of

The Promise of the Mosque   25

the Egyptian state. King Fuad wishes to lay the foundation stone of this *temenos* himself during his impending visit to our country. We request that this draft law be considered with the utmost urgency and be passed on a single reading. (Sidheris and Sifneos 1934:1404)

Nevertheless, the deteriorating health of King Fuad, coupled with the slow progress that local authorities were making in Kavala and the liberal approach to deadlines of Konstantinos Dimitriadis, the Paris-based sculptor of Muhammad Ali's statue, resulted in the postponement of the visit and, ultimately, the project. By 1936, King Fuad had died. As for Dimitriadis's statue, it eventually made it to its destination but would stay obscured by a tarp throughout the Second World War until it was officially inaugurated by the Egyptian prince Amr Ibrahim in 1949.[9]

Colonial Modernities

I soon shared my findings with Vassilios Christides, a professor of Arab history and an Egyptiot (a member of the Greek diaspora in Egypt). He brought to my attention that Greece was by no means the only state pursuing these kinds of reciprocal relations with Egypt. The Regent's Park Mosque (or the Islamic Cultural Centre and London Central Mosque, as it is officially termed), for example, was purchased with funds given by the British government to reciprocate the gift of a site by the Egyptian government for an Anglican cathedral (Holod and Hasan-Uddin 1997:230; Serageldin and Steele 1996:165–166). "Even though nowadays," Christides explained, "the building of mosques is usually viewed as a purely internal issue in most Western countries, for quite some time projects of this sort were considered a matter of foreign policy."

Like the mosque of Athens, the one in Regent's Park had also remained an unrealized project for many years. The idea of building such a structure can be traced back to the 1920s. However, the enterprise was seriously promoted only when Lord George Lloyd, the former high commissioner to Egypt (and chairman of the British Council), and Nashat Pasha, the Egyptian ambassador to London, "began to campaign for it during the Second World War" (Crinson 2002:86). When construction finally began in the late 1970s it had become clear that the project also reflected "important changes in the political and economic relationships between the oil-rich Middle Eastern states and the oil-dependent Western countries" (Crinson 2002:88).[10] Its fruition depended on resolving bureaucratic complications and establishing effective communication between subsequent committees of Muslim ambassadors, the London County Council, the Fine Arts Commission, and the architect Sir Frederick Gibberd (Crinson 2002:86).[11]

Most sources discuss the case of the Regent's Park Mosque together with that of the Grande Mosquée de Paris—given that these two projects set precedents for the construction and administration of central mosques and Islamic centers in Europe and North America (Holod and Hasan-Uddin 1997:230). The history of the Grande Mosquée, however, is significantly longer than that of the Regent's Park Mosque. Even though the commemorative plaque on the building's façade identifies 1920 as the starting date of construction, this project first went unrealized for a good century and a half. The project's origins are to be found in a treaty signed in 1767 between Louis XV and Moulay Ismail of Morocco, which was to "allow mutual places of worship in their respective cities but which was never carried through" (Bayoumi 2000:275–76). A century later, in 1895, the construction of a mosque in Paris, this time in Ottoman-Turkish style, was agreed upon with the Comité de l'Afrique française. Nevertheless, unforeseen events, namely the Ottoman massacres of Armenians between 1894 and 1896, resulted in public outrage and the project's postponement (Bayoumi 2000:276).

The Grande Mosquée was finally completed in 1926 in recognition of the sacrifice of some three hundred thousand soldiers from the French colonies who had died during the Great War and also as "a symbol of pro-French loyalist Islam that could function as a counter weight to anti-colonial Muslim movements in North Africa" (Maussen 2005a:54). There was, however, an important ideological issue that threatened the very foundations of this initiative: how is it possible for a secular state to operate a place of worship and also fund its construction? The solution was that the Grande Mosquée de Paris would be built not solely as a place of worship but as part of an "Institut musulman" ("Mosque and Muslim Institute" as per its official name). In this way, explains Bayoumi, "it was a site of learning, and as such, it was asserted, it became part of the great French tradition of education. It was thus modernist in ethos, if traditional in form. Furthermore, by opening the café and *hammam* to the general public, the city council was ensuring the public use of this institution and not simply funding a minority religion" (2000:284).

As was the case in the universal and colonial expositions of the nineteenth and early twentieth centuries, the Grande Mosquée was not only a space of Muslim worship but also a familiar piece of Moorish architecture providing

Figure 4. The café in the Grande Mosquée. Author's photograph.

visitors opportunities for both education and recreation. It recalled, for the French, the architecture of colonial pavilions and the concept of a *cité musulmane* (Bayoumi 2000:275; Holod and Hasan-Uddin 1997:228). It was in many ways reminiscent of the Palace of Algerian Attractions, the Egyptian Pavilion, the much photographed Algerian Quarter, and the Official Palace of Algeria (Benjamin 2003:107; Çelik 1992:125–130), where the French could encounter the indigenous and classical antiquities while enjoying the palace's wine bar, or even visit a mosque "set up as a coffee-house, where Egyptian girls performed dances with young males and dervishes whirled" (Mitchell 1991:1). Simply put, it brought the Orient home.

Nevertheless, for the French administration the Grand Mosquée was also a structure necessary for monitoring the activities of the North African immigrants who were settling in Paris and the nearby suburbs in large numbers after the end of the First World War (Bayoumi 2000:286). To draw from Bayoumi once again: "the need for the metropole to develop an official Islam, the French felt, became acute—not just to create a representation which it would control, but to counteract the seeds of sedition against empire that would be orchestrated in the name of Islam (or communism, or—worse—both). This is how the mosque must be understood: its putative purity of North African form within the fifth *arrondissement* was an attempt to force the presence of colonial North African subjects into visibility and containment" (Bayoumi 2000:288). At the time serious concerns were being expressed regarding the need to safeguard the colonial *mission civilisatrice* from the newcomers, and this led to the establishment of the infamous Service des affaires indigènes nord-africains (SAINA). Its agents attended public protests and attempted to infiltrate the Communist Party and Étoile nord-africaine, an anticolonial movement, in an attempt to study the immigrants' character and spy on their activities (MacMaster 1997:153–171; Simon 1998:52–57). To further its mission, SAINA went as far as to establish its own health clinic within the "Institut musulman."

While the French petit bourgeois enjoyed steam baths and Turkish coffee, SAINA's agents operated in the very same space, thus turning the Grande Mosquée into an architecture of surveillance, though without much success. The city's impoverished immigrants preferred the places of worship they had already established in their workplaces (Mouriaux and Wihtol de Wendent 1997:11). As MacMaster (1997:106) notes, "The avoidance of the Paris Mosque and other forms of 'official' religious provision was not a sign of declining religious faith but of political opposition to all manifestations of colonialism."

As we will soon see, this idea of containing Islam through architecture has some telling parallels with how many Greek officials thought of Muslim presence in the country from the late 1990s. The making of a central mosque in Athens was indeed considered through the intersection of diplomatic relations, religious rights, and security concerns. This situation is, no doubt, reminiscent of what Bayoumi (2000:271) described as "colonial modernity": the moment in which the colonial subject—only nominally a full citizen—settles in the country of the colonizers, only to realize that modernity's "redistribution of political, social, economic, and cultural authority away from the capricious whims of absolute power and into the hands of the body politic (thereby redefining subjects as citizens through the expansion of individual rights)" does not fully apply to his case.

An Arab Alliance

Despite my efforts to retrieve information regarding the Athens mosque in state archives and newspapers from the years that followed the promulgation

The Promise of the Mosque   29

of Law 6244, the issue seems to vanish from public documents until 1948. Yet, when it resurfaces, it is again connected to the state's efforts to reestablish Greece as a tourist destination for Egyptians and, most importantly, to facilitate the Greek diaspora's "readjustment" (as many Egyptiots would say) to the postcolonial realities in Egypt. A letter sent by the General Secretariat of Tourism to the Ministry of Foreign Affairs reveals that, between 1931 and 1940, 78,814 "Mohammedans" had visited Greece, and that the Greek diaspora in Egypt intended to fund the building of a mosque in Lutraki—a popular resort that was home to a casino and a hot spring but, rather predictably, lacked any Muslim infrastructure (DHAGMFA/CS 1948d). Already by that time the 1934 idea of building a new mosque and an Egyptian Institute in Athens had been abandoned. The government was now pursuing a new cost-efficient plan to reuse the Ottoman Fethiye Mosque located within the Roman Agora in central Athens, attract Muslim tourists to the country's hot springs, and prevent the emigration of Egyptiots (many of whom were considered communists) to Greece. In this regard, the date of the above communication is important. The letter is sent amid the Greek Civil War and months before the expiration of the twelve-year transitional period that the Montreux Convention (Regarding the Abolition of the Capitulations in Egypt) stipulated. While diplomats, lawyers, and leaders of the Egyptian diaspora were drafting "a treaty of establishment" to safeguard the presence of the Greek diaspora in Egypt, "offsets had to be invented and offered to the Egyptian side" (Dalachanis 2017:29) to bring the impending negotiations to a successful conclusion.

While Greek officials were waiting for Egyptiots to secure the necessary funds, the Ministry of Foreign Affairs contacted the embassies in London and Paris. Diplomats in Athens were eager to enquire over the architecture and operation of mosques in Europe, making clear in this way that only Western Europe—not the Ottoman past—could provide valuable models for the project. As the ambassador explained, Woking's mosque in the suburbs of London had no minaret, and the muezzin's call was not heard outside the mosque, a privilege that his Parisian counterpart enjoyed on Fridays (DHAGMFA/CS 1948b, 1948c). A few months later, the government had to face the harsh reality: the fundraising campaign for the mosque had failed and the size of the diaspora continued to shrink (DHAGMFA/CS 1948e). A more pragmatic approach was urgently needed. In 1951, the wedding of King Faruk gave the authorities an excuse to scrap the plan for the mosque in Loutraki altogether and offer the Fethiye Mosque to the Egyptian sovereign as a wedding gift (DHAGMFA/CS 1951). The Egyptian Revolution of 1952 put these plans on hold as well.

30   Chapter 1

Four years later, when Greek diplomats proposed, in view of Gamal Abdel Nasser's visit to Athens, that the Fethiye Mosque become operational, the geopolitical landscape had substantially changed together with the priorities of Greek foreign policy. While the well-being of the diaspora in Egypt was still a concern, the country was also looking for allies among Arab countries in the United Nations to push for *enosis* (the unification of Greece and Cyprus) and trying to cultivate relations with the oil-producing countries and ensure the unobstructed crossing of the Suez Canal by Greek ships (Dalachanis 2015:87–88; MCERA 2015). The connection, however, between the new foreign policy goals and the use of an Ottoman mosque in the greater Acropolis area by diplomats and businessmen was not understood by everyone; the all-powerful Archaeological Service found the idea appalling and quickly rejected it. As a seasoned diplomat told me in an interview, "Unfortunately, archaeologists lack international outlook."

Yet the possibility of reusing Ottoman mosques as a means of improving relations with the Arab world was now an idea to be entertained. In 1965 the government allowed the deposed Saudi king Saould bin Abdulaziz Al Saud (known as Ibn Saoud in Greece) and his entourage to pray in the Fethiye Mosque and turned the event into a media spectacle. Newspapers published countless articles on the prayer, which was led by an imam from Western Thrace and attended by students from Sudan, Jordan, and Libya, and the luscious meal that followed (e.g., *Eleftheria* 1965), while the newsreels screened at the cinemas presented the event as a jet-set extravaganza right before a fashion show. "For the first time in 130 years," said the newscaster, "the voice of the muezzin has been heard again in the old mosque in Monastiraki. The former King of Saudi Arabia, Ibn Saoud, is praying in the mosque together with members of his family and amongst Mohammedan students of the University of Athens from Libya, Sudan, and Jordan" (HNAVA 1965).[12]

A couple of years later, on July 24, 1971, amid military rule, Konstantinos Kourkoulas, the secretary general for religious affairs and a keen supporter of Zoi (Life), an influential pietist organization, sent a letter to the Ministries of the Presidency and Culture demanding that the necessary actions be taken "in order to make the Fethiye Mosque operational" (Tsatsi 2003b).[13] His request, too, was outright rejected. On October 5, 1971, the archaeologists of the Ministry of Culture made clear what kind of past was to be valued and protected by the state: "We would like to inform you that the allocation of the Fethiye Mosque next to Kiristos Clock for the fulfillment of the devotional needs of Muslims passing through Athens is not possible, for on the one hand this is

The Promise of the Mosque   31

located on the archaeological site of the Roman Agora, and on the other there are other reasons against the operation of a mosque under the Acropolis, a location of historical and monumental character" (Tsatsi 2003b). Despite the attempts of high-ranking officers of the military regime to present Greece as a jet-set destination and boost tourism—declared as the country's main industry at the time—by opening up to Arab authoritarianism, the project was again abandoned. Ottoman mosques were never used again. In the meantime, discussions regarding the establishment of a *temenos* in Athens continued.

In 1976 Prime Minister Konstantinos Karamanlis, who had spent eleven years in self-exile in Paris and was certainly familiar with the Grande Mosquée, followed up on earlier discussions between Greek shipowners and the Saudi authorities and promised to Arab ambassadors the building of a mosque in Athens (MCERA 2015; Andoniadhou 2008). Three years later, in February 1979 during an official visit to Riyadh and a discussion with Crown Prince Fahd over Greece's oil deficit, Karamanlis brought up the issue.[14] The recorded exchange made clear that such an initiative still constituted a gift that the Greeks were offering to the Arabs not only as a token of friendship but also as a means of sealing an important financial agreement:

> *Konstantinos Karamanlis:* We have a consumption of 10,000,000 tonnes per year. This year we are 2,500,000 tonnes short. I would request that, if you can, you make good this deficiency through an interstate agreement, and that, if possible, you enter into another interstate agreement for five years to cover a portion of our needs . . .
> *Fahd:* Thank you for your proposal. Unfortunately, the Minister of Oil is not here. I will make sure that I learn what the situation is and I would be happy to accommodate you as a friendly country . . .
> *KK:* I would also like to add that the Greek Government offers space free of charge for the erection of a *temenos*. We have many tourists from Arab countries and, in this way, we hope that we will accommodate the performance of their religious duties. (Svolopoulos 1993:49)

Research in the late prime minister's archive revealed that on May 11, 1979, Karamanlis sent a follow-up letter to the crown prince, which he ended by referring yet again to the mosque:

Figure 5. Karamanlis in Riyadh, 1979. Konstantinos Karamanlis Archive, Athens.

Concerning the matter of erecting in Athens a mosque for the religious needs of the Arab Moslems living in Greece, which we discussed during our meeting, I would like to inform you that the necessary work for the implementation of the project is carried on normally. The Greek government has already selected the site where the Mosque will be erected. The small delay which has occurred is due to the fact that the legal form of the recipient of this donation has not yet been defined.

I hope, nevertheless, that the necessary details will soon be taken care of and the building of the mosque will begin. In the meantime, the Greek Government has taken the appropriate steps for a provisional arrangement which will permit to our Moslem visitors to satisfy their religious needs until the building of the mosque is completed. (KKA)

The Promise of the Mosque

At the same time, the Council of the Arab States' Union in Athens (which was later replaced by the Council of Arab Ambassadors in Athens), a diplomatic structure similar to that which was involved in the making of the Regent's Park Mosque, began negotiations with the Greek government (Tsitselikis 2004:286–287) and a year later, in November 1980, the deputy minister of foreign affairs, Theokharis Rendis, stated in parliament (in response to a question posed by a Greek Muslim MP from Western Thrace) that "there will be an allocation of a plot of land to Arab governments for the construction of a mosque in Athens" (Tsatsis 2003b).

Despite these public assurances, the project never got underway. Even though throughout the 1980s it continued to be discussed among Arab ambassadors and Greek diplomats, and several possible sites were proposed for the mosque's construction (such as Alimos, Khalandhri, Marusi, Markopulo, and Koropi), nothing concrete happened (Zoulas 2006; *Mesoyiakos Tipos* 2006; MCERA 2015). In the early 1990s yet another prime minister, Konstantinos Mitsotakis, who thought that a mosque in Athens would lure investors from Kuwait (given Greece's participation in the first Gulf War), instructed Virginia Tsoudherou, the deputy minister of foreign affairs (1991–1993), to resolve the issue (*Monitor* 2003). Even though there is evidence to suggest that Mitsotakis's government feared potential local reactions, in my discussions with Tsoudherou she mentioned only existing legislation as the main hindrance to her plans to establish an official place of worship for the capital's Muslims (primarily Arab diplomats and students and Pakistani workers; see Tsatsis and Spiropoulou 2000). The problem, she claimed, was legislation dating back to the Metaxas dictatorship in the late 1930s. More specifically, pursuant to Emergency Laws 1363 and 1672 (GG 1938:1989–1992, 1939:841–842),[15] the establishment of non-Orthodox churches and places of worship had first to be requested by at least fifty families and required a governmental permit issued by the Ministry of National Education and Religious Affairs. All of this was supposed to follow a decree provided by the local Christian Orthodox episcopate.[16] Any church or place of religious assembly built and operated without authorization was liable to be closed and placed under seal by the police. Those responsible for unauthorized establishments would be prosecuted, imprisoned, or fined. "You see, on top of everything else I would also have to convince a bishop," she said. "This was taking a lot of time and then, as you know, Mr. Antoniou, our government collapsed."[17]

The issue became prominent again first during the terms as foreign minister of Theodore Pangalos (1996–1999)[18] and then George Papandreou

34 Chapter 1

(1999–2004). Both found themselves in the unfortunate position of having to respond to serious allegations regarding religious freedom in the country made by human rights organizations, the U.S. State Department, and the European Union and endlessly reproduced by news agencies around the world.[19] This kind of domestic and international pressure, coupled with the government's attempt to project a new image of the capital city as being sufficiently modern, European, and multicultural to host the 2004 Olympic Games, likely explains why the issue of building a mosque in Athens resurfaced with intensity toward the end of the 1990s.

The 2000 Bill

The government of the Panhellenic Socialist Movement (henceforth PASOK) understood that the making of a mosque in Athens could be used by the parties of the opposition to attract attention and create public outrage. As an opposition deputy revealed during the proceedings of June 15, 2000, PASOK's ministers of environment and culture had delayed the discussion of the issue until after the elections of April 9, 2000, had taken place, so that the government could avoid incurring "political cost" (PP 2000).

When the bill finally reached parliament, after PASOK's reelection, the government attempted to avoid widespread controversy by presenting the construction of a mosque as necessary infrastructure for the impending Olympics. For this reason, the initiative's discussion was placed in the context of a bill titled "Issues of Preparation of the Olympic Games 2004 and Other Provisions" (polling had shown that there was overwhelming popular support for the Olympic Games), and the word *temenos* (as well as the colloquial *dzami*, a Turkish word that is widely used in Greek to refer to a mosque)—so prominently used in previous laws—was carefully avoided. It was likely for this reason that Article 7 of the bill called for the building of an "Islamic Cultural Center" in the capital's outskirts (GG 2000:2279).

More specifically, the Ministry of Foreign Affairs, which was handling the issue, suggested that the center be established in Kambos, in a plot of 35,000 square meters, property of the Ministry of Agriculture. The location was designated by the capital's Planning Organization (*Orghanismos Rithmistiku Shedhiu Athinas*) not only due to its proximity to a new highway connecting the suburbs to the city center, which was already scheduled for construction (i.e., *Attiki Odhos*; see Chapter 4), but also because polling had corroborated

The Promise of the Mosque 35

the Church's position that a Greek cannot bear the sight of minarets in the center of Athens (Verousi and Allen 2021:6; *Monitor* 2003; Tsatsi 2006; Tzilivakis 2002; see also Chapter 5).

Government officials had envisioned that the Islamic Cultural Center would be supervised by the state and subsidized by a wealthy Arab state (Saudi Arabia and Kuwait were repeatedly mentioned during these sessions by several deputies).[20] As for its language of operation, it would be Arabic—"the language of the holy Koran," as several MPs repeatedly told journalists.

Despite the government's efforts, its wish to keep the issue out of the public arena was frustrated right from the beginning. Even before the bill reached parliament, most newspapers had already published long articles under titles such as "Green Light for the Mosque" or "Disagreements Continue over the Mosque in Kambos," completely overlooking the proposed center's official name. No matter how hard officials tried to present this initiative as leading to the establishment of a complex that also included a cultural center, a library, and a café, the image of the mosque prevailed.

PASOK had also not taken into account its own nature as a broad political formation. Even though a group of so-called modernizers (*eksinkhronistes*) with open attitudes toward religious pluralism had assumed control of the party under the leadership of Kostantinos Simitis in the mid-1990s, it included politicians with diverse conceptions of socialism, not always free from nationalist sentiments, and very eager for publicity. Indeed, from the very moment the government's intention to establish an Islamic Cultural Center became known, some PASOK deputies made statements notable enough to attract the media's attention. One of them, for example, proposed that the Turks "hand the keys" of St. Sophia in Istanbul to Greeks, while another, less concerned with Greco-Turkish reciprocity, claimed that the new mosque had the clear potential "of becoming a shelter for international terrorism" (PP 2000).

The opposition, meanwhile, expressed serious objections to the project. But the objections were not so much directed at the mosque itself—something that most journalists and scholars overlooked—as to the government's handling of the issue. Clearly the discussion of the initiative was shaped by an expectation that Greek politicians would strongly oppose the government's decision and the belief that the "state . . . has been totally unprepared to provide equal religious rights to the new Muslim populations of immigrants" (Skoulariki 2010:302). In this context it became impossible to consider the opposition's concerns as expressions of a calculated strategy that catered to both the initiative's opponents (through the media's focus on objections) and

36 Chapter 1

its supporters (through the acceptance of the government's wish to build a mosque in principle). In the discussion of the mosque debate, every objection voiced in parliament was evident of a "strong essentialist view of Greece as a coherent Christian Orthodox nation, where the presence of Islam is perceived as a threatening alterity, a familiar yet rival cultural marker, potentially destabilizing" (Skoulariki 2010:302). But what exactly were the opposition's objections to the government's initiative?

The main opposition party of the center-right, New Democracy (ND), disagreed, for instance, with the proposed location and argued that there had been no prior study of the suitability of the area and the needs of the capital's Muslims. Especially when the plenary sessions were broadcast on TV, many New Democracy MPs accused the government of hiding the initiative (by incorporating the draft law into legislation involving the Olympics) and spoke of a complete lack of transparency regarding the project. During the four days that the bill was discussed, New Democracy posed a great many questions and called for immediate answers. Would a wealthy Muslim country finance the project? Was it true that the minister of foreign affairs had met with a committee of Arab ambassadors on February 16, 2000, and promised to give them a draft charter of the proposed legal entity, and if so, why had this development not been brought to the attention of parliament? Would the government deal with this sensitive issue in a democratic manner by including in the negotiations the people of Kambos and the county council of eastern Attica? And finally, why was it mentioned in the draft bill that this initiative was being taken not only to serve the devotional needs of the capital's Muslims, but also to "serve the country's foreign policy objectives and fulfill its international obligations" (PP 2000)?

As for the Greek Communist Party (KKE) and the Coalition of the Left and Progress (*Sinaspismos*, "coalition" in Greek—an alliance between small leftist parties and initiatives to secure parliamentary representation), they also objected to the proposed location and suggested an area in the center of Athens, Gazi, where many Greek Muslims from Western Thrace resided, as an alternative site (PP 2000; see Chapter 3).[21]

Despite the criticism, on June 20, 2000, the ruling government approved for the fourth time in the state's history the building of the first mosque in the capital. Ten days later Law 2833, "Issues of Preparations for the Olympic Games 2004 and Other Provisions," was published in the Government Gazette; Article 7, entitled "Placement of Islamic Cultural Center," stated:

The Promise of the Mosque

"Space for an Islamic Cultural Center that also includes a place of worship is allocated in a plot of land that is granted by the Ministry of Agriculture in the location Housmouza of the municipality of Kambos in Attica. . . . The conditions and restrictions of construction will be determined by a common decision of the Ministries of Foreign Affairs, Environment, and Public Works and Culture" (GG 2000:2279).

The Media Plane

The issue of the mosque in Kambos appeared, disappeared, and reappeared in the Greek and international media for a number of years and on several occasions. It seemed that every time a human rights report was published, whenever there was new information regarding the issue, or simply when there was no news at all (as is often the case during the summer months), the mosque controversy would resurface in the newspapers, TV shows, and so forth. As time went by without construction starting, I found myself collecting a large number of press clippings and video recordings of morning television shows.

In reviewing this material, I noticed that even though nothing concrete was happening, the Greek Ministry of Foreign Affairs remained active on this front. I was also able to confirm what New Democracy MPs had said in parliament regarding the meeting of the minister of foreign affairs with Arab ambassadors (*Monitor* 2003). More specifically, it was by now common knowledge that the ambassadors of Morocco, Jordan, Saudi Arabia, Lebanon, and the PLO representative had been drafting a statute in cooperation with Greek diplomats since 2000, and also that Prince Fahd had agreed to provide the funding necessary for the project (*Monitor* 2003).[22] Originally the committee of ambassadors had suggested that both the mosque and the cultural center be presided over by a fifteen-member board of Arab ambassadors, Greek officials, and a representative of the Organization of the Islamic Conference (*Monitor* 2003).

The 9/11 attack changed everything. As fear of Islamic terrorism spread, the government wanted to have full control of the new complex (*Monitor* 2003) and suggested that it be presided over by an eleven-member board consisting of six Greek officials and five Arab ambassadors (Mikhas 2005). Eventually the two sides reached an agreement toward the end of 2004 (Mikhas 2005). In the final draft charter, it was stated that the mosque and the cultural center would be a public benefit foundation, presided over by a twelve-member board. Six of the board members would be state officials, including a professor of Islamic studies, the director of religious affairs of the Ministry of Education, the head of the Directorate of Cultural Relations of the Ministry of Culture, and a legal advisor. The other six members would be the head of Saudi Arabia's diplomatic delegation in Athens, who would be the permanent president of the board, and five other ambassadors (Mikhas 2005). Simply put, no serious decision could be made without the support of the Greek board members.

Interestingly, in that version of the charter, it was specifically mentioned that the Muslim side would be represented by heads of diplomatic delegations "exclusively and only from Arab Muslim countries" (*apoklistika kai mono ton aravikon musulmanikon khoron*) (Mikhas 2005)—phrasing that was evident of Greece's decision to exclude Turkey from the negotiations. Given the state of religious affairs in Western Thrace, this practice could hardly come as a surprise. For many years the Greek state had been promoting Saudi involvement in the minority's religious affairs in an effort to counter Turkey's intervention in Greece's domestic affairs (*Monitor* 2003; see Chapter 3). In 2003 the Greek journalist Tasos Telloglou elaborated on this policy in a television documentary about "the Athens Mosque." For Telloglou, Saudi Arabia's involvement in the project was part of the very same Greek policy that allowed the Saudi state to provide €400,000 for the restoration of the Hayriye madrassa in Western Thrace.

Telloglou's documentary also incorporated interviews with a Middle East expert working for the Greek Ministry of Foreign Affairs and concerned about the existence of unofficial mosques and the possibility that Muslim immigrants living in Athens were "lost in a sea of Islamic interpretations" (*khameni se mia thalassa islamikon erminion*). In this respect, he continued, a central mosque could play a role in steering the community away from extremists, since it would provide a "religious reference point" for Muslim immigrants and defuse resentment. As the documentary clearly suggested, the expert found the situation of Islam in Athens problematic, since the state was totally incapable of monitoring the activities of the capital's Muslims.

This discourse was also reproduced by certain Muslims themselves, thus showing that experts were not the only ones worrying about "underground" mosques. In the same documentary, İbrahim Şerif, a state-appointed mufti in Thrace,[23] also claimed that the construction of a central mosque would enable the state to have some sort of control over Athenian Muslims, since "who knows what the Muslims do in the basements" (*pios kseri ti kanun eki i musulmani sta ipoyia*).[24]

In the months that followed, many similar productions were broadcast on television and many newspaper articles published, most of them using cliché phrases and provocative titles such as "Athens is the only European capital without a mosque" or "Villagers try to block Athens mosque plan" (Smith 2003). The closer it got to the Olympics, the more often the BBC, CNN Türk, Australian ABC, and Al Jazeera would bring crews to Athens to document the mosque controversy. The Greek capital, it was always stressed, should not be associated only with the Parthenon, Zorba, moussaka, and sirtaki, but should also be thought of as a modern metropolis facing the challenges of Muslim immigration and religious terrorism.

Meeting the Expert

A few months after Telloglou's documentary was broadcast I scheduled a meeting with the Middle East expert, who, as I had found out, was involved in preparing the draft laws that were discussed in parliament.

When we finally met, I was taken aback by his welcoming attitude. Unlike an older generation of Greek diplomats, he did not see the issue from the lens of Greco-Turkish antagonism. He was a liberal intellectual who considered the construction of a mosque a human right and an opportunity to address the sorry state of Islamic studies in Greece. Contrary to the way he was depicted in Telloglou's documentary, his support for a "French solution" along the lines of the Grande Mosquée or Institut du monde arabe—a mosque that would coexist with a café, a library, and possibly a museum—resulted from a belief in the necessity of creating a "common point of reference for Muslims, a place that would set the tone" (and by that he didn't mean that existing unofficial places of worship should be closed down), and the importance of familiarizing the public with the scholarly study of Islam (at the time he was also pushing for the establishment of a master's program and an institute of Middle Eastern studies). To his mind, the case of Western Thrace offered opportunities for creative thinking regarding the administration of Islam in Greece and the role of state-appointed religious functionaries (such as the muftis) in guiding Muslim immigrant communities. "How could it be," he asked me, "that the Muslim minority in Thrace never experienced any problems with religious radicalism?"

40 Chapter 1

During that first visit, the expert did not represent the nationalist state that, like so many other scholars, I expected to encounter. Rather he seemed genuinely interested in the well-being of immigrants and trying to critically assess the anxieties of the state's security apparatus concerning "Muslim invisibility," the activities of the Muslim Brotherhood in the country, and in particular the operation of unofficial mosques in Athens.

To frustrate my expectations even more, the expert carefully reviewed a chronology of events that I was compiling and added an important piece to the obscure story of the Athens mosque: in the 1970s the project was used to approach members of the Arab League and the Organization of the Islamic Conference to secure Muslim support in the UN after Turkey's invasion of Cyprus. He also confirmed that the committee of Arab diplomats with which the ministry was negotiating was a diplomatic structure modeled on the way in which the British government negotiated the establishment of the London Central Mosque at Regent's Park.

"So when will the mosque be built?" I asked.

"Soon, I believe," he responded, "even though politicians always calculate the 'political cost' of this initiative and your compatriots in Kambos don't make things easy either. In any case, be mindful of the way opinions are presented in the media. I am not so 'security oriented' and, frankly, I don't think that the Arab diplomats care that much."

The Mosque Once Again

Six years after Law 2833 was passed, in early November 2006, the mosque issue resurfaced. The very same people who had expressed serious concerns over the handling of the issue as members of the opposition were now introducing a new bill titled "Islamic Place of Worship of Athens and Other Provisions" (*Islamiko Temenos Athinon ke alles Dhiataksis*), with the intention of solving the century-old issue once and for all. The bill stipulated that a nonprofit legal entity named the Governing Committee for the Islamic *Temenos* of Athens be established in the municipality of Athens, operating under the supervision of the Ministry of Education and Religious Affairs (PP 2006). As was widely reported, the government had identified an appropriate location in the area of Votanikos, property of the Greek navy, which would be allotted for the establishment of the mosque (Lialios 2006). In this way, government officials thought, unnecessary tensions with municipal authorities would be avoided.

A month later the draft bill, its supporting documentation, and the minutes of the relevant parliamentary discussions became available, and with the assistance of Apostolos, the librarian, I got hold of the material. Together with the preamble (HP 2006) and the reports produced by the parliament's Second Directorate of Scientific Studies (HP/SDSS 2006) and the Standing Committee on Educational Affairs (HP/SCEA 2006), the document I was given was almost forty pages long (and extremely densely written).

A couple of things became immediately clear. First of all, Kambos was no longer considered the ideal location for the building of the *temenos*. Second, the Ministry of Education and Religious Affairs introduced the bill (the issue was now considered a purely domestic one) and, in particular, the director of religious affairs handled the case (*Mesoyiakos Tipos* 2006:16), not the Middle East expert, who had since left the Ministry of Foreign Affairs for a career in academia. As Marietta Giannakou, then minister of education and religious affairs, made explicit in parliament: "First, this proposal has nothing to do with the country's foreign affairs and with the Ministry of Foreign Affairs, as you have seen. To be more precise: [the mosque] does not constitute an item of infrastructure that will be established after negotiations and discussions with other countries. It constitutes a duty of the Greek state toward Muslims living in Greece, without taking into account whether they are Greek citizens or not" (PP 2006:895). During the plenary discussion all parties described the building of a *temenos* in Athens as necessary. Again, it was repeated that "Athens is the only European city without a mosque" (PP 2006:881) and that the building of such a structure was a precondition for closing down existing Muslim places of worship, which operate without official permits.

When discussion moved to Articles 5 and 6 of the proposed bill, intense disagreement sprung up between the New Democracy government and PASOK. According to these articles the "Islamic Place of Worship of Athens" would be under the strict control of government authorities and be managed by a board of directors presided over by the general director of religious affairs. The board would consist of officials from the Ministry of Education and Religious Affairs and the Ministry of Economy and Finance, two representatives of the municipality of Athens, and an Islamic studies scholar from a Greek university, along with two members from officially "recognized and

42   Chapter 1

representative" Muslim associations of the greater Athens area (HP/SCEA 2006:1–2). It was this board's responsibility to appoint an imam and exercise administrative and financial control. Now it was PASOK's turn to express concerns over the particularities of the proposed bill. Will Muslims have a say in the operation of the central mosque? Were they ever asked to comment on this initiative? Is the government aware that Islam is by no means homogenous? (PP 2006:882, 889).

These questions aside, a few comments made during the plenary session really caught my attention, due to my fascination with the way issues of immigration intersect with older administrative structures regulating the activities of the indigenous Muslim population and the history of the Grande Mosquée de Paris. "We have to differentiate," claimed one MP, "the possibility of centrally appointing the imam of the proposed mosque from the state's appointment of the muftis of Western Thrace." The latter, he implied, was rightly a prerogative of the state since their status is defined by the provisions of the Lausanne Treaty. By contrast, "We have here [in the Athens mosque] an imam who has an exclusively religious role and not judicial, administrative, and other state-related competences. This imam has nothing to do with the mufti of Rodhopi or Ksanthi" (PP 2006:886). Another MP criticized this kind of state interventionism, but from a different perspective, which was reminiscent of Bayoumi's research on the Grande Mosquée: "Let me remind you of one thing. According to the bill the Greek state is responsible for the mosque's maintenance expenses. This means that since the Greek state accepts responsibility for the maintenance expenses of this *temenos*, tomorrow and for reasons of constitutional equality, the very same request and demand may be posed—and very rightly so—by the Bishop of Zihnon, a poor diocese, and he will come and ask you to cover the churches' maintenance expenses. And herein lies the issue . . . this provision creates constitutional inequality" (PP 2006:900). If the state were to provide financial support for the maintenance expenses of a mosque, shouldn't the same policy be followed for the funding of churches? But wasn't it for this exact reason that the French authorities named the Grande Mosquée de Paris an *institut musulman*, so that an otherwise inevitable discussion around issues of secularism and the state could be avoided?

Notably, in the proposed bill there was no provision for the building of an Islamic Cultural Center. This model as well as any aspiration for monumental architecture had now been abandoned. Nevertheless, the Greek government was still looking for "Western" examples to emulate. As had been stated in

Figure 6. The Islamic Center in Washington, D.C. Author's photograph.

parliament, the project was supposed to follow a different model, that of the Islamic Center in Washington, D.C.: a large structure with no cultural center attached to it and with the board allocating space to different Muslim communities.

According to Holod and Hasan-Uddin (1997:233) the Islamic Center in the American capital is the earliest representational mosque, "established by a group of ambassadors from Muslim countries and completed in 1957." The rationale behind this initiative was "to promote a better understanding of Islam in a country where the Muslim religion was not well known and as a vehicle by which to improve relations between the United States and the Muslim World" (Holod and Hasan-Uddin 1997:233). There was even a connection between the Regent's Park Mosque and the Islamic Center in Washington: "The Washington project was roughly contemporaneous with that of the London Central Mosque (initiated four years earlier by Hassan Nashat Pasha, Egyptian Ambassador to the court of St James). Moreover, it is not improbable that the undertaking in England may have influenced events in Washington, as Muhammad Abdul-Rauf, the mosque's imam, has suggested"

(Holod and Hasan-Uddin 1997:234). What Greek officials had not taken into account was that the model of allocating the same space to different communities and of centrally appointing a single imam had not been particularly successful. In the case of the Islamic Center, "disputes between Shiite and Sunni users of the mosque and the resulting occupation led to a number of appointments of shorter-term imams, and the job was divided so that by the mid-1980s there was a Director and an imam, as well as visiting imams" (Holod and Hasan-Uddin 1997:238).

Thus the question remains: why did New Democracy move away from the model of a cultural complex? Apparently, this change echoed the position of the Orthodox Church, which from the late 1990s supported the government initiative on the condition that no cultural center be built. In "The Muslim Complex of Attica," an article published in *Ekklisia*, the Church's official magazine, the Holy Synod's disapproval of the building of an Islamic Cultural Center is explained: "A crucial issue is the planning of the parallel construction of an Islamic Cultural Center. Regarding this issue the Holy Synod has on occasion expressed its disagreement and intense concerns. What is the purpose behind its establishment? Is it not evident [that it should not be constructed], given the activities of such centers in other European countries, where they operate as meeting points for every marginal, criminal, and terrorist element?" (*Ekklisia* 2003:593–594). There seemed to be a widespread perception, I discovered, that the Church played an important role in the decision-making process. It was perhaps for this reason that the parties of the left this time approached the building of the mosque through the prism of church-state relations. Both the Sinaspismos and KKE MPs referred to and criticized the lack of separation between church and state. To their mind, the institutional predisposition of state authorities to become involved in the administration and operation of the Orthodox Church (instead of promoting self-management) was also reflected in the Ministry of Education's wish to maintain full control of the mosque's steering committee.

A great many opinions were expressed during the parliamentary debates, as more and more MPs became convinced that the mosque issue was controversial enough to ensure them airtime on TV. Yet what was not explicitly mentioned is perhaps the most important thing. The opposition parties expressed criticism of the location, lack of Muslim participation in the decision-making process, and church-state relations. Through their silence, however, they

The Promise of the Mosque 45

seemed to accept that a single mosque was enough for the capital's Muslims and, in the post-9/11 era, a necessary precondition for the society's security—an idea that the new Law 3512 was meant to realize in the immediate future (GG 2006a: 2811–2812).

The Limits of a New Field

As years passed without a mosque being built, journalists and scholars increasingly arrived at the conclusion that the structure was doomed to remain notional. Governments, they claimed, always calculate the "political cost of their actions," while locals and the Church would react to any sign of Islam—suppositions that I explore in subsequent chapters. In reviewing the literature on the mosque, it becomes clear that most authors considered the project a chronic case of intentional state failure to accommodate religious alterity.

The story of the mosque, however, is incomplete if told solely through a Greek perspective or a liberal lens as part of a linear narrative of institutional unwillingness to honor religious rights, which suddenly ends with establishment of a mosque in Votanikos. While it would be wrong to overlook continuities in the project's conception (noticeable in the phrasing of bills and the administrative structures that they stipulate), the proposals to erect a mosque in 1890, 1934, and 2000 or to use an existing Ottoman one are best understood as a series of interrelated and yet independent initiatives, products of an interstate symbolic economy in which the promise of a mosque is intended to set a cycle of reciprocity in motion.

Like their European counterparts, Greek diplomats and politicians understood well that building a mosque in Athens carried high symbolic value and could become the means of achieving foreign policy and economic objectives. This is clearly affirmed in Laws 1851 and 6244, the provisions of the Treaty of Athens, newspaper publications of 1932, the Foreign Ministry's correspondence over the future of the Greek diaspora in Egypt, Karamanlis's talks with Prince Fahd, and, most recently, the 2000 bill, which explicitly states that the establishment of the "Islamic Place of Worship of Athens" is supposed to "serve the country's foreign policy objectives and fulfill its international obligations." In all these cases the mosque is considered a collective gift on behalf of a nation that constitutes a "token of friendship" toward empires,

46   Chapter 1

kings, or nation-states. However, to maintain its diplomatic usefulness over a long period of time, it has to remain unbuilt.

What happens, though, when the making of a mosque becomes a domestic issue? Departing from existing scholarship on the mosque, I show how examining the debate that took place in Greece from the late 1990s until 2006 through a broader historical and geographical lens brings to light striking similarities between Greek authorities' imagination of a central mosque and colonial practices of containment and surveillance. Adding to existing literature on the colonial dimensions of Greek governance (e.g., Herzfeld 2002; Hamilakis 2007; Plantzos 2012) I have referred to Venizelos's civilizing visions and described in some detail the cases of the Grande Mosquée de Paris and the Regent's Park Mosque, enterprises that are colonial both in terms of aesthetics (by re-creating a *cité musulmane* reminiscent of colonial expositions in the heart of Paris) and politics (by offering a symbolic incorporation of colonial subjects into the host society and attempting to secure a Western presence in the colonies). My interest in their cases lies in the fact that these structures set a precedent for the establishment of similar centers in many other parts of the world, including Greece. Looking at their history and the administrative, architectural, and geopolitical concerns that informed their establishment allows us, I contend, to map a larger discursive framework in which to place the making of a mosque in Athens, while seeing the project's development in dialogue with Greece's Ottoman past.

Already in 1932 there was clear awareness that the new mosque in Paris might represent a valuable model for Greece in its attempts to lure Egyptian tourists to Ipati. Two years later, Law 6244 of 1934 explicitly refers to an "Egyptian *institut*" (using the French term instead of the Greek for "institute," *idhrima*), echoing French attempts to portray such an initiative as being educational, while in 1948 Greek diplomats were asked to report on its architecture and investigate its operation. Like the French, who were desperately trying to safeguard their presence in Algeria, Greek governments were striving to protect the Egyptiots (who were believed to be willing to undertake the cost of building a mosque in Greece) and the international presence of the Orthodox Church. Until 2000 the Greek state did not seem to move away from the idea of building a larger complex with several nonreligious functions (educational and recreational). If we are to believe what the Foreign Ministry expert told me, the state considered the Institut du monde arabe a possible model for the capital's Islamic cultural center, which would familiarize Greeks with another religion and the intellectual achievements (structurally represented by the library) and habits (spatially represented by the café) of the Arabs. When the Greek state finally decided to construct a space for worship alone with no cultural center attached, a question that echoes French tensions regarding secularism was raised: should a state build and operate a mosque?

Finally, there is indeed something strikingly similar between early twentieth-century discussions on the activities of colonial subjects and contemporary security considerations concerning Muslim activities in underground mosques. Bayoumi's discussion of how SAINA used the Grande Mosquée as a base of operations and a means of monitoring Muslim activities is indeed reminiscent of contemporary Greek and international discourses on security as expressed by the Middle East expert ("Muslim immigrants are lost in a sea of Islamic interpretations"), Thrace's "pseudo-mufti" ("Who knows what the Muslims do in the basements?"), and members of parliament who viewed the *temenos* as necessary architecture for bringing Islam above ground and surveilling it ("We do not refuse to allow the use of a space or apartment—which the government should know about—under the conditions and regulations for the performance of religious duties, until a *temenos* is established," PP 2006:904).

These security considerations also explain why the Greek state ultimately assumed full control of the project and no longer negotiated with the committee of Arab ambassadors. In fact, from the early 2000s onward their places seemed to have been taken by a diverse group of individuals appointed by the media as the government's unofficial interlocutors on the subject. These included a certain Kostis, a vociferous medical doctor from Kambos; Samir, the representative of an immigrants' association; Hassan, a Sudanese imam; Halil-Latif and Gökhan, two Western Thracian Muslims; and Dora, a university lecturer who was somehow connected to the previous two. In contrast to the ambassadors, all of the above were fluent in Greek, readily available to participate in morning shows and the evening news, and, most important, strongly opinionated. Time and again they were interviewed by journalists from across the globe and had to respond to the same cluster of questions. How many Muslims live in Athens and where do they come from? Is a single mosque sufficient for them? What do the people of Kambos think, and what is the position of the Church? As the years went by, however, without a mosque being built in the capital's outskirts, all these questions were overshadowed by another one: why had the mosque not been built?

It is this simple question that I myself ask these individuals in the following chapters. The examination of their responses calls for different kinds of contextualization and makes for a story that moves from the premises of immigrant associations to coffee shops, friends' homes, a doctor's waiting room, and ultimately to the offices of academics, journalists, politicians, and pollsters. As the research unfolds, the story of the unbuilt mosque of Kambos becomes the pretext for exploring political cost, democratic governance, and, ultimately, what it takes for projects to fail or succeed. It starts, however, with an interfaith research project and my meetings with Samir and Hassan.

CHAPTER 2

The Making of "Muslim" Subjects

> [Exile] is a tough job, because there are three sacred things
> for me: work, love, and the residence permit. All three of
> them are most of the time hard to find. But especially the
> last one often replaces erotic passion. However, for the
> last eight years I couldn't get it and I was scared to dream
> about it even in my most drunken dreams.
>
> —Gazi Kaplani

The Project

In early May 2007 I returned to Athens, after a year as an exchange student in the United States, to continue fieldwork research and meet with Samir and Hassan, prominent members of the Muslim community who had participated in the debate over the establishment of a mosque in Kambos. By then the project had been abandoned and a different mosque was now slated to be built in Votanikos—a perfect time, I thought, for reflection on the project's failure. It was then that I found out through friends at ELIAMEP that an old acquaintance, the sociologist Kostas Vlakhou from the Center for Migrant Workers of the Orthodox Church of Greece, had enquired about my whereabouts.

The two of us had met by pure coincidence in April 1999, when I found myself sitting next to him on a flight to London. It wasn't long before we embarked on a discussion about immigrants, the Greek state's attempts to regularize their presence, and the tough lives of those who had settled in Athens. I recall asking him a great many questions regarding those who had first entered the country after the collapse of the communist regime in neighboring Albania in 1992, such as their religious identity and their possible interaction

50 Chapter 2

with migrants from Western Thrace and other immigrants coming from South Asia, the Middle East, and North Africa.[1] I also enquired about the total number of Muslims living in Athens. "No one quite knows," Vlakhou responded and explained that the regularization program that Greece implemented in 1998 (following the example of Spain, Italy, and Portugal) did not include any questions regarding religious affiliation. For him, however, it was important that I kept the larger picture in mind: almost 400,000 immigrants submitted applications for residence and working permits, and almost 150,000 immigrants who could have participated in the program did not.[2]

As the years passed and I moved abroad for graduate studies, Vlakhou and I lost touch, even though there were certainly many issues to discuss: Greece had implemented two additional regularization programs in 2001 and 2005 (Pavlou and Christopoulou 2008:5) and thousands of immigrants had found themselves unemployed by the end of the Olympic Games, while parts of central Athens were now considered by many the territory of prostitutes, drug dealers, and junkies. The impact of the wars in Iraq and Afghanistan on the city's human geography also became clear, as refugees appeared in Omonia, Platia Kodzia, and Kumundhuru, some of the capital's main squares. Racist attacks against immigrants were frequently reported, and groups of young fascists (many of them members of the ultranationalist group Khrisi Avyi, Golden Dawn), with the toleration of the police, assumed control of children's playgrounds and public squares. The city was undergoing transformations almost unthinkable in the preceding years, and the optimism of the Olympic Games was gradually being replaced by a widespread sense of insecurity and decadence.

When Vlakhou and I finally reconnected, in Moni Petraki, the Church's headquarters, he informed me that the European Union had allocated substantial financial resources for the study of Islam in Greece already from 1999 (he was referring to the project "Muslim Voices in European Union"; see Chtouris, Psimmenos, and Tzelepoglou 1999), and in the years following 9/11 more funding had become available. In particular, the Center for Migrant Workers, an entity originally established to support Greek workers returning from Germany (where he had studied and observed how different Christian churches conducted research on Muslim immigrants and created structures for their integration; see Nielsen [1992] 1995:33–34) had successfully applied for a project on Christian-Muslim relations. Vlakhou wanted me to participate as the principal investigator and gave me the chance to include in these funded investigations questions about the mosque in Kambos and to use the center's contacts to approach Muslim community leaders.

The project was titled "Realms of Coexistence" and aimed to investigate the role of religion in discriminatory practices against immigrants in Athens. According to the proposal, the center would conduct, record, and transcribe twenty in-depth semi-structured interviews with Muslims; cooperate with the immigrants' association Agora to map existing places of worship; organize information sessions for Orthodox clergy and meetings between imams and priests; create a website; and produce brochures summarizing the project's key findings.

It was only once I had overcome my initial excitement that I began considering the endeavor's challenges. The Ministry of Labor and Social Protection, which was monitoring the progress of this research, made clear that note-taking was not considered adequate and that all interviews had to be recorded as a means of proving that they had indeed taken place. They also insisted that research on Athenian masjids, apartments, and warehouses that had been turned into places of worship by immigrants should be as detailed as possible, with information on their location featured on the center's website, which could subject immigrants to unwelcome publicity. The information sessions and interfaith meetings, though a common practice in Germany, would constitute an unprecedented initiative for the Greek Orthodox Church, with the clear potential of creating more problems than they could address. Most important, I had to stick to the timeline. "There are no extensions for deliverables," I was told by Dina, Vlakhou's assistant, time and again.

In revisiting my participation in this project, which lasted nine months and introduced me to the complexities of Muslim urban life, I focus on four key moments: my first interviews with Samir and Hassan, and two interfaith meetings that didn't quite go as planned. I situate Samir's and Hassan's responses to the question of why the mosque in Kambos was never built in the context of a research economy that produces measurable deliverables, rigid narratives, and monolithic identities. Yet, as the three of us discussed the project, who counts as Muslim, and where Islam is currently practiced, what we all ended up asking is if religion is a useful lens for understanding the making of a mosque in Athens.

Agora

With the help of the center, a meeting was soon arranged with Samir, the president of Agora and a frequent participant in televised debates concerning the mosque, at the association's headquarters. When the day of the meeting came, I left my house in the suburbs two hours before and was surprised at arriving within an hour and also finding a parking spot. After locating Agora, I headed toward Filis Street, a nearby area of ill repute, where I had heard that brothels and masjids coexisted. The idea that the making of a central mosque should be accompanied by the closure of all unofficial Muslim places of worship to prevent the spread of terrorism had gained particular prominence at the time, and I thought it was only right to wander, even for a while, in a neighborhood with "illegal" mosques. Soon I came across a group of young Bangladeshi men standing outside a subterranean apartment which, as I was told by one of them, was one of the four masjids to be found on the same street, named after Hamza al Muttalib, a renowned warrior and paternal uncle of the Prophet Muhammad. They were in good spirits and perfectly at ease with the fact that some of their compatriots were obviously opting for the other services offered on Filis. Simply put, brothels and masjids seemed to have overlapping followings and, at least for the locals, their coexistence did not seem paradoxical. As it turns out, due to the rigidities of Greek legislation, both establishments operate without permits and occupy spaces that few would rent, while those running them are often subject to extortion.[3] In the words of one of the street's madams whom I met on my walk, "On this street . . . we are all *paranomi* (illegal) . . . while we bribe everyone . . . the cops, municipal employees." I must have looked rather out of touch with realities on the ground to her, since she suggested, with an undertone of mockery, that I also visit gay saunas, video clubs with private cabins, and the *tsondadhika* (porn cinemas) of Omonia Square, if I was truly interested in the lives of Muslim immigrants.

At five to nine, I enter Agora's premises, an old two-story mansion whose beautiful façade is easy to overlook when visiting the neighborhood for the

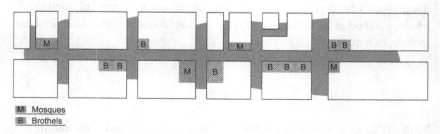

Figure 7. Masjids and brothels on Filis Street.

first time. As I climb the stairs I hear loud discussions and quickly realize that Agora is a busy place frequented by Greeks and immigrants alike. In the large lounge area, which has a big wooden table in its center and is also used as a classroom, there are people of all ages and appearances. Young Greek volunteers, women speaking Russian, others wearing hijabs, several Pakistanis or Bangladeshis whose orange and deep red shirts I cannot help noticing, one or two Albanians, and a young man around my age whom I later overhear saying in broken English that he has just come from Moldova and whose anxiety about establishing himself in Athens somehow vanishes in this chaos. This first floor feels very welcoming. It has nice wooden floors, freshly painted walls decorated with children's drawings, and high ceilings—a cheerful place.

In the lounge I am greeted by Anuar, a Pakistani immigrant wearing a gray pullover in midsummer who informs me that my meeting with the president will be postponed for another quarter of an hour or so. I tell him that I am involved in a project on Christian-Muslim relations and writing a dissertation on the nonexistent mosque. Anuar doesn't seem at all surprised by my interests. He is, I understand, used to being asked all sorts of questions by individuals conducting research on Agora's premises and quickly shares with me a condensed version of his life. He tells me that he came in 1995 and that, in contrast to most Pakistanis in the country, he comes from Karachi and not the greater Gujarat region.[4] Until early 2005, I am told, he worked in a textile factory and mastered the art of sewing together the different parts of a pullover in less than six minutes. "Of course," he tells me, "now my condition in Greece has improved."

"Of course, of course," I reply.

"I now work here," he says, and his eyes convey pride and enthusiasm.

Echoing the state's attempts to link the mosque to a Muslim cemetery in nineteenth-century Piraeus, Anuar tells me that a *dzami* must be built, as this would result in the establishment of the infrastructure necessary for the preparation of the deceased for burial. "This you cannot do in an apartment," he continues, "the washing of the deceased, having an imam chant a prayer, wrapping the body in the *kafan*. Greeks are afraid of the dead and complain when they see a coffin being carried in and out of a block of flats."[5]

On the more personal front, Anuar informs me, there are two main sources of sorrow in his life: *khartia*, "papers," a term encapsulating all of an immigrant's anxiety about securing a legal presence in the country and the stressful and unending dealings with Greek bureaucracy to acquire work and

54 Chapter 2

residence permits, and also the absence of a female companion with whom to share the hardships and achievements of his life, a condition shared by many Pakistani and Bangladeshi immigrants (IMEPO 2004:5; Leghari 2009; Evergeti and Hatziprokopiou 2013:180).[6] He worried over the fact that almost every year he has to queue for hours on end, and all that at the crucial age of thirty-five, a time of transition, as he says, in every man's life. Marriage is a concern not only for my interlocutor but also for his elderly father, who often reminds Anuar that family should be given priority over any profession and financial security. But for that to happen he would have to return to Karachi, something that he very much doubts will ever happen.

The idea of Agora, I learn, goes back to the early 1990s and the first Athens Antiracist Festival, organized by immigrants and political parties of the left. It was then that some established figures in the immigrant community envisioned an organization that would bring together and represent all immigrants living in Greece. Agora, claims Anuar, has managed to navigate successfully the complicated micropolitics of the various immigrant associations, which are otherwise fragmented and particularly hostile toward each other, to emerge as an umbrella organization that enjoys the support of the Greek state and of many communities. It is considered the main immigrant organization in Greece, and its activities range from offering Greek classes to legal support for those applying for residence and work permits, and even interreligious dialogue, "a new," as he says, "and very promising thing."

Samir

Even though Samir is one of the most influential members of the immigrant community, he retains an appreciation for modesty, which is manifested in his insistence on sharing an office space adjacent to the main hall with two other Agora employees. He smokes constantly in an environment frantic with loud conversations, constant phone calls, and smoke, a lot of smoke. We begin by talking about Sudan, his country of origin, his studies in classical philology in Athens in the late 1970s, his work as a translator and journalist at *al-Dafatayan*, the capital's Arabic newspaper, and his family. He informs me that his "funny" looks, which combine brown skin with a white mustache and short white curly hair, are the outcome of a Middle Eastern mixture of peoples, a kind of diversity that the Western world has neither realized nor embraced. This diversity transcends appearances, he notes, and extends to religion. "Take my own family, for example. One grandfather is from Syria; the other comes from Egypt. Half of the family is white, the other half black. Half Muslims, half Christians."

After these introductory remarks, our discussion shifts to the history of Middle Eastern immigration to Greece, which, he tells me, started in the 1970s. Back then, says Samir, Arabs (Egyptians, Sudanese, Lebanese, Syrians, and Jordanians) constituted the vast majority of the capital's Muslim population, and this continued to be the case in the 1980s. Nowadays, he tells me, these demographics have radically changed. Arabs number twenty-five thousand, while Pakistanis (who had a small presence in the country already from the 1970s; see Tonchev 2007) and Bangladeshis exceed sixty thousand and have established the most masjids. To these figures, suggests Samir, one must also add five thousand to six thousand Muslims from Western Thrace who have settled in the broader Gazi area. "Their case is very different, however, as they are Greek citizens," he notes (see Chapter 3).

As a prelude to our discussion of the mosque in Kambos, I relate to Samir a particular childhood memory about a small, prefabricated mosque on top of the Caravel Hotel in central Athens, which I used to see from the back seat of my family's car when we would visit an aunt who lived nearby.[7]

"Did you ever visit that mosque?" asks Samir, who seems to have enjoyed this childhood memory of mine. "But you were very young then, weren't you?" he adds. He then goes on to explain that the mosque I remember was an "elite mosque," hardly ever visited by immigrants since they would have had to order a coffee or tea to make use of the facilities. Instead, they quickly organized their own spaces of worship without involving diplomats or state authorities. Rather expectedly, according to Samir, "no one bothered them. The Greeks did not touch them at all. As usual, they just left things as they were."

"What about you?" I ask. "Is there a particular mosque that you usually go to? How often do you go?" Having immersed myself in Samir's persona as presented by mass media, I was convinced that religion was a determining factor in his life, so I did not anticipate his answer.

"I think," Samir begins, "the majority of immigrants don't go to masjids, and even those who do go pray for only a few minutes. They get inside, they pray, and they leave immediately. Generally speaking I don't do it."

"But when you do go, which one do you use?" I persist.

"Any one," he replies.

"Any one?" I repeat in astonishment. "What about sectarian and ethnic differences? What about differences in language? Sunnis and Shiites?"

56 Chapter 2

"Dimitri, this is a problem in Christianity, not in Islam. The most important consideration for me is whether a masjid is near me or not."

"So would you then go to a Pakistani mosque?" I ask again in an attempt to provoke a fuller answer from him.

"Of course," says Samir with a smile and asks why anyone would go out of his way just to pray or, for that matter, leave the city center to visit a mosque in Kambos. For Samir, the geography of existing places of worship should primarily be understood along lines of convenience, real estate availability, and access to public transportation. In that respect, the case of the masjids of Omonia is indeed telling; they are close to a metro station, with affordable rent, and are frequented by Muslims of all nationalities who just "hop in and out."

I was not the first one with whom Samir shared this perspective. As he tells me, in the early 2000s, when the making of a mosque in Kambos was debated in parliament, PASOK asked his opinion. His insistence on portraying Muslim immigrants as rational actors who wouldn't lose a day's income to pray in the suburbs fell on deaf ears. This reluctance on the part of state authorities to consider an immigrant's viewpoint led him to believe that the making of a central mosque was a story for the outside world. In this respect, not much had changed. As in the nineteenth century, when the state tried to erect a mosque to smooth relations with the Ottoman Empire and later to safeguard Greek presence in Egypt, the more recent iteration of the project constituted, for Samir, yet another case of internationalism.

Yet the mosque debate also pointed to something much larger: the political irrelevance of the immigrants. As long as those categorized as Muslim immigrants did not have a path to citizenship and voting rights, no politician, journalist, or pollster would ever take them seriously.[8] From this perspective, it is quite understandable, he explains, why the mosque in Kambos remains notional. Local opposition and Church reactions aside, there is no voting constituency to lobby effectively, and politicians see no cost to the project's constant postponement. "To provide you with a different insight," continues Samir, "I would say that the main issue here is not so much the creation of a central mosque, which is important, but the issue of *khartia* and the eventual legalization of all existing places of worship. For initiatives of this kind would convey the message to the immigrants that Greece doesn't wish to be transformed into a nation of illegals."

In the days that followed my first interview with Samir, I began transcribing our exchanges; in doing so, little by little, certain words, phrases, and, predispositions in our thinking that seemed only natural at the time began to

The Making of "Muslim" Subjects   57

stand out. Like most scholars and journalists writing on the mosque of Kambos, we too kicked off our discussion on the capital's Muslims with numbers: 25,000 Arabs, at least 60,000 Pakistanis and Bangladeshis, around 5,000 to 6,000 migrants from Western Thrace. As I realized in the course of our subsequent meetings, these figures were based on intuition more than anything else. They excluded Albanians as well as immigrants disconnected from the communities of the city center. Given that the national census takes place every ten years and the numbers of those without *khartia* are always subject to a politics of speculation, it is understandable how the capital's Muslim population was estimated as from 100,000 to 200,000 (Anagnostou and Gropas 2010:92), from 200,000 to 300,000 (Skoulariki 2010:305), or 450,000 (Imam and Tsakiridi 2003:24) in the literature on Muslims in Greece.

Crucially, these figures result from the subtle translation of national citizenship into religious identity.[9] In the absence of specific data about religion,[10] it often seems perfectly logical to consider an Egyptian immigrant or an Iraqi refugee as Muslim, which survey research usually describes as an "indirect method of quantifying Muslim presence based on geographical/cultural association" (Brown 2000). In fact, most works on Muslims in Greece and Europe employ this logic, which, with few exceptions, goes unquestioned.[11] It is through this very move that Muslim subjects are constructed, making it possible to explore otherwise secular aspects of the immigrants' everyday (housing, personal finances, etc.) through a religious lens.[12] Yet Samir's suggestion that many Muslims "don't go to masjids" raises a basic question that I take up in the next section: how religious are the subjects in question or, simply put, what exactly makes a "Muslim immigrant" Muslim?

Hassan

The world of the immigrants, vast and impersonal as it may appear to outsiders, is also a microcosm in which major players know each other. In this regard it wasn't surprising to find out that Samir was an old friend of Hassan and that he could put me in touch with him. After all, they were compatriots who had studied at the University of Athens at the same time in the 1970s.

As in the case of Samir, I was familiar with Hassan not as a result of an actual encounter but through seeing him on television so many times. For many Greeks, I thought, Hassan epitomized a "Muslim cleric," and during the televised panel discussions on the mosque in Kambos he was often introduced

58   Chapter 2

as such. His appearance also corresponded to what most Greeks would expect such a figure to look like—brown skin and a long gray beard, and always wearing a small embroidered skull cap.

The meeting is scheduled for an early afternoon in July outside the masjid that he had established many years ago, but I am unsure if I have come to the right place. I find it hard to believe that such an establishment could look so much like a warehouse.[13] From the outside all I can see are a curtain heavily faded by the sun and stacks of boxes. Who knows, I think, it might well be the case that even neighbors believe that this is a storage space or the dilapidated offices of an obscure company that only hires Arab immigrants for a few hours a day. I glance once again at my notes. The address, written in brown paint right next to the entrance, offers some reassurance. This is indeed 87 Eleftherios Venizelos Street.

From afar, I see Hassan coming toward me with a gentle smile on his face. He welcomes me inside the masjid, which is clean and tidy, in stark contrast to its exterior appearance. There is a thick green carpet that extends to the very back of the room, a small book collection by the metal staircase, and behind the façade's windows even a mihrab. We take off our shoes and sit on the floor. "*Bismi'llah*" (In the name of God), says Hassan, and after this invocation we are ready to start the interview.

It is quite possible that Hassan thinks that this is my first contact with Muslims and Islam. I am told that we are all brothers and have a common ancestor, Adam, that both Christianity and Islam respond to man's existential questions, and that Islam constitutes a continuation of previous revelations to Jews and Christians. To make the discussion less theological, I ask him how he came to Greece. He tells me that he arrived in Athens to study medicine in 1974. There was no Muslim place of worship at the time, and soon he and a few other students started praying in an empty room at the Medical School "without experiencing any problem from fellow students and university authorities." But after ten years, in 1984, when he was doing his specialty training, he no longer felt comfortable with that ad hoc arrangement.

"So how did you establish this place?" I ask, curious to see if his answer will confirm the widespread belief that the Greek state doesn't allow the operation of mosques because it doesn't respect the religious rights of the non-Orthodox. In response he tells me the story of his masjid, his failed attempts to operate it legally, and his meetings with bureaucrats reluctant to make a potentially costly decision and therefore fully engaging in the art of buck-passing (*efthinofovia*).[14] The latter included a meeting with the mayor of

The Making of "Muslim" Subjects   59

the municipality of Zoghrafu, who claimed that no permits were necessary as long as the police was informed, and then a visit to police headquarters, where he was referred to the Directorate for Followers of Other Doctrines and Religions (*Dhiefthinsi Eterodhoxon ke Eterothriskon*) at the Ministry of National Education and Religious Affairs. Rather than asking Hassan to apply for a "house of prayer" permit (see Chapter 1), the head of the directorate assured him that there would be no problem with the masjid and suggested that he establish a Greek-Arab association—a recommendation that he didn't follow.

After all these years operating a masjid in Athens, Hassan is convinced that there is something particularly convenient, almost calculated, in the state's reluctance to legalize existing spaces of worship. Such a practice, he thinks, makes immigrants potentially vulnerable to the authorities (the police, the fire department, the local planning office) and creates relations of obligation to anyone who has the power to prevent the closing down of a masjid. When the discussion turns to the central mosque in Athens, Hassan claims that a single mosque would simply "not suffice." "People go to their neighborhood mosque to see their friends, for community support, to ask around for jobs, certainly not only to pray." In no uncertain terms he makes clear to me that the idea that Muslims in Athens pray in subterranean apartments because there is no single proper mosque—so very prevalent in the press and scholarly analysis—is naive. To my surprise, he suggests that Muslim states should work with Greece to create multiple mosques for their respective communities. "Given the large number of masjids currently operating in the capital, a central mosque is necessary mainly for symbolic reasons," he explains, since it would signify acceptance and the prospect of integration into the host society. As for the reasons behind its delay, he tells me that one shouldn't seek complex answers: the ambassadors involved in the long-term negotiations with the Greek state are "completely secular," while politicians are always susceptible to pressure from the Church.

How do we know that all these immigrants called Muslims practice Islam, I ask.

"Most of them don't," he assures me. "They are called Muslims because they come from Pakistan, as you're considered Christian because you're Greek." He goes on to describe how, especially after 9/11, he can only have a place in the Greek public sphere as a Muslim. The television news shows inviting him to panel discussions on the mosque are solely interested in his perspectives on terrorism, the nature of jihad, and, always, his numerical

60 Chapter 2

estimations of Muslim immigrants, but never in his personal situation—his constant anxiety about the *khartia* and residence permits for his children, and his immense frustration at not finding a permanent job in a state hospital.[15] "Do you know what I ask myself sometimes?" he offers. "Could it be that all these things happen to us because of our religion?"

"But the Albanians, the Poles, and the Bulgarians have the same problems," I respond, telling him that everybody complains about the *khartia*.

"Yes, Dimitri, but when did these people come to Greece and when did we? Do not forget this! That's why I am telling you that a mosque in Athens will show the good intentions not only of the Church, but also of the state. It will not solve our problems, but it will show that here, in the cradle of democracy, the foreigner does not remain a foreigner forever!"

The Conference

In the months that followed my first meetings with Samir and Hassan, the Center for Migrant Workers documented all Muslim places of worship operating in Athens. This research would have been impossible to carry out without the crucial assistance of Agora's president, who was able to mobilize within minutes armies of young immigrants on scooters to take us to locations none of us had visited before and provide us with contact details of several imams. In this way we managed to estimate the number of masjids in Athens (not including Piraeus) at twenty-six.

We were asked to present these research findings, together with information on immigrants' everyday life in the capital, at a conference organized by the center and hosted by the diocese of Peristeri, one of the capital's most densely populated neighborhoods, where many immigrants reside. According to the program, the conference was to consist of short presentations by all those who had been involved in the research: priests, scholars, community leaders, and church administrators. The aim was fairly straightforward: to expose Orthodox priests to the new multireligious reality of the capital and challenge widespread stereotypes and misconceptions about Islam at a time when the government had reaffirmed its intention to build a mosque, now in Votanikos, and the debate over the issue seemed to have picked up again.

On the day of the conference, the bishop of Peristeri arranged for us to be given an extensive tour of the diocese's headquarters before we were shown to the auditorium, which was packed with some two hundred priests. The

The Making of "Muslim" Subjects 61

meeting commenced with a prayer and a brief welcoming speech by the elderly bishop, who seemed to be in full control of his diocese's clergy. A single glance by him was enough to initiate activity or to stop it completely. "I welcome you all," he began, "and wish you a happy Christmas." "Happy Christmas," replied the crowd in a single voice. "This is an important day, for we have the honor of hosting distinguished scholars and learning from them. For my part, I will only say that in our days everything has changed. People from different parts of the world live among us. These are the people we hire to build our houses and take care of our elderly parents. Now the time has come for us to think of them, learn about their religion, and help them in any way we can," said the bishop, whose voice by the end of this short speech had grown stronger, more determined, and certainly more strict.

The presentations commenced with Dina introducing the research. Samir was the third to speak, after a certain Patikas, a professor of theology, gave a lecture on the tenets of the Muslim faith. We were seated on a wooden platform facing the audience and had an unobstructed view of everything that was taking place in the conference hall. Even from the first minutes of Dina's presentation I could see that most of the priests were profoundly uninterested in the topic of the conference. They would exchange notes, talk to each other, giggle, and mock the speakers. Whenever one of them brought up the issue of terrorism or Turkey in the Q and A session that followed each presentation, the others would clap in support, and it was only through the bishop's intervention that they would stop. Their attitude did not change even when a fellow priest talked passionately about his attempts to help Afghan immigrants and to organize some joint events in his parish, or when Samir gave his presentation, which included all the data we had collected on masjid establishment in Athens.

Unlike what I was told by Agora's president during our initial meeting concerning the transcendence of ethnic boundaries in the masjids of Athens, his presentation to the priests painted a more fragmented picture of the capital's Muslim religious landscape. As he explained, a great deal had changed since the establishment of a mosque on top of the Caravel Hotel. First, a great number of masjids had been established, this time not by wealthy businessmen but by immigrants from the Middle East and South Asia, who quickly moved from praying in private houses to renting affordable spaces (for the most part basements, storehouses, garages, and small shops) in downgraded neighborhoods.[16] These places operated without proper permits and varied in size, the languages used in prayers, and the style and topic of the sermons; they were divided along lines of ethnicity, the general rule being that Muslims of Arab origin would never mix with Afghan, Pakistani, or Bangladeshi immigrants. Socioeconomic differences were also easily observable among worshippers; Arab diplomats and businessmen would gather on Fridays in the masjid of the Libyan school in Paleo Psihiko, one of the most affluent areas of Athens, where most of the embassies are located, or rent ballrooms in hotels for prayer and iftar during the month of Ramadan, whereas Arabs of a lower socioeconomic status would gather in Hassan's masjid, the Arab community's masjid in Ambelokipi, or a new one in Moskhato. As for the Albanian immigrants, there was absolutely no sign of them in the spaces that we visited.

As Samir noted in his talk, those not familiar with the life of the immigrants wouldn't know that almost all of their masjids had names: ar-Rahman (The Beneficent), al-Salam (Peace), al-Ghoraba (The Strangers), al-Ikhlas (Sincerity), al-Taqwa (Piety), Tawhid (Oneness), as-Salihin (Good People), Ali, Ka'ba, Dar al-Salam (Abode of Peace), al-Jabbar (Powerful), al-Malik (The King), Bilal, and Bait al-Mokarram (The House of the Honored), to name but a few. These names were indicative of the emphasis placed on particular figures in Islamic history and theological traditions by imams and the communities they serve. Most outside the community also wouldn't know that the establishment of such places was often the result of an initiative taken outside of Greece. Some had been established with the support of international organizations, such as Lahore Ahmadiyye, Tablighi Jamaat, Jamaat-i-Islami, Minhaz-ul-Qur'an, or Da'wat-e-Islami, engaged in missionary work for different Sufi orders or at the request of religious leaders stationed in England, Pakistan, or Saudi Arabia.[17]

With a few exceptions, these places were administered by imams who lacked proper theological training and attended by young, often illiterate men. As we were told on many occasions, those acting as imams are *hafiz* (one who has memorized the Koran) at best, and certainly not *'alim* (a theologian). They are paid by their respective communities through a system of voluntary contributions, by international organizations, or by their countries' embassies in Greece. There is thus a microeconomy at work that results in the continuous establishment of more places of worship, since in this way some immigrants make a decent monthly salary (cf. Salvanou 2013:15). These practices are common knowledge among community members and are also the source of intense gossip, rivalry, and mutual accusation.

Presenting some preliminary findings of this kind, Samir tried to challenge widespread perceptions of the practice of Islam in Athens that understand

The Making of "Muslim" Subjects 63

the building of a central mosque as an initiative capable of putting an end to "dangerous" practices of underground worship and the ongoing establishment of new masjids. "The diversity and fragmentation characterizing Muslim communities in Athens would not disappear," said Samir; he continued the presentation with an analysis of Greek tendencies to associate Islam with Turkey and then the project's key finding: religious discrimination against immigrants does not seem particularly prevalent in Athens. While most interviewees felt that they were considered foreigners, this perception, they believed, had more to do with the color of their skin or their dress than their Muslim faith.

After a short break, the conference resumed with me as the first speaker of the afternoon panel. I tried to show that knowledge of Muslim theology is not always helpful in understanding the complexities of the immigrants' lives and explained that the use of religious classifications overlooks the obvious fact that people have plural identities.[18] I invited the priests to think of all of the affiliations an individual may have—a fan of a soccer club, a gardener, an Orthodox Christian, a father—which are prioritized differently depending on context and cannot be reduced to a single one. In this sense, I claimed, one shouldn't approach immigrants from Asia or the Middle East primarily as religious beings. Rather, as our research had indicated, we should also think of them as ordinary people primarily concerned with the harsh realities of everyday life and especially bureaucracy—an issue to which most Greeks could easily relate. After all, everyone involved in the project had noticed that our "Muslim" interlocutors wanted most to speak about the *khartia*, which they viewed as their main problem. I asked the priests, "Would it make sense to you if someone tried to understand your housing and financial preferences in terms of the Gospels?"—a question that they perceived as a joke. Right after the conference ended, Samir approached me. We chatted about the research and our payment. I told him that I was falling behind with the interviews and complained about the priests, while he seemed used to situations in which "diversity," as he said, "is not wholeheartedly embraced."

The Interfaith Meeting

The final act of the center's project took place in a small chapel at the city center in December 2007. This was supposed to be the culmination of a research project that had lasted for more than six months, and it surely was.

The meeting's location had been carefully selected by the center's personnel, because Father Epifanios was known for his eagerness to promote liberal approaches to the challenging issue of immigration. "A progressive priest," as Dina would describe him.

The meeting was scheduled to begin at seven, and I brought my mother along. We arrived a few minutes early, and to my surprise I saw that at least fifty people had already gathered. This was an unusually mixed crowd. Quite a few of the attendees were friends and relatives of the center personnel, and research associates who had given me the impression that their connection to religion had ended many years ago.

This was surely not the case with the second and much smaller category of attendees, elderly people living in the vicinity and a few middle-aged women who thought of St. Marina as an extension of their own houses (cf. Hirschon [1989] 1998:190). My mother and I entered the chapel. I introduced her to Dina, and Dina introduced her to her own mother. "Father Epifanios will say a few words at the beginning, followed by Patikas, and then Hassan will give his presentation," Dina told me. We took our seats, which had a direct view of the speakers' table placed right in the middle of the chapel—a peculiar arrangement that I had never encountered before.[19]

The meeting was about to begin. The speakers had already taken their seats at the central table, and Father Epifanios was ready to welcome us to St. Marina when George Papandreou, the leader of PASOK, together with the president of the Hellenic Migration Policy Institute, appeared.[20] "Please take a seat among us," the priest said in polite excitement. With some hesitation Papandreou, who had come without a politician's usual entourage of journalists and cameramen, accepted the invitation and sat between Hassan and Father Epifanios. This would have been the perfect snapshot of the multicultural Greece he himself envisioned: a future prime minister sitting between a priest and an imam.

The meeting started with Patikas giving the same talk on the basic tenets of Muslim faith and the differences between Sunnis and Shiites. Hassan's presentation was equally encyclopedic. Throughout these presentations an old man behind us never stopped muttering. While he did not do it in a loud voice, it was still loud enough to test the tolerance of those around him. "You must be ashamed of this, all of you! Had you known the Turks, you would not. . . . These are the plans of the new order!"

"Could you stop?" I asked him, and my mother intervened to prevent an even louder disagreement. "Let's hear what these people have to say," she said

The Making of "Muslim" Subjects 65

quietly. Even though his respect for me was apparently limited, he had no choice but to comply with the polite suggestion of a woman of some age, and for some time the commentary stopped.

Both Patikas and Hassan confined their presentations to a general and somewhat abstract account of Islam and Christian-Muslim relations. I did not know Patikas well, but having met with Hassan several times, I knew that he had wonderful human stories to narrate, which would have been much better understood in this context. Without being aware of it, they appeared to support the idea that racism and Islamophobia[21] stem from a fear of the unknown, conditions that they thought they could remedy by means of information.

Papandreou, on the other hand, who seemed to have enjoyed the presentations, refrained from giving a long speech when his turn came. He referred briefly to political cost that prevented many Greek governments from building a mosque in Athens and he welcomed comments and questions on issues of religious tolerance and immigration. In an attempt to give Hassan the opportunity to address larger issues and draw on his personal experiences, I asked him to speak about the main challenges that immigrants face in Greece. Hassan raised the issue of the *khartia*, and Papandreou acknowledged how important it is for the state to attend to the needs of the second generation, which at the time had no preferential access to citizenship.

All this time I had failed to notice a middle-aged woman wearing a gray pullover on top of a purple shirt, a long skirt, and glasses, with her hair in a ponytail (signs of devotion). "I would like to ask something," she said all of a sudden in a loud voice.

"Of course, Mrs. Dharioti, what is it that you would like to share with us?" Father Epifanios responded in a soft and welcoming voice.

"It is obvious," she started, "that none of you has ever read the scriptures, the Gospels, none of you has ever read the Revelation of St. John the Divine so that you avoid the trap of heresy into which you have all fallen. Lord, what more is there for us to witness? Prostitutes in a church? Homosexuals being married? Is this really what you think Orthodoxy is all about?"

"Please, please," said Father Epifanios, approaching her in an attempt to calm her down.

"Don't touch me!!" the woman screamed. "This is my church too, you have no right to tell me to leave."

"But I didn't," said Father Epifanios.

Chaos ensued. The old man behind me started shouting that he knew a marine who had died during the Turkish invasion of Cyprus, the woman was repeating verses from the Apocalypse, other older women started yelling "*Dropi, dropi*" (shame, shame), while others reproached them. The interfaith meeting had clearly come to an end. Papandreou stood up, approached me, thanked me for my question, shook the hands of Father Epifanios and Hassan, and left.

I felt bad for Hassan and his young son, who had been carrying a video camera to record his father's speech. This was supposed to be an afternoon worth remembering, signifying a moment of acceptance. I enquired about the boy's studies and introduced Hassan to my mother, who was equally sorry about what was still taking place, since Mrs. Dharioti continued complaining and talking to herself in a loud voice. It was obvious that no one really knew how to behave. For most attendees it was now a matter of honor not to leave the church prior to Mrs. Dharioti's departure. We gathered at the back of the chapel, where Father Epifanios had prepared a small buffet.

"Oh, just shut your mouth. This was supposed to be a celebration, Mrs. Dharioti, and you ruined it," Father Epifanios proclaimed.

Counting Muslims for a Central Mosque

While it might be easy to understand why the making of a mosque in Athens was connected to a discussion of the capital's masjids, it is less obvious why every single scholarly and journalistic article on the matter attempted to count Greece's Muslim population. To understand this phenomenon, I suggest considering the new economy of research that emerged in the post-9/11 world at the intersection of security considerations, integration concerns, and the prioritization of religious affiliations in scholarly analysis and, quite often, at the level of grassroot community initiatives.

In the year that followed the research project "Places of Coexistence," several articles about Muslim immigrants in Greece and the mosque controversy were published—many of which were in English and constituted "deliverables" for projects funded by the British Arts and Humanities Research Council (Hatziprokopiou and Evergeti 2014), the European Commission (Triandafyllidou and Gropas 2009), and Greek public benefit foundations (Salvanou 2014). To access funding, establish an international presence, participate in pan-European projects, and cater to the needs of policymakers and private donors interested in the peaceful coexistence of diverse people, scholars wrote prolifically on Islam in Greece. In that context, they also engaged in the

The Making of "Muslim" Subjects   67

creation of Muslim subjects, even if that entailed translating national citizenship into religious identity and, sometimes, counting secular Albanian immigrants. The effects of this practice are not only observable in uneasy interfaith meetings in conference halls and churches. They also take the form of rather paradoxical assertions that proliferate in the scholarship. As a sociologist of migration acknowledges, "Albanian Muslims . . . have not become an organized group, have not identified themselves as Muslims, nor have they raised any claims regarding the accommodation of their religious needs" (Triandafyllidou 2010:205), while another sociologist argues that because "they have left an atheistic regime which lasted for many decades, [they] are not as religious as the other Muslims and perhaps that is why they are more easily converted into Orthodox Christianity by being baptized" (Sakellariou 2011:78).

In addition to numerical validation, the making of Muslim subjects often entails the employment of rigid research methodologies and narrative frameworks in which immigrant informants can appear adequately Muslim. Samir's and Hassan's cases are particularly illuminating in this regard. The former has extensive knowledge of the challenges immigrants face, and the latter is a protagonist of Muslim life in Athens. Both have suggested that the building of a central mosque, even though it might silence domestic and international criticism, would certainly not result in the disappearance of existing places of worship, contrary to the suggestion of experts, politicians, and journalists—a belief that the state de facto accepted, as we will see, when a mosque was finally built in Votanikos. Muslim presence in Athens, as they have pointed out, is so diverse that it cannot possibly be accommodated by a single place of worship. When the two men are faced with the question of why the mosque in Kambos was not built, they refer to local reactions, the role of the Church, the inability or unwillingness of ambassadors to argue effectively for its construction, and the lack of political participation by immigrants. Their tidy and quick answers to my question seem to them self-evident and reproduce aspects of the media discourses that they have helped shape.

Yet when they answer more open-ended questions, religious classifications become less relevant. At that point the Athens mosque loses its religious specificity and emerges as a site for the negotiation of citizenship, inclusion, and hospitality. Samir, for example, does not think of the Muslim immigrants whom I study as being particularly religious—if they visit a masjid, they just pray briefly and leave immediately, he says—even though Agora participates in and thus benefits financially from a research project on Christian-Muslim relations. Hassan, like so many others, is primarily concerned with the issue

68   Chapter 2

of *khartia* and links the making of a central mosque to democratic governance in Greece and the symbolic acceptance of immigrants.

In this regard, the Filis Street madam's suggestion—that I pursue a different kind of research that would challenge not only the basic parameters of my fieldwork, as initially conceived, but also a whole body of literature dedicated to the study of the human condition through a religious lens—becomes particularly pertinent. An alternative approach to studying these same "Muslim" subjects might involve, for instance, visiting brothels, gay saunas, porn cinemas, and video clubs with private cabins—testing the usefulness of categories such as "Muslim immigrants" that prioritize religion over many other affiliations that an individual may have (relating to gender, sexuality, level of education, place of origin, and so on). This kind of exploration is something that investigators of the "Muslim" everyday would either not pursue or not mention in the "deliverables." It is at that very moment of editing that a pure Muslim identity is created at the level of fieldwork and textual analysis, where a focus on religion produces research subjects depicted as praying incessantly.

Problematic as this depiction may be, it is certainly not new to Greece, and moreover it opens up economic and political opportunities. The exchange of populations that Greece and Turkey undertook in 1923 was organized along lines of religion and clearly demonstrated the tremendous impact that religious classification of former Ottoman subjects as simply "Muslims" or "Christian" had on the life of individuals. In her ethnography on borders in the Greek north, Olga Demetriou describes the case of Eleni, a Turkish-speaking Orthodox Christian who explains how those who agreed to prioritize their religion over their language found themselves having to leave their homelands and move to the territories of the Greek state: "'*Dilimizi verdik, dinimizi vermedik*'" (We gave our language, we did not give our religion) (2013:36). Yet these taxonomies, rigid as they may be, can also be used strategically. As we will see in the following chapter, three other protagonists of the mosque debate, Dora, Halil-Latif, and Gökhan, understand quite well how a place in the public eye and an opportunity to challenge the state can be predicated on a Muslim identity and engagement in a debate over the making of a mosque.

CHAPTER 3

Islam as a Path to Democracy

News

While in the 1890s the issue of making a mosque in Athens was clearly connected to Greek-Ottoman relations, the Greek-Turkish War of 1919–1922 and the subsequent Treaty of Lausanne in 1923 recognizing the existence of a "Muslim minority" in the country made Greek officials question the role of their eastern neighbor in the project. The treaty not only granted minority members access to Islamic family law, representation through muftis, and the self-management of *vakifs* (charitable endowments), but also linked their well-being to Turkey's treatment of its Rum communities through the emphasis on reciprocity. Most important, however, the treaty did not specify where exactly that Muslim minority was located—an omission that became crucial after the annexation in 1947 of the islands of Rhodes and Kos, which also had Muslim populations.[1] Should Greece allow Turkey to emerge as protector of all Muslims living in its territories? Should all Muslims in the country enjoy the rights stipulated by the treaty or, as was eventually decided, only those in Western Thrace?

As the archival record shows, these concerns very much shaped the state's thinking about the making of a central mosque in the capital city. When, for example, the government began to consider the reuse of the Fethiye Mosque in Athens in the 1940s, it was quite aware of the possible complications arising from the fact that, tourists aside, there were other Muslims in the country who were Greek citizens and had to be treated equally. In 1948, amid the Civil War, the minister of education Andonios Papadhimos wrote to the Ministry of Foreign Affairs that he did not object to the use of the Fethiye Mosque by "Muhammad's faithful." Yet, he suggested, "the impression that this allotment would make on the Turkish Minority [of Thrace] or

70 Chapter 3

the Turks of the Dodecanese must be carefully examined as it [i.e., the allotment] will be compared to the tactics applied to them by the Greek state up to now" (DHAGMFA/CS 1948a). Some sixty years later, in 2006, an MP would warn his colleagues in a plenary session, "We have to differentiate the possibility of centrally appointing the imam of the proposed mosque from the state's appointment of the muftis of Western Thrace." As for the scholars and international reporters writing about the mosque in Kambos, they always acknowledged the existence of an indigenous Muslim population that constituted the country's "old Islam" (e.g., Tsitselikis 2012) and represented an enduring Ottoman legacy.

With this broader geographical and historical context in mind, it is by no means surprising that one of the protagonists of the mosque controversy in the early 2000s was a certain Halil-Latif from Western Thrace. I first met him in April 2002, at a time when the government was still intending to construct the mosque in Kambos, and few could ever imagine that such a structure would be eventually erected within Athens in Votanikos. I was following up on an article in *Eleftherotipia*, the most popular newspaper of the left at the time, that described the impoverished situation of "Greek Muslims" in Gazi—the neighborhood proposed by some MPs for the mosque. Drawing on a report produced by an NGO, the article noted:

> Without knowing how to read or, for many of them, even communicate in Greek, [they] are inevitably enclosed within Gazi's boundaries, incapable of working outside. . . . Cases of social marginalization are constantly multiplying. This is a result of unemployment, poverty, and despair. . . . Many men spend the whole day in coffeeshops. . . . The percentages of alcoholism and drug use, especially among the youth, are constantly rising. . . . Intense incidents of hostility take place among those who possess feelings of religious fanaticism and those who, in identifying Greek Muslims with foreigners, exhibit racism and xenophobia. (Skordilis 2002)

Wondering who these "Greek Muslims" were, I called the newspaper and explained the nature of my interest in the article. I was advised to get in touch with Halil-Latif, the president of Solidarity, the Muslim Association of Greece; and Ios, a group of investigative journalists with a rich archive on minorities and their treatment by the state. I called Halil-Latif that same afternoon. It was he who would eventually lead me to two other protagonists

The Visit

of the mosque debate: Dora, a university lecturer, and Gökhan, another Western Thracian community leader. Through our meetings, I came to examine how minority politics shaped approaches toward a central mosque, identify popular assumptions regarding the agents of and obstacles to government initiatives, and realize that the controversy over a nonexistent site of worship was—at least for them—more about inclusion, citizenship, and, ultimately, the practice of democracy in Greece.

The Visit

Solidarity's offices were situated on the ground floor of an apartment building in the multiethnic district of Patisia and overlooked a Pakistani masjid—a very appropriate location, I thought, for what *Eleftherotipia*'s journalists had described as a grassroots Muslim organization. I stood outside for a while ringing the bell and trying to reach Halil-Latif on the phone and was finally able to enter because someone held the door open for me as he was leaving. Cautiously, I knocked on Solidarity's door, which was soon opened by a woman wearing a black headscarf. "Good afternoon," she said, showing me in.

The office consisted of two rooms with two desks in each, several chairs, and a small sofa. "Hello, Antoniou," said Halil-Latif, who remained seated at his desk amid a cloud of smoke and refrained from introducing me to the woman working in the next room. Without giving me any time to introduce myself and my research, the president, as he was called by the woman with the headscarf, handed me a pile of documents that I "needed to study carefully" if I was to grasp the initiative's importance.

In a rather melodramatic manner Halil-Latif presented me with a chronicle of the calamities that had befallen Western Thrace and that he had somehow survived. He took pride in everything he had achieved against all odds, amid profound discrimination and "state cruelty." He had been among the few from his village to finish high school in Istanbul, where he also studied economics and political science. After his return to Western Thrace and an unsuccessful attempt to become an MP in early 1990s, he moved to Athens, where he established Solidarity. His sister had lost her Greek citizenship and stayed in Turkey, and Halil-Latif had married a Christian woman—showing his compatriots that he was a "free spirit," as he put it.

"I know exactly what you're thinking, what you really want to ask me," he continued. "'Is he Turkish, Greek, or Pomak?' thinks Antoniou now. I am

72   Chapter 3

whatever the hell I want to be: Rodhopian, European, Greek citizen, whatever I feel like."

I had been rather silent up to this point and thought that I had better say something. "I read in *Eleftherotipia* about the people in Gazi," I said, trying to avoid using any ethnic categorization.

"Yes, yes, I will call Gökhan," said Halil-Latif, then lifted the receiver and dialed a number: "How are you? . . . I'm fine too, thanks. I've got a student of mine here. He's doing research, yes, on Gazi, he's going to ring you tomorrow, ok? Sure, sure." "I've arranged for you to meet the president of the Society of Thracians, call him tomorrow," Halil-Latif said and gave me the number, which I was still trying to note down as he walked out of the office. The woman who had shown me in approached, smiled, and asked me whether I wanted coffee. I smiled back, thanked her, and started smoking. Soon we found ourselves chatting about her life in Western Thrace and her current ill health, and I felt somewhat more welcome.

Eventually the woman working in the next office, who had remained focused on her work throughout Halil-Latif's loud monologue, emerged from the pile of papers in which she had immersed herself. "I'm Dora," she said with a gentle smile, and I seized the opportunity to sit on the chair facing her desk.

"Do you work here?" I asked with some hesitation.

"As a volunteer," she rushed to clarify and informed me that she was a social scientist and the vice president of Solidarity's scientific council, that she had been working with Muslims for the last ten years and had conducted numerous interviews, and that immigrants and refugees face all sorts of problems and were daily subjected to various forms of discrimination.

"So do you rent spaces for them to use as mosques, do you organize classes for the study of the Koran, do you bring imams from Thrace, do you put pressure on the government to set land aside for a Muslim cemetery, and what about the mosque in Kambos?" I asked with excitement.

My interlocutor seemed surprised to have been asked all these questions, and with a gentle smile and shake of the head put an end to my enquiries. "As an NGO we have many activities," said Dora, "but I am mainly referring to the assistance we offer with regard to *khartia*," going on to explain how imperialist politics "have created the current situation: a humanitarian catastrophe on an almost unthinkable scale and the daily displacement of thousands of people in the Middle East and in Afghanistan."

"But what about the religious rights of the immigrants and refugees who come to Greece?" I asked.

"Solidarity supports the Muslims' right to have places of worship, a proper mosque, if that is what you are asking, and we will surely stand against the Church and the locals, even though we don't necessarily believe that Kambos is the right location. You see, it is far away from the city center and there are no Muslims living in that area—most of them reside around here and in [the suburbs of] Peristeri and Ayios Ioannis Rendis. In any case, I don't think anything will happen, because this is the sort of initiative that attracts a lot of negative publicity. 'It has political cost,' as politicians would say. But to return to our activities, let me also tell you that as a Muslim federation we participate in protests against the war in Afghanistan, antiracist festivals, and various international fora supporting the Palestinian struggle."[2]

"It's interesting that you referred to Kambos as I come from there," I told her.

"Then you know exactly what I'm talking about. Who is that person appearing on TV all the time? You know, this doctor. This is the sort of person I am talking about: fanatical, nationalist, racist, dangerous. And you know what? He is believed to represent Kambos."

"You're right," I concurred, "he does give that impression."

"You talked about several initiatives that enjoy the support of the left, and I am now tempted to ask you whether you identify yourself as a leftist," I asked.

"Oh absolutely," said Dora.

"I understand your support for the Palestinian struggle and the rights of the immigrants and refugees," I assured my interlocutor, "but then again why do you need a Muslim federation like Solidarity for this?"

"What are you getting at? Are you implying that leftists should have no respect for other people's religion?"

"But it's not about respect," I responded, "Given that you place yourself on the left, shouldn't you talk about class solidarity, workers' rights, the global proletariat, and so on? Again, why do you need to support a Muslim federation to oppose American imperialism?"

"But I do talk about class, and social marginality, and structural inequality," protested Dora, who then went on to explain how Islamophobia is a by-product of late capitalism and new forms of colonialism and therefore makes an alliance between the Left and Muslim immigrants both strategic and necessary.

"Would you ever participate in a gay pride parade as a member of Solidarity then?" I asked.

74 Chapter 3

"Personally, I wouldn't mind at all marching in a gay pride parade," answered Dora, "but it is completely misplaced on your part to expect a Muslim organization to engage in such a struggle."

The tone of the discussion had changed. Both of us were getting agitated and I felt bad for having managed to upset an important contact in our first meeting. I apologized and Dora gallantly assured me that everything was fine.

A (Personal) History

Because I found so many of Halil-Latif's remarks confusing, I began to explore the history of the "minority" in a more systematic manner and put together a list of questions: Why did Halil-Latif describe himself as European and Rodhopian but not as Greek or Turkish? Who are the Pomaks? What were the policies that made him speak of "state cruelty"? Why did he study in Turkey, and why did his sister lose her citizenship?

The literature at the time rarely drew on archival and ethnographic research,[3] relied extensively on conflicting demographic data, and posed emphatically a question that a few years later would take on a new urgency for scholars of Muslim immigrants in Greece: how many are there? Baskın Oran (1994), for example, claimed that the minority numbered 120,000 and was composed of approximately 85,000 Turks, 30,000 Pomaks, and 5,000 "Gypsies." Not surprisingly, these estimations significantly differed from those of Greek authorities, which in 1991 had counted the Muslims of Western Thrace at 98,000. Fifty percent of them were of "Turkish origin" (but not "Turks"), 35 percent were "Pomaks," and 15 percent were "Athinganoi," a neoclassical term lumping together all sort of people that seemed "Gypsy" to the state's eyes (Kostopoulos 2003:60).

Throughout the literature the Turkish element was described as predominant in Western Thrace, and yet most Greek scholars primarily focused on the Pomaks—people who inhabited the Rodhopi Mountains well before the creation of national states and spoke a language akin to Bulgarian. After the Treaty of Lausanne settled the issue of borders in the eastern Balkans, they found themselves living in territories belonging to Greece, Bulgaria, and Turkey and posing a challenge to their respective states' discourses regarding national identity—and therefore constituting a security threat. Greek officials, conditioned to loathe Bulgaria already from the late nineteenth century, feared in particular that the Pomaks would embrace communism due to their familial and linguistic connections to the neighboring country. In the aftermath of the Civil War (1946–1949), during which both the government forces and the communist rebels constantly tried to recruit the Pomaks to join their ranks (the rebels even had plans for the creation of an "Ottoman battalion"; see Featherstone et al. 2011:204–207), the state pursued a policy of "Turkifying" the Pomaks as well as the Roma. It preferred to identify the Pomaks with the Turks of Western Thrace and Turkey (which had also joined the NATO by that time) over communist Bulgaria (Brunnbauer 2001). This policy was facilitated through compulsory minority education, which was stipulated by Articles 40 and 41 of the Lausanne Treaty and now strongly promoted Turkish as the minority's lingua franca. In this way, the policy opened the way for Pomaks to pursue higher education in Turkey (Tampakis and Plati 1997:49–53) and the compulsory replacement of the term "Muslim" with "Turkish" in the names of local schools, clubs, and associations.[4] Despite the rising tension between Greeks and Turks in Cyprus as well as the outbreak of violence against the Greeks of Istanbul in 1955, the primary enemies of the state were still the communists and Warsaw Pact Bulgaria, and to a lesser extent the nominal NATO ally Turkey (Demetriou 2004:105–106).

The state pulled back on this policy of Turkification in the late 1950s when it became clear that interethnic conflict in Cyprus was spiraling out of control and that the remaining Greeks of Turkey were now emigrating to Greece in large numbers.[5] A letter that the ministry sent in 1957 to all local authorities captures an important shift in Greek minority politics: "The only right name of the minority in Western Thrace and according to article 14 of the Treaty of Sevres and 45 of Lausanne is 'Muslim minority'" (Iliadis 2013:411). From then on calling this population "Turkish," as Venizelos and so many state officials of his time used to do (Tsitselikis 2012:16), came to be seen as treasonous.

Recent research has revealed the establishment in 1959 of a secret state organization, the Coordinative Council of Thrace, controlled by the Ministry of Foreign Affairs, whose aim was to systematically undermine a Turkish identity in Western Thrace and ultimately alter the area's ethnic composition, a process that had commenced in the early 1920s with the settlement of thousands of Christian refugees in the area (Iliadis 2013). It is in this context that we should understand the gradual definition of the minority as a Muslim one comprising three categories—the "ethnic Turks," the "Pomaks," and the "Gypsies" (evident in the writings of Foreign Ministry advisors and diplomats

76   Chapter 3

such as Hidiroglou 1990 and Alexandris [1983] 1992). Even though many minority members were completely secular and had fully embraced Atatürk's modernist vision, this designation, which echoed an Ottoman religion-based understanding of identity very much present in the Treaty of Lausanne, was employed as a discursive means of severing ties between the "Pomaks" and the "Turks." These complex classificatory politics most likely explain Halil-Latif's sensitivity to categorization. Pomaks were now considered Greeks, and this even led to state-sponsored campaigns aimed at proving that they were Islamized Christians of Greek descent (Demetriou 2004:106–107).[6] To further facilitate the separation of Pomaks and Turks, the council also expanded the "military surveillance zones" originally established in 1936 to counter a possible Bulgarian invasion (Labrianidis 1990, 1999) to include most Pomak settlements and thus prevent any unregulated contact between them and Bulgarians. This was part of a new "Pomak policy," which was well known to Greek diplomats handling the Athens mosque issue. This policy included the establishment of basic infrastructure in the area, the creation of medical offices and new mosques (à la the Grande Mosquée), the promotion of Arabic as the most appropriate language for indigenous Muslims, and the creation of a network of salaried collaborators.

As for the other members of the minority, especially those who openly professed a Turkish identity, the Coordinative Council had other plans in store. Every time that Turkey would harass its citizens of Greek origin, show signs of aggression in Cyprus, or actively promote a Turkish consciousness through the activities of the Turkish consulate, the council would implement retaliatory and discriminatory measures—anything from not issuing licenses for operating tractors to property expropriations and systematic police investigations of sports clubs and professional associations (Anagnostou 1999; Brunnbauer 2001:48; Clogg 2002:206; Yağcıoğlu 2004; Iliadis 2013:411). Greece now interpreted the principle of reciprocity—so prominently featured in Article 45 of the Treaty of Lausanne and intended to protect those exempted from the exchange of populations—in the most perverse manner (Bonos 2008:363; Akgönül 2008). These practices continued even after the restoration of democracy in 1974, due to widespread and deeply embedded fears that "Turkey harbors expansionist designs against Greece" (Alexandris 2003:128) and that Western Thrace would become a "second Cyprus" (Demetriou 2004:107).[7] In 1983, after the "declaration of independence" of the Turkish Republic of Northern Cyprus, the policy of Turkification was completely reversed, and the state banned the term "Turkish" and its derivatives for referring to anything related to the minority population. Yet by that time many Pomaks had moved to urban areas and had undergone Turkish education. When a new generation of social scientists began fieldwork in the area, it quickly became clear that identities usually described as rigid and unmalleable by state actors were in fact quite situational, used strategically by minority members, and prioritized according to context (Tsibiridou 2000; Trubeta 2001; Demetriou 2004; Davis 2012; Evergeti 2006).[8] Depending on the interlocutor, "Pomaks" and "Gypsies" might well describe themselves as "Turks."

In the aftermath of the destruction of many minority-owned shops by a Greek mob mobilized by the local Orthodox bishop in January 1990, and the fear that Turkey might intervene to protect the minority, the situation in Western Thrace considerably improved.[9] Yet Greek state inconsistencies and decades of discrimination had left their mark on the minority and, together with the economic underdevelopment of the area, contributed to several temporary or permanent migrations to urban centers as well as emigration to Germany, Holland, and Turkey (Antoniou 2005:94; Notaras 1995:46).[10] The emigration trend did not go unnoticed by Turkish diplomats, who feared that if it continued, the "Turkish minority of Greece" would soon disappear and they would lose substantial leverage in their negotiations with their Greek counterparts. Thus, beginning in the 1960s, Turkey no longer provided Western Thracian immigrants with residence and work permits, making their settlement in the country extremely difficult (Aarbakke 2000:32; Alexandris [1983] 1992:315; Bahçeli 1987:112). Even though students from Western Thrace were welcome to study at Turkish high schools and universities, it was expected that they would eventually return to Greece proud of their Turkish identity.

In view of Turkey's reluctance to facilitate their permanent residence, many who went to Turkey decided to return to Greece. Some of them, however, were now categorized as "stateless" persons, including Halil-Latif's sister.[11] This was due to Article 19 of the Greek Citizenship Law of 1955, originally introduced to prevent the return of communist rebels who had found refuge in the Eastern Bloc after the Civil War and then used against minority members: "A person of non-Greek ethnic origin leaving Greece without the intention of returning may be declared as having lost Greek nationality. This also applies to a person of non-Greek ethnic origin born and domiciled abroad. His minor children living abroad may be declared as having lost Greek nationality if both parents or the surviving parent have lost the same. The Minister of the Interior decides in these matters with the concurring

78 Chapter 3

opinion of the National Council." In 1998, following years of pressure from the Council of Europe, the article was finally abolished. Yet this development did not mean much for the hundreds who had already lost their citizenship.[12]

The Manifesto

From the many documents that Halil-Latif gave me to study, it was clear that Solidarity saw itself as an organization representing all Muslims living in the country regardless of ethnic or national origin. More specifically, some of its press releases mentioned that most of its members, whose number supposedly exceeded two hundred thousand, were of Pakistani, Afghani, Bangladeshi, Egyptian, Iraqi, and Kurdish origin.

In stark contrast to what I saw on my first visit, when the woman with the headscarf constituted the only obvious sign of religiosity, Solidarity was described as a highly industrious and indeed powerful Muslim organization with extensive contacts with members of the European Parliament and international Islamic organizations such as the Muslim World League (Rabita al-alam al-islami), controlling and also in the process of establishing several masjids in Athens, organizing seminars for the study of Arabic and the Koran, bringing imams from Thrace, arranging the transportation of the deceased to Muslim cemeteries in Ksanthi and Komotini, providing legal counseling to asylum seekers, and offering food and hospitality to more than 2,500 immigrants and refugees in apartments located in Patision, Omonia, Platia Vathis, Metaxuryio, and other areas of the city center.[13]

The exaggeration evident in Solidarity's description of its membership and range of activities was also reflected in the very way these documents were written. The language was a bizarre mixture of vernacular and Foucauldian terminology—words such as "heterotopia" and "biopolitics" were used together with expressions such as "*ki omos oi Musulmani to khorevun to sirtaki*" (indeed Muslims do dance sirtaki)—which made me dwell on the possibility that Halil-Latif and Dora had coauthored the press releases.

I turned to Celia Kerslake, professor of Turkish and my thesis supervisor, for help translating an open letter addressed to "*Müslüman Kardeşlerimiz*" (Our Muslim Brothers) that Halil-Latif described as the "manifesto" and told me was distributed in thousands of copies in Athens, in Western Thrace, and also in Germany and Holland. Neither of us could have predicted that translating a single page would take so long. "The text was obviously written by a

Islam as a Path to Democracy

79

non-native speaker," said Dr. Kerslake after a minute or so. "The sentences are long, pretentious in style, difficult to follow, and, in all honesty, poorly formulated." The manifesto, it turned out, announced the establishment of Solidarity in 1997 and its aim to unite members of the minority ("regardless of ethnic origin"), side with other minorities and "all people facing problems" in Greece, fight against discrimination and economic underdevelopment, and, if necessary, appeal to European and international organizations for the protection of its members' "religious obligations in the way our exalted God demands."

It was only after several long meetings at Solidarity that I began to see any value in the "manifesto" and understand that it offered a glimpse into Halil-Latif's political cosmology. As I came to realize, hidden in long and uninviting sentences lay ideas that captured the spirit of a new era. Already in 1997, as Greece was becoming integrated into European structures, he saw the new opportunities arising as the country received thousands of immigrants and refugees classified by scholars, the press, and national and international institutions as Muslims. His vision transcended Western Thrace and Greek-Turkish animosity. It placed a rather local predicament, hardly considered by most Greeks, in an international liberal context, where religion was defended as a human right even by nonbelievers.

Preparations

In tandem with my exploration of the literature on Western Thrace and Solidarity's manifesto, I began preparing for my meeting with Gökhan, the president of the Society of Thracians, whom Halil-Latif had called during our meeting. Knowing little about his community, I first reached out to Thalia Dragona, chair of the Department of Early Childhood Education at the University of Athens, for guidance. Together with Anna Frangoudaki, from the same department, she had implemented a pioneering program in the area for the integration of Muslim children into the local school system and knew Gazi well.[14] Dragona told me that the Greek Muslims settled in the area in the late 1970s and early 1980s, when the gas plant (thus the name "Gazi") was still in operation. "Keep in mind that in those days this was one of the most polluted and downgraded neighborhoods.[15] Many people of your age only go there at night and know Gazi as a fashionable destination, full of bars and restaurants. Next time you go try to notice the people selling beers after the concerts, collecting aluminum cans from the streets, and living in the

80   Chapter 3

old houses with the satellite dishes. It was the children of these people that we tried to bring back to school. Marianna Oikonomou's film will give you a sense about their lives," she said, handing me a copy of *The School*, a 2001 documentary that examined "intercultural education" at the eighty-seventh primary school and the teachers' efforts to create a welcoming environment for local Muslim children. The documentary offered an introduction to Gazi's Muslims, presenting a community that was Roma, largely illiterate, renting old houses with yards, and living in grave poverty.

My next step was to meet with Dimitris Trimis and Tasos Kostopoulos, *Eleftherotipia*'s "Ios" columnists. They eagerly shared with me all the material they had collected over the years concerning the community: articles they had authored for various leftist newspapers and magazines (such as *Rizospastis*, *Skholiastis*, and *Prosanatolismi*), news clippings, pamphlets circulated by workers and solidarity associations, works of economic history (Petraki 1993, 1997), and even essays written by students volunteering for local organizations (such as *Nomarhiaki Epitropi Laïkis Epimorfosis*, NELE) for introductory sociology classes (Tseloni 1984).[16] As Trimis and Kostopoulos explained, these materials painted a far more complex picture of Gazi's Muslims, according to which they came for the most part from the Rodhopi prefecture in Western Thrace and began to settle in the area (in the neighborhoods of Gazi, Ruf, Keramikos, Profitis Dhaniil, and Votanikos) as early as the 1960s as part of larger internal migration movements to industrialized areas. In typical chain migration fashion, more of their co-villagers followed them in the mid 1970s. Yet few from that second wave settled in the Gazi/Votanikos area, as they tended to find employment as manual laborers in the districts of Avlona, Dhrapetsona, Tavros, Ayios Ioannis Rendi, Elefsina, Lavrio, and outside Athens in Thiva, Khalkidha, Inoi, and Inofita. This latter trend continued throughout the 1980s and picked up in 1985–1989, when the policy of *metadhimotefsi* was introduced by the alternate minister of foreign affairs Yiannis Kapsis. This policy aimed to numerically and politically weaken the minority population by encouraging their resettlement in cities outside Thrace with the promise of employment in the public sector and low-interest loans for housing (Trimis 1986; Avramopoulou and Karakatsanis 2002).

Contrary to what I had understood from *The School*, Gazi's Muslim community wasn't homogenous. It consisted in part of Turkish speakers who, at least to their observers, seemed more secular and integrated into metropolitan life (authors would often stress that some of these Muslims lived in apartments and dressed in "European" fashion), as well as another community, often described as "Turkish gypsies" by the first group, who were much poorer and conservative, but, to some social scientists, appeared equally uninterested in religion.[17] "If religious identity is not important to them, why are they described as Muslims and involved in discussions about the mosque?" I asked Trimis and Kostopoulos, who explained that the use of the category seemed to be the only kind of identity marker on which members of this diverse community could agree (having rejected the labels "Greek" and "Turk"). As for the mosque, they continued, they agreed with the Sinaspismos parliamentarians, who had proposed that it be established in Gazi, a central and convenient location, even though, Kostopoulos pointed out, "for such a structure to be built it will take years, *many years*. This is an issue for us to discuss, but not a priority for the government. If there is some reaction, it [i.e., the endeavor] will instantly stop and Muslims will remain without a mosque."

"Why is this issue important to you?" I followed up. "Why does *Eleftherotipia* publish so many articles on the mosque and the situation of 'Greek Muslims'?" (In fact, it had published more articles on Muslim immigrants, their living situation, and the mosque controversy than any other Greek newspaper; see Triandafyllidou and Gropas 2009:967.) "Why do groups primarily defined by religion manage to attract the attention of a newspaper of the left?"

"It is surely not a common belief in the necessity of religion," Trimis rushed to reply, and explained how the systematic persecution of the Greek Left for decades had created "a powerful collective memory that is nowadays recognizable in the form of support for every individual or community mistreated by a state that remains nationalistic to this day." He also reflected on how Greek anti-Americanism in the past had often created sympathies for various Islamic movements, and mentioned the late prime minister Andreas Papandreou's support of the Palestinian struggle and Muammar Qaddafi in Libya.[18] Ultimately, and on this issue Trimis and Kostopoulos were adamant, the issue of the mosque and any discussion of the lives of Muslims in Greece is intimately connected to questions about what it means to be Greek today, basic rights, and democratic governance.

Meeting with Gökhan

It was only when I went to meet Gökhan in Gazi that I noticed the Turkish graffiti on walls and benches and the old houses with the enormous satellite dishes. Gökhan came almost half an hour late on a Vespa that looked like it

Figure 8. Gentrified Gazi 2024: Remnants of a refugee house with a satellite dish. Author's photograph.

was about to fall apart and was producing noise completely disproportionate to its size. "Get on," he said, "let's go to the coffee shop, it's my treat!"

"If you've had coffee already you should get a beer," said Gökhan, when we reached our destination.

"*Olabilir* (that's possible)," I replied, in a clumsy attempt to show that I spoke some Turkish. "Perhaps Halil-Latif has already told you that I'm a student, studying Muslims in Athens. I want to talk to you about this neighborhood, yourself, the Society of Thracians, the masjids, the mosque in Kambos."

"Bravo, bravo," said Gökhan. "Antoniou, I am an open man with nothing to hide."

"An interview? An interview?" Gökhan was asked by a man from the next table.

"Go fuck yourself," said my host, and then turned to me with a big smile: "We are all friends here!"

"Let's talk about the mosque," I said, after a short pause.

"We don't have one, don't you know that?" answered Gökhan immediately.

"What about a masjid then," I followed up. "Is the Society planning to establish one?"

"Antoniou, listen, we are poor people. I am the most educated here because I finished primary school and work in the public sector. Where are we going to find the money for rent, water, electricity?"

"What about the new one in Kambos? Would you go to it?" I asked.

"Do not believe them!" said Gökhan. "Nothing will happen. There will be some fuss, the TV channels will gather, and the politicians will get scared.

After all, how are we going to get there? A journalist from ANTENA [a TV station] asked me the same question some months ago and I told him that it's a cemetery that we need more than a mosque, so that we don't pay money all the time in transportation [i.e., to cemeteries in Western Thrace]."

"I was told that Solidarity has set up many masjids in Athens. Why don't you go to one of those?"

"It's not the same," said Gökhan, "we are not the same, you know. Antoniou, they are Pomaks, they have dealings with the Arabs."

This was an answer I had not anticipated, and in an attempt to keep the discussion going I told Gökhan that the next round was on me and that I was not going to take no for an answer.

"Bravo, bravo," said Gökhan, "you're a good kid, you come from a good family, I can tell!"

"How did you come to Athens?" I asked.

He answered at length:

I came to Athens in 1985, when I was twenty-five. Before that I was living in Gümülcine [Komotini], where I grew up. At that time, I had economic problems. I had worked for many years with other Muslims as a sailor, but I was tired of it. Fortunately, in 1985 I was approached by people working for the social services, who told us they could find a job for us in Athens, in the public sector. I had nothing to lose, so I came with my family. I was hired as a porter in a branch of the National Bank of Greece, where I work to this day. I was clever. Others from Gümülcine who were also offered jobs decided not to come to Athens. They were too afraid that they would have to wear a cross, that they would become Christians. I was not afraid of that. I knew from the very beginning that this would not happen. I was telling them, "Aren't we Greek citizens? Why should we be afraid?" When I went back to Gümülcine the next summer, all these people found out not only that I was still a Muslim, but also that I had a good job and that I had bought an apartment with an interest-free loan from the government. Of course, I was not the only one offered a job in the public sector. Many of my friends also found jobs in banks, hospitals, etc. When other people in Gümülcine found out that we have a good life here, they decided to move to Athens too. But they could not find jobs. So they moved to these old houses. They were stupid. . . . They did not say "yes" from the

84 Chapter 3

very beginning. Now they complain. They say to me, "You have a job, a big apartment, you're rich." And I reply, "You morons. The state fucked [i.e., assisted] once and it's not going to be fucking forever."

I continued to visit the area and meet with Gökhan and many others regularly for several months, and throughout this time the community of Gazi never appeared particularly religious to me. I was thus surprised to read, a year after that first meeting with Gökhan, an article published in the Turkish newspaper *Zaman* about the proposed mosque in Kambos and the religious life of the Gazi migrants, who were portrayed as suffering from the lack of a Muslim infrastructure. The article described residents as Muslims and incorporated interviews on the problems they face in their daily practice of Islam and their religious dependence on Western Thrace and Turkey:

> Because there is no imam to perform the funeral rituals, our deceased have been traveling an 800-kilometer distance to Gümülcine or to Iskece [Xanthi] for years. . . . There is no one who would teach our religion to our children. I know two *suras* [chapters of the Koran], that is all I grew up with, my children perhaps know one. But their children neither know Turkish nor their religion. We bought books from Turkey with our own money and we made photocopies, but it is not enough. . . . Nowadays we only listen to the Glorious Koran from cassettes, because we do not know how to read it. We also chant the *Mevlid* using cassettes that we bring from Turkey.[19] (Arslan 2003)

When I spoke to Gökhan about the article and enquired about the identity of the journalist's informant, he suggested that I not pay any particular attention. "*Ase re Dimitri ke mia kuvenda na tin pari o aeras*" (Let it go, Dimitris, just some words in the wind).

The Documentary

When I visited Solidarity's offices for the second time, the small apartment was now full of people waiting to meet with Halil-Latif. After almost an hour, everyone else had left and I approached Halil-Latif's desk. He said he had had a long day and that the situation with the immigrants in Athens was getting out of control. I myself was tired, it was getting late, and I didn't pay much attention to these words at first. I told him that I had studied the documents that he had given me during the first meeting and also that I had translated the manifesto into English.

"Good, good," said Halil-Latif, "So what do you want?"

"I would like to talk to you about the challenges posed by Muslim immigration to Greece. Do you think, for instance, that the provisions of the Treaty of Lausanne might be used by immigrants in the future? Should indigenous Muslims have a say in the administration of Islam in the capital city? If, let's say, a mosque is finally built, do you think that prayer should be led by a Western Thracian imam [as was the case in Rhodes and Kos]?"

"Antoniou, are you completely insane? Who do you think we are? You talk to me as if I am Osama bin Laden!"

"So have you never thought about these issues?" I asked again.

"Come to your senses, my boy," he replied and offered me a cigarette.

Given Halil-Latif's reaction to my framing of him as a Muslim activist, I was somewhat surprised when, two days later, I read an *Eleftherotipia* article presenting Solidarity's president as the founder of the first mosque in Athens and solely dedicated to the creation of religious infrastructure for both indigenous and immigrant Muslims. At a time when discussions of the capital's mosque were quite intense, the implications of the article were clear: if the state hesitated to fulfill its own legislation, Muslim organizations would take matters into their own hands and, as in the case of Solidarity, convert of a three-story building into a center with a masjid, a library with "books on the history and theology of Islam," and classrooms for learning Greek and Turkish. While Halil-Latif was the article's most prominent figure (he was photographed wearing a skullcap and praying next to young Muslims), Dora was also mentioned. As a social scientist and head of Solidarity's scientific council, said the authors, she works with seventeen other Christian volunteers to help Muslims with the many pressing legal, social, economic, and educational issues that they faced.

After the article's publication, both Halil-Latif and Dora began appearing on TV to comment on Muslim immigrants and the making of a mosque in Athens. In those panels they would usually be asked to converse with ultra-Orthodox activists and priests, who would claim that a mosque in the capital city would be a sign of the country's Islamization and a hotbed of terrorism. An argument would usually ensue. Within a few months they had become publicly recognizable figures—a great advantage, I realized, to my

86 Chapter 3

own research. Entering the public sphere gave them access to church officials (Halil-Latif even met with the archbishop), community leaders, government representatives, journalists, and researchers—contacts that they happily shared with me. Yet I had something to offer in return, especially when the making of a mosque in Athens acquired an international dimension.

More specifically, a few months before the Olympic Games, in May 2004 I received an unexpected phone call from Steven, a friend from college, who had embarked on a career in journalism and now worked freelance for various news agencies. "There is a lot of interest in the situation of Muslims in Athens. Your research is really 'hot' now," he said. "To get to the point, I have been asked by Mark [a well-known Australian journalist] to help him with a documentary on Islam in Athens. I want you to help us contact the right people."

With a certain feeling of guilt, I told Steven that the Muslims I knew weren't many and that I had been mainly studying the debate over the making of a mosque, and I suggested that he contact Halil-Latif and Gökhan.

Less than a month later I received a copy of the documentary. Right at the beginning the Australian journalist tells viewers that they will be given a tour of the rough neighborhoods of Athens and the underground mosques that tourists never see, and that they will be introduced to immigrants who have been working on the various construction sites during the months preceding the Olympic Games' opening ceremony on August 13. "Greek immigration laws are so tough," Mark reports, "that it is almost impossible for these people to be given a Greek passport. They are expected to work for low wages and they will always be denied citizenship because of their Muslim faith." Over images of a baptism ceremony in an Orthodox chapel, the narrator continues: "In Greece the Church is an all-powerful organization dictating the state's attitude towards foreigners and other religions. Yet Islam is not completely unknown to present-day Greece," he says, as a Pomak village in Rodhopi appears on the screen. A woman in a headscarf is shown helping her husband harvest tobacco. "This is a dying industry, and for many years locals who suffered decades of discrimination had no option but to emigrate to Turkey or search for a better life in the center of Athens."

At that moment Halil-Latif appears on screen walking the streets of Omonia and greeting immigrants. He is described as a man "building bridges between the people of Thrace and the Muslim immigrants." The views he expresses perfectly fit the journalist's attempts to underline the backwardness of the Greek Church and the state's fears of Islamic fundamentalism. Solidarity's president says that the government has tried to keep Muslims in

Islam as a Path to Democracy

ghettos, out of public sight, and conveniently confined to particular areas of the capital where they can be controlled. Yet this plan was doomed to failure since, he estimates, the capital's Muslim population exceeds 450,000, out of which 200,000 pray on a daily basis.

"[It is] a sensitive demographic," says Mark, that Greece "tries to ignore."

At that point the mosque issue is introduced. After a short appearance by the doctor mentioned by Dora in our meeting, who shows the journalist a white metal cross that he has erected on top of the hill where the Kambos mosque was supposed to be built, Halil-Latif is shown standing in Monastiraki Square in front of Tzistarakis *dzami*. "This belongs to my grandfather," says Halil-Latif, "and it has now been reduced to a museum of ceramic art." Like many Turkish journalists who emphasized the existence of an Ottoman architectural heritage in Athens (cf. Batur 2003; Kırbaki 2003; *Hürriyet* 2003), he too suggests that Ottoman mosques be used instead of erecting a central one hidden in the suburbs. He also claims that the Church was responsible for the project's nonmaterialization and that a mosque in the city's outskirts would be too far away for Muslims to use. The twenty-five-minute documentary comes to an end with Halil-Latif showing the journalist a coffee shop that he had opened some years ago in central Athens but had to close because of his daily mistreatment by the police. "Now," he says, "I am using this space to store copies of the Glorious Koran that I receive from the cultural center of the Iranian embassy in Athens." He opens one copy and chants a sura. He then closes the holy book, kisses the cover and in a sign of devotion touches it with his forehead.

"Despite all he has suffered," Mark narrates, "Halil-Latif remains a peaceful man. But is this also going to be the case with the next generation of Greek Muslims?"

To my disappointment, Gökhan and his disarming honesty make no appearance. Steven later told me that the crew did not find his appearance to be adequately Muslim.

The next day I called Halil-Latif. "I saw the documentary," I said without losing any time introducing myself.

"Was it good?" he asked.

"You never told me that you don't want the mosque to be built in Kambos," I complained.

"In any case it's not going to happen, there are reactions," he replied, and continued: "This time I did not restrain myself and talked about the Church too. There is no hope with [Archbishop] Christodoulos. When he opens his mouth, politicians lose votes! You know what these people want, Dimitri? They want Halil-Latif to keep his mouth shut, and now they will try to punish me for having said all this on a foreign channel!"

I did not want to enquire about my interlocutor's enemies—we had discussed this in the past without reaching any agreement. "In any case," I said, "I have to congratulate you! You looked very Muslim!"

"What did you expect?" Halil-Latif asked.

Over Ouzo

In January 2006 I met Yiannis Kapsis, the PASOK minister who had conceived of and implemented *metadhimotefsi*. Kapsis had published a memoir revisiting his work as a journalist and a politician, which I had read and was carrying with me. When we met at Brasserie, a busy spot in central Athens only a few hundred meters away from the Ministries of Press and Foreign Affairs, he was in fine spirits. Kapsis introduced me to his company, and when they left he suggested that we conduct the interview "over ouzo." I explained to him that almost all academic and journalistic discussions of the Athens mosque mention Western Thrace, and that his name had come up in several discussions I had about the Gazi community. Without hesitation Kapsis admitted that *metadhimotefsi* was his idea, which he didn't at all regret. As he put it, the poorest members of the minority population were subject to exploitation by Greek and Turkish mafias and were better off leaving Thrace. For him this was a humanitarian policy and he vehemently denied the accusation that it was meant to weaken the minority population. "Did you ever talk to these people?" he asked me. "You should visit the Thracians in Dhrapetsona. All of them still vote in Western Thrace! What are you talking about?"

Listening to him recounting his time as the alternate minister of foreign affairs, it quickly became clear how knowledgeable he was of the mosque issue and how much minority politics in Western Thrace had shaped institutional approaches to the initiative. It wasn't only that diplomats handled both issues ("all these people are friends, they talk to each other, they work on the same floors at the Ministry"), knew that a mosque in Athens could serve Thracian Muslims, and were consulted by civil servants and municipal authorities on this potentially "sensitive issue." The making of a central mosque clearly reflected the idea that promoting Islam over Turkishness was patriotic and, in particular, that Arab involvement in domestic Muslim affairs would keep Turks at bay. Preventing Turkey's involvement in the country's religious affairs was for Kapsis a key objective of Greek foreign policy that would take considerable time and effort to be achieved, since the connections between Turkey and local Muslims run deep—"you should read the Treaty of Athens, which acknowledges the jurisdiction of the Ottoman Sheikh ul-Islam over Greece," he suggested.[20]

"Why was the Kambos mosque not built?" "Why is the government making plans for a mosque in Votanikos?" I asked Kapsis, and he immediately laughed. As with all my interlocutors, to him the answer was obvious. Seasoned in Greek politics, he remarked that such an endeavor is not about Muslims and Islam, but rather about (both domestic and international) power struggles and publicity opportunities. "Everyone enters this debate with his own agenda," he said.

I left the lunch wondering what Halil-Latif's, Dora's, and Gökhan's agendas were. My meetings with them, which continued once I began collaborating with Samir and Hassan on the Church project, were full of moments of awkwardness, disappointment, and confusion, and instances when Halil-Latif and Gökhan simply did not appear as "Muslim" as I would have expected—something that at the time caused me significant frustration. In retrospect, however, I could recognize that the central issue was not whether Halil-Latif, Dora, and Gökhan presented themselves in a selective manner and whether their actions perfectly corresponded to their discourses. Rather, it was what "Islam," "Muslim," and "mosque" signified, their frustration with the fact that the rights of non-Christians depended on assessments of political cost, and whether they could have entered public discourse to address larger issues of citizenship, justice, and democratic governance outside of a Muslim identity or framework. Would Halil-Latif have appeared in the Australian documentary had he only been described as an activist fighting for equal opportunities and the integration of immigrants? Would Gökhan ever have given a TV interview had he not been identified by *Eleftherotipia* as a "Greek Muslim" suffering from discrimination due to his religious identity? Would Dora have attracted the same kind of attention if her research did not focus on "Muslim" immigration and social marginality?

The story of the documentary is instructive in this regard as it shows the snowball effect of publicity: someone is quoted in a newspaper who then becomes the subject of anthropological research and then a protagonist in an Australian documentary. Yet the very same documentary also reveals the economy of stereotypes on which news production and, as we will see, state decision-making are based. Mark did not have the time or interest to question the main analytic category that he employed nor to examine the many affiliations of his informants. His documentary was about Muslims in Greece, and all those participating had to reinforce the stability of this identity through specific performances and a series of well-organized shots: Halil-Latif standing in front of the mosque, greeting immigrants in the dirty streets of Athens, and reciting the Koran and kissing it at the very end. As for Gökhan, he simply did not look Muslim enough to be included.

Throughout all of this, my persistent question "Why was the Kambos mosque not built?" is usually met first with an exasperated smile. I seem to be enquiring over the obvious. Like the Middle East expert, Samir, Hassan, and George Papandreou, Halil-Latif, Dora, and Gökhan imagined a hesitant state impeded by anticipated reactions. Halil-Latif referred to the role of the Orthodox Church, which he perceived as a powerful organization, capable of blocking the decisions of a democratically elected government. Had the Church so wished, the mosque in Kambos would have been a reality, he suggests in the documentary. Dora accuses both the Church and the locals as represented by the doctor on TV, whereas Gökhan alludes to a fear of politicians over "fusses," a term that in this context describes local reactions featured on TV. It is to these broadly shared ideas about the reasons behind the nonmaterialization of this government initiative that I turn to in the second part of *Why Not Build the Mosque?*—the role of the locals, the position of the Orthodox Church, and the notion of political cost.

PART II

Answers

CHAPTER 4

The Locals

Kambos

Up until the parliament approved the construction of an "Islamic Cultural Center" in Kambos on June 20, 2000, and the "locals" started to be discussed in newspaper articles and television panels as uniformly opposed to the project, public interest in the town was limited. Even when the controversy broke out, not much was said about the history and identity of Kambos. For most Athenians it was merely a village in the city's outskirts with fine retsina and picturesque tavernas. Locals, of course, saw themselves differently, as members of one of the most prosperous towns in Attica,[1] and they would say with pride in the *platia* (square) that Kambos was wealthier than nearby Merenda, Viethi, and, most certainly, Viliza.[2] There is some truth to these beliefs. Decades of work in the vineyards, the area's fine climate, and extensive endogamy had created powerful families who controlled vast areas of land. By the late 1950s most *dopii* (locals) were related to one another and owners of substantial property Their wealth explains how the town's cathedral was painted by Greece's finest (and most expensive) iconographer; why Ernst Ziller, the patriarch of neoclassical architecture in Greece, was involved in the restoration of its dome after a cataclysmic rain in August 1915; and why some of the city's youth pursued university education in Graz, Aachen, and Bochum in the 1960s and 1970s, when many Greeks lived in poverty.[3]

The air of cosmopolitanism brought to the town during the summer months, when these students would return from abroad dressed in bell-bottoms, miniskirts, and colorful shirts, didn't make the town any less conservative. When it came to politics, the town overwhelmingly supported the Right, the royal family, and, in the late 1960s, the military dictatorship. These political preferences are to this day reflected in the streets named either after locals who died in military campaigns, royalty (e.g., Vasileos Pavlu, Dhiadhokhu Konstantinu, Vassilisis Fridherikis), or dictators (e.g., Ioannou Metaxa). As older people sometimes say among themselves in bitterness, many of those who now criticize the 1967 junta had shouted that year at Easter, *Khristos anesti, i Ellas anesti* (Christ is risen, Hellas is risen).[4] They also recall the great ceremony that the municipality organized in honor of the dictator Stylianos Pattakos, who visited the town in the spring of 1973 and was welcomed by hundreds of people as well as the town's first mayor; the director of customs; and a war hero, the late Dimitris Antoniou, my grandfather. Pattakos had promised that Kambos would finally be connected to the capital's water network, and this indeed happened. Meanwhile, the town had recently been upgraded to a more significant administrative unit with a new library, new premises for the scientists' club, and many asphalt roads, and it proudly held the Dhimosthenia, a local festival in honor of Demosthenes, who also originated from the area. For the local intelligentsia, there was no question that Kambos had to reconnect to the classical past through a festival celebrating the great orator. Such an initiative, however, was the result of a process that had commenced decades earlier.

In 1915 local teachers, priests, and doctors had successfully petitioned the state's Commission for the Toponyms of Greece to replace their village's Albanian name with that of Demosthenes's ancient hometown.[5] In this way they took it upon themselves to Hellenize the area and thus conceal the fact that the village's knowledge of the Greek language was fairly recent and that they themselves were Arvanites, descendants of Christian clans from Epirus that had settled in Attica between the fourteenth and sixteenth centuries, who spoke Arvanitika, an Albanian dialect.[6] The advent of national education in the area had facilitated linguistic integration into the Greek nation-state, but to my grandfather's mind there was more to be done. He thought that Arvanitika should not be spoken (at least not in the presence of outsiders) for *ethnikus loghus* (reasons of national interest).[7] For him this dialect represented a troubling knowledge, and its use could be misinterpreted by those who were not aware that "Arvanitika-speaking populations did not see language as a defining criterion of their Greek identity and that their sense of identity relied upon their adherence to the Greek Orthodox Church, their sense of localism with ties to the land and their sense of kinship" (Gefou-Madianou 1999:420).

At the same time, amateur historians also attempted to create an appropriate local history for Kambos that would firmly correspond to state narratives

Figure 9. Dhimosthenia, 1973 (Dimitris Antoniou is in the back row, second from the right, and Stylianos Pattakos is in the middle row, literally on the far right). Author's personal archive.

of continuity with ancient Greece by manufacturing connections between an idealized classical past and a more recent revolutionary one. In this context, the etymology of Albanian toponyms was challenged. Georgios Hatzisotiriou (1973:311), a doctor with an interest in local history and folklore, argued that those connecting the village's old name to the Albanian term *liopa* (cow) or to a prominent member of a clan carrying that name should also consider the alternative Greek etymology *iliu opsis* (a place facing the sun). It was the same man who some years before had published a monograph on the contribution of a local Arvanitika-speaking warlord, Yiannis Davaris, to the Greek War of Independence and his involvement in the Acropolis siege (Hatzisotiriou 1971, 1973). The times in which the two local heroes Demosthenes and Davaris lived are separated by over two thousand years. However, this did not prevent the celebration of both men's memory as if they were outcomes of a single historical continuum. Local discourses, as Herzfeld (1987:93) puts it, "encapsulate and exploit history for their own strategic ends," and in this case they never allowed for the open discussion of obvious questions: how was it

96 Chapter 4

possible for the local warlord to forget the language of the great orator and what had transpired in the years separating the two men?[8]

History (actual or imaginary) aside, the capital's growth eventually did reach Kambos. By the 1990s land belonging to the established families was transformed into desirable real estate, and many locals made substantial profit by selling property. The cultivation of the land was gradually abandoned and *dopii* maintained only a few vineyards to which the older generation was attached. Those who had any property left had good reason to hope that it would be expropriated by the government for the construction of *Attiki Odhos*, the new expressway connecting the airport to the suburb of Elefsina, offering remunerations of €100,000 per *stremma* (1,000 square meters). It was thus only a matter of time before daily jobs were abandoned and many locals could focus solely on hunting, betting, and watching soccer.

Despite its rapid and often anarchic development, Kambos kept some of its old charms intact. The town's center had beautiful houses with big gardens, wide roads with trees on both sides, and hardly any traffic. Many intellectuals and artists had settled in the surrounding hills: Vassilis Fotopoulos (who won an Oscar for set design for *Zorba the Greek*), Fleri Dantonaki (the favorite singer of composer Manos Hatzidakis), two prominent art collectors, Dr. Kalfas (the personal physician of Haile Selassie), and two renowned British horticulturalists studying Mediterranean flora. All of this gave Kambos a certain touch of cosmopolitanism and constituted yet another source of local pride.

For some Athenians these features made the town an ideal residential location, and they started settling in the area. They bought property on Kambos's periphery, but only a few managed to mix with the *dopii*. It was only those of a certain financial standing or those who married locals who managed to penetrate the town's microcosm. Their settlement continues to this day, and it is now believed that they have come to outnumber the "indigenous" population. Even though children of both groups attend the same schools the *dopii–kseni* (outsiders) divide remains. *Kseni* own property in the area and return to Kambos after their day jobs, but their connection to the town, their contacts with its people, and most importantly their appearances in the *platia* are limited.

The subtleties of local life were of course unknown to the press, including Richard Galpin from the BBC, who, on an early afternoon in July 2003, when the mosque issue was being discussed with particular intensity on Greek TV, decided to embark on a trip to meet the locals. When he finally arrived in

Kambos he found the *platia* empty and the few coffee-shop patrons reluctant to talk to a journalist. Within a few days a long article appeared on the BBC website relating the story of the proposed mosque: "[Kambos] is an unremarkable place, and an air of boredom hangs over the central square." Galpin then goes on to cite the mayor, who claimed that "almost 100% of the population here is opposed to the mosque."

This certainty over the content of Kambos's public opinion, based at best on information retrieved over the course of a couple of hours in its central square, was indeed representative of national and international beliefs concerning local stances to the mosque. In addition to the Middle East expert, Dora, Samir, and most journalists, scholars writing on the issue also reproduced media depictions of Kambos as a site of resistance and often referred to the negative role of the locals and their mayor, whose reactions "took the form of protection of local identity against Islamic invasion" (Roussos 2010–2011:159; and similarly Angelidhis 2011:70; Methenitis 2015:63; Rikou 2008:122; Skoulariki 2009, 2010:306). In the aftermath of 9/11 it seemed perfectly reasonable that, as in so many other places in the world featured in the literature on mosque controversies (e.g., Allievi 2009; Cesari 2005; Dunn 2005; Eade 1996; Landman and Wessels 2005), the Christian population of a small town would react to the project with exclusionary understandings of the nation and a distorted image of the impending structure informed by the globally circulating imagery of Islamic radicalism. At the time of my fieldwork, in particular, the media would often cite the local bishop Agathonikos (more on him in Chapter 5), whose sermons on the impending structure supposedly captured local imagination. His descriptions of the "Islamic Center" were first presented in the local press but soon enough were reproduced by national and international media as representative of local fears of a gigantic mosque built on top of a hill (with the Arvanitic name Housmouza), dominating the landscape with its minarets and giving tourists landing in the nearby Athens airport the impression that Kambos and Greece are now Muslim.[9]

In this second part of the book, I delve deeper into the public history of the state's attempt to construct a central mosque in Kambos and investigate the three main assumptions regarding the project's failure that my interlocutors have previously identified: local resistance, church opposition, and political cost. By following this line of inquiry I will not only answer why this particular mosque was never built but also, in the conclusion, why the mosque in Votanikos was, and, ultimately, reflect on what it takes for things to happen in Greece. Like the journalists, I start my research in Kambos's

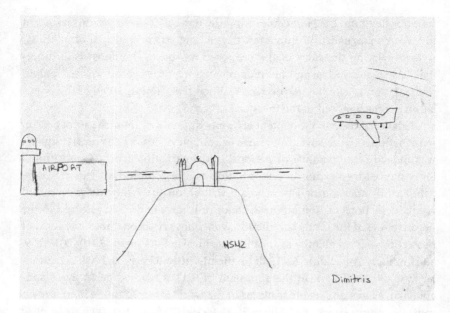

Figure 10. My drawing of the mosque in Kambos—a clumsy attempt to depict local opposition.

platia, to examine the locals' opposition to the mosque and whether they imagined it through the lens of radical Islam. I first consider what kind of insight into local attitudes the *platia* provides. Then I explore how friends, family, and coffee-shop patrons think about the controversy, using drawings that I asked them to produce of the notional mosque.[10] I gave participants a blank piece of paper (except when I only had sticky notes or napkins on hand) and a blue pen and asked them to sketch Kambos's mosque. Despite some initial reluctance related to a lack of confidence in their artistic abilities and skepticism over the effective translation of mental images into sketches, everyone I asked eventually produced a drawing. Ultimately, one hundred locals participated in what they saw as a "fun" activity and, in my eyes, was the communal production of meaning.[11]

Out of this investigation, a rather different picture of Kambos emerges. The eight drawings that I present, along with their corresponding ethnographic episodes, challenge key assumptions regarding local imagination and stances toward the mosque. Most important, they shed light on the processes by which local and national governments assess popular resistance and

The Locals 99

potential political consequences, and the ways that such assessments produce what come to be seen as unquestionable "facts."

The Square and the Cafés

At the level of both geography and popular conception the *platia* constitutes the epicenter of socialization, the place where the heart of the town beats, where contact is facilitated, business deals are made, and news is exchanged. If something is discussed there, it is de facto public, and it is then only a matter of time before an exchange among coffee-shop patrons reaches a great many households. What seems to be a simple act of having a coffee or a drink is actually in many ways an act of "deep play." Locals tend to be careful as to how they behave, what they say, and what they wear, for they know that any divergence from social norms defining proper public conduct and appearance, any careless utterance, any peculiar look might be discussed and judged by their fellow locals.[12]

Like most cafés in Greece, those in Kambos serve coffee during the day and alcohol at night. In other words, what transforms a café into a bar is the transition from day to night, as well as the customers' mood (in the sense that one can order cognac or *tsipuro*[13] even in the morning, and indeed many do). Local practices have assigned specific hours of operation to some of these establishments and almost twenty-four-hour service to some others. In this sense, Ora (Time), the café that the town's youth frequented the most during my fieldwork, witnesses a continuous circulation of customers from 10 a.m. until roughly 2 a.m. Other cafés, however, like Epimelos (Diligently), Belier, and Noby, are popular in the morning among older male patrons and almost empty in the evening. Sinandisi (Meeting), a café-restaurant, and Selini (Moon), a café-bakery, are particularly popular among families, who spend significantly less time there than regular coffee-shop patrons. In this sense, going to Belier at 10 p.m. might well constitute a definitive statement. Some people visit different cafés at different times of the day or simply move from one place to another. When night falls, the human geography of these establishments changes drastically. Younger people who still have to return home at a reasonable hour leave, while others who only go out at night make their appearance.

The coffee shops in Kambos (and indeed in many other areas) implement a policy of segregation seldom noticed by their Greek patrons, which greatly impacts the *platia*'s human geography. In the late 1990s the prospect of having

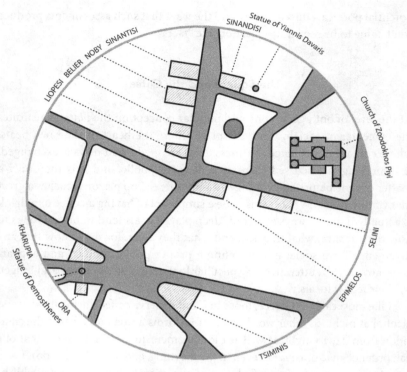

Figure 11. Kambos's *platia*.

to serve coffee and drinks to Albanian immigrants who had settled in the area terrified many owners. The immigrants were people of modest means working on construction sites and in the fields, who lacked both the clothing and the manners of locals and were conceived of as a potential threat to customers. "You have not seen them drunk," I was told by a coffee-shop owner once when I noticed that he wouldn't take an order from two Albanians. "If I serve them, tomorrow they will come with all their friends harassing the girls and trying to pick fights. What would I do then?" he asked me. "Should I call you, perhaps?" This exchange made me further investigate the issue, and to my surprise I discovered that almost every single coffee-shop owner had developed elaborate techniques to discourage Albanians from entering his shop. Sometimes they were overcharged, sometimes their orders were desperately delayed, and in some extreme cases they were bluntly asked to drink their coffee and leave. These harsh attitudes changed over time as the second generation of Albanians made a careful appearance in the town's *platia* and usually in the company of Greek friends. Their fathers, however, hardly ever frequent coffee shops such as Ora, Belier, and Epimelos and are served only by the more traditional *kafenia*, like Tsiminis and Kharupia, establishments where alcohol is consumed from early in the morning, which mainly cater to the needs of construction workers and old men playing *prefa*[14] and have now installed large TVs for watching soccer matches.

Nikos

Among the first to participate in my research was Nikos, a university student whom I met by chance in Noby one early morning. It so happened that he sat next to me at the bar while I was discussing soccer with the barista. This, as I soon realized, must have been a favorite topic of discussion for Nikos, who had a lot to contribute concerning referees, the fact that both Panathinaïkos and AEK, two of the capital's most popular clubs, use the same stadium, and also that Olimbiakos, the soccer club of Piraeus, enjoys "privileged support from the state."

This was a discussion that I could not maintain for long, and when the opportunity appeared I enquired about his studies and his family. As I found out, Nikos was a graduate student of business administration whose parents had moved to Kambos only a few years ago.

"What about you?" he asked.

I live abroad, I responded, currently writing a thesis on the mosque in Kambos; I went on to inform him that I was intending to collect as many mosque drawings as possible. Would you like to sketch one? I asked with some hesitation.

"Sure," said Nikos and started drawing from the upper left side toward the bottom, then to the right, and then up again. He paused for a moment and then brought the process to an end by sealing the sketch with what appeared to me to be a lid. Within a minute or so, he had managed to produce a slightly disfigured rectangle.

It seemed to me that Nikos didn't wish to spend much time remembering or imagining a mosque. What was the drawing's message? Did it reveal a lack of interest in my research or a lack of basic knowledge of Muslim architecture? Was this a failure of execution, as was perhaps the case with my own drawing, or a failure of imagination?

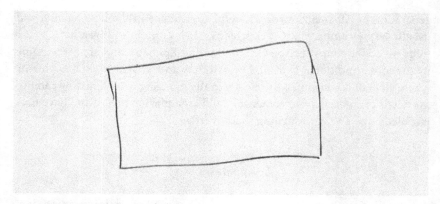

Figure 12. Nikos's drawing.

When, some moments later, I asked Nikos whether he had ever seen a mosque in his life, he responded that he had certainly seen one but had forgotten what it looked like.

"Have you heard anything about the mosque that the government is planning to build here?" I asked, trying to start a conversation.

"I think my dad mentioned something, but I didn't pay much attention. I don't have time for these things."

Among Cousins

During fieldwork in Kambos I was able to reconnect with many cousins and friends whom I had not seen for some time. Twenty-year-old Kalomira, a distant cousin of mine and a server at Epimelos, was one of them. The coffee shop where she worked was usually busy until noon, and when one day I made an unexpected appearance around 3 p.m. I found myself the only customer, and Kalomira very happy to see me. "*Ela re manari mu pu ise?*" (Come on, my *manari*,[15] where are you these days?), she greeted me in a playful manner and as only Arvanites would.

"I'm here, *moi dioloth*,"[16] I responded, picking up the joke and using the few Arvanitic words I knew. I sat by the bar, ordered coffee, and we started chatting about our families before I told her about my research on the mosque." My reference to "research" caught Kalomira's attention.

"That's fucking awesome (*ghamato!*)," she said. "When I get my degree, I want to do research too."

"So what about if you help me with my project," I said, seizing the opportunity, "and you give me an interview."

"What would I have to do?" asked Kalomira.

"Let's start with your thoughts on this whole 'mosque issue,'" I said, trying to sound relaxed and informal.

After some deliberation, Kalomira replied that she had heard some "bad things" about it.

"Like?" I asked.

"Well, that they're going to make a mosque around here . . . that immigrants are going to settle and that this will create problems," she replied.[17]

"But many immigrants have already settled in the area," I reminded her, and gave her an example: "On my street alone there is an Egyptian family, and I know many Pakistanis who work in the fields or in greenhouses in Merenda. They have been around for some time without creating any problem so far. On the contrary. . . . The fact that they don't appear in the square doesn't necessarily mean that they don't exist." I continued with yet another question: "If some immigrants have decided to live in Kambos, shouldn't they have the right to a mosque?"

Kalomira seemed to deliberate over it. "I guess if I were in their position I would like to have a church." She paused once again. "Damn, I haven't thought at all about this issue," confessed my cousin, somewhat embarrassed, and I felt bad for having put her in a difficult position.

"What about if you draw me a mosque?" I said, and offered her paper and a pen.

"Yeah, sure, I'll do one," she replied hesitantly. "It's just that, you know, I can't think of one right now."

"Just draw whatever comes to mind," I insisted.

"In any case it's going to look stupid," warned my cousin, and drew a simple block structure with four windows and a door.

Some days later I showed this sketch, along with some others that I had collected, to one of my local mentors, Dimitris Hatzis, a former professor of allergology, well versed in psychoanalysis and with an eye for the seemingly trivial. "You can go about this material in all sorts of different ways, but my advice to you would be to stick to the stories. As we say in our trade, nothing can match a detailed patient's record!"

Figure 13. Kalomira's drawing.

Hatzis, a man of gravitas whose professional achievements and integrity were always admired by his peers and whose advice was often sought, had stated in the *platia* during a discussion with the mayor Nikolis that he did not oppose the building of the mosque. He alerted me to the fact that most people thought it would be established right in the center of Kambos and not outside the town on a hill overlooking Attiki Odhos. "This seems to me a strategic mistake on the part of the government," he said. "Everyone identifies with his hometown, but few with an expressway." He suggested that the whole initiative should have been phrased differently. A mosque built on Attiki Odhos would have caused no reactions.

When I presented him with Kalomira's drawing he suggested that it may well stand for the archetypal home—an intriguing observation that, I thought, echoed Kalomira's phrase/statement: "I would like to have a church." With these words, she seemed to put herself in the position of an immigrant who resides in a foreign land and retains a symbolic connection to the homeland (represented by the archetypal house) through visits to a church. In this case the church serves functions that transcend the domain of the sacred. By metonymy, it stands for a country of origin and its culture and brings to consciousness notions of domesticity. Thus one might well claim that Kalomira with her drawing provided Muslim immigrants with a place to inhabit and a space to exist. Looking at her sketch and thinking of her words, I was tempted to believe that in reality she seemed to have been saying, "Give them a home."

When, however, Vassilis, a middle-aged publisher, entered Belier, where Hatzis and I were discussing Kalomira's drawing over drinks and cigarettes,

The Locals   105

he offered a radically different interpretation. "It looks like a prison. There are no windows at the level of the door that could provide a view to the outside world. The person who sketched this space accepts the presence of immigrants only in designated spaces."

"Now he ruined it for us!" Hatzis exclaimed.

"Voltron" and the Drawing Meeting at Vicky's House

Konstantinos was a childhood friend and a neighbor whom I would meet in Ora café at four o'clock every afternoon during my research for a shot of espresso. These appointments were destined to take place, since I could never resist the temptation of drinking yet another coffee, and Konstantinos would hardly ever divert from his routine. Unlike me, who would leave Kambos for long periods, he never considered living away from his birthplace, and for good reason. He was the only son of a family with strong financial interests in the area who loved him unconditionally and taught him everything necessary for the management of the *periusia*, one's property. This not only entailed studies in agronomy (for the effective management of the family's vineyards), but also daily observation of the performance of power hierarchies and careful participation in the life of the *platia*. This was effectively his day job; trivial as it could appear to Kambos's outsiders, it was a very significant one. Under the guidance of his father, a respected fixture of the *platia*, Konstantinos had learned, among many other things, how to acquire information without being intrusive and avoid certain discussions while remaining pleasant and talkative and, most important, what can be said and what cannot.

When, for example, discussions at Ora would shift from soccer, TV shows, and Formula 1 to my research, Konstantinos would listen carefully without saying much. Whenever I inquired about his views on the mosque in the presence of Yiorghos, the coffee-shop owner, he would respond diplomatically: "According to the constitution, they [i.e., the Muslims] have the right to establish a mosque." His restraint was understandable. A close relative was involved in local politics and was known for his opposition to the project. If word got to him that Konstantinos was openly questioning his publicly expressed views, a *pareksiyisi* (literally, a misunderstanding), an element of strain, or even a permanent severance of familial ties could occur, for which Konstantinos would have been held responsible.

106 Chapter 4

It was only when we moved away from the coffee shops and found ourselves at a drawing party that I had organized at my friend Vicky's house that Konstantinos finally opened up about his views on the mosque. In principle he did not mind, but he would still oppose the enterprise due to his distrust of state agencies and municipal authorities' capacity to handle sensitive issues.

In affirmation of these remarks, Ghrighoris, an architect also present at the party, intervened: "If you think the central government is corrupt and inefficient, then you really don't know how horrible the situation is with the local government. Take Kambos, for example. The people elected here have no clue about public administration. They don't even know what the term 'project' means. They just attract the votes of their kin. Your uncle gets the votes of the Antonious, his uncle [turning to Konstantinos] the Chountas, and so on." Ghrighoris's remarks reminded me how politics in the area had worked for many years: large patrilineal groups would operate as a single voting entity and support particular candidates, who would try to include prominent members of different families on their tickets—a strategy that was becoming increasingly ineffective as more and more *kseni* were settling in the town.[18]

After these remarks, the drawing commenced and Konstantinos presented me with a sketch that was very different from the ones that I had collected up to that point. It was obviously produced by an individual who had seen mosques on a number of occasions and had a clear idea of how they tend to look. His sketch depicts a structure situated in time, making use of electricity, with four loudspeakers attached to the minarets so the voice of the muezzin can be heard from afar. It is also one of the six that incorporates written text: the Greek inscription at the entrance to the mosque reads "Mahmout's Mosque."

We all thought that Konstantinos's drawing was by far the funniest (mainly due to the reference to the widespread Greek stereotype of "Mahmout" as a typical Muslim name), and we also laughed a lot about the fact that a thirty-year-old would sign his sketch with the name "Voltron."[19] Jokes aside, Konstantinos was eager to enquire about my interpretation of what he had just produced.

"Well, I'm not a psychoanalyst," I said, "but I can certainly tell you how your sketch fits into my research. It reminds me of a frequent argument against the establishment of mosques, regarding the 'grave consequences' of sound pollution,[20] and also a discussion I had recently with Fatuma, an Ethiopian immigrant whom I had naively asked whether she missed her homeland.

Figure 14. Mahmout's Mosque.

There are two main things that Fatuma misses in Athens," I told Konstantinos. "The first is *iftar* [the evening meal breaking the fast during Ramadan] with her girlfriends in Addis Ababa and the second is the voice of the muezzin saying 'Allahu Akbar.' Here is what I first think when I see your drawing: the same iconic sign can trigger different trains of thought. For non-Muslims the sight of a minaret with loudspeakers attached is sometimes associated with sound pollution. For Fatuma, on the other hand, the same image brings to mind the *azan* [call to prayer] and its effect in terms of Islamizing a particular urban space and endowing it with acoustic memories of the homeland."

"Now why don't you tell me more about the inscription," I asked, and Konstantinos responded that "Mahmout" or "Mahmood" is for him a typical Turco-oriental name. "Again, interesting that you say that," I said in all seriousness, "because if the name is spelled with a *t* then it is modern Turkish, if with a *d* it is Ottoman or Arabic. It is a name of ambivalent nature, if you like. It is both Turkish and Islamic, or to be more precise, it condenses the 'Turkish' and the 'Islamic' into a single word. In Turkish it is only the declination of the name that uncovers an unexpected *d* (e.g., Mahmoud'a) in the dative, thus revealing an Arabic origin. It is in a way reminiscent of the Kemalists' attempt to erase the Islamic tradition that insists on resurfacing."

"*Bravo Profesora!*" shouted Ghrighoris, who must have found my interpretations far-fetched and somewhat pretentious.

Rambo and His Brother

Far from the one-man army "John Rambo" known from the Hollywood films, the person behind the following drawing was an even-tempered seventeen-year-old high school student and a first cousin of Konstantinos. In his sketch, which he made for me one afternoon while we were all sitting outside a friend's beach house, he presents a mosque with a dome standing between two minarets. The drawing also depicts two rectangles created by an extension of the same lines that form the main building, which seem to constitute—as the diagonal hatchings suggest—depictions of two water channels on which the sun's light is reflected.

Where could Rambo have seen such a structure that dominates the landscape and is surrounded by water elements?, I asked Konstantinos while the artist was engaged in a long telephone conversation with his girlfriend.

"Probably everyone thinks of a mosque he has seen at some point in his life," answered my friend. It could have been an Ottoman mosque in Ioannina they had visited some years ago; "a mosque in the Turkish part of Cyprus,"

Figure 15. Rambo draws the Taj Mahal.

as Giota, a twenty-five-year-old Cypriot student, suggested; a picture of St. Sophia in Istanbul; or in Konstantinos's case, "a mosque in Adrianoupolis, which I could see through my binoculars when I was doing my military service in Evros."[21]

"I guess there is a certain predeterminism concerning the production of fantasies," I responded, "in the sense that our imagination is not as free and wild as we would sometimes like to believe. That is to say that the production of mental images is based on what we already know," I said, thinking of the possibility of projecting Kirmayer's (1996) insights concerning "landscapes of memory" onto the imaginary.[22]

"*Re puso re*" (shut up), said Rambo's brother in Arvanitika, thinking that Konstantinos and I were about to miss an obvious point. "It's the Taj Mahal," he said, looking at Rambo's sketch. "Are you saying that what we think about the mosque is connected to the way we draw it?"

"Not necessarily," I answered, and explained that this whole exercise usually generates interesting discussions and interpretations. "But what do you think about the mosque?" I asked him.

"It shouldn't be built, the Turks have fucked us," he said, trying to tease me.

"How exactly have we been fucked?" I tried to clarify with yet another question.

"Do they have churches there?" he asked.

"Sure they do! There is one in Kadiköy, the place where I used to live—Konstantinos, you saw it when you visited me," I replied.

"Let it be built then!" Rambo's brother said, and burst out laughing.

"You're a prick," said Konstantinos, "we're having a serious conversation here."

Anthi

Anthi was a neighbor in her late fifties, living with her elderly mother, Kyr'Asimina, and making a living by selling family property, organizing presentations of clothing and Tupperware in different households, and *mesities*.[23] All of the occupations that Anthi practiced over the years were telling of her outgoing character and her impressive ability to establish networks of acquaintances throughout Greece who were ready to perform all sorts of favors for her.

When immigrants started to settle in Kambos in the early 1990s, Anthi, like many others, saw an opportunity for a flexible and inexpensive labor

110 Chapter 4

force and offered a part of her house to an Egyptian family on the condition that they help her look after Kyr'Asimina, who suffered from Alzheimer's. This embrace of an immigrant family did not pass unnoticed by the neighbors, who were quick to comment that Anthi simply wanted *na kani ti zoi tis*, to live her life, without the burden of looking after an elderly relative. This responsibility now belonged to the Egyptians, and more specifically to Suzana (Salihah), wife of Andonis (Adn) and mother of Maria (Noha) and Makis (Hakim).

This might indeed have been the original reason for Anthi's hospitality. Nevertheless, as the years went by, Noha and Hakim, or Maria and Makis as they had been socially baptized by their Greek neighbors,[24] became the children she never had, while Andonis and Suzana provided steady company, capable of looking after not only the elderly mother (who was called *yiayia*, grandmother, by all members of the Egyptian family), but also their host. After all, Anthi herself had started to believe that, physically speaking, she was not quite the person she used to be. She was getting tired more easily and had also started worrying about her health. However, her real concern, I thought, was of a different nature: sooner or later her mother, a source of constant concern yet the only other living member of her family, would die and Anthi would be left alone, or at the mercy of her neighbors and friends' free time. In this sense, there was a lot more to the family's moving into her house. Their presence was filling not only unused space in the house but also an existential void in her life. When one day Andonis decided to take the family back to Egypt, Anthi was in a way relieved but also overtaken by sadness. Andonis's conservatism (he wanted Noha to be circumcised), ill health (he had recently discovered that he had hepatitis and was in need of a liver transplant), and erratic behavior had made him intolerable. But she truly loved the children and Souzana. What will happen to them when he dies, how are they going to make a living, how easy will it be for the kids to feel comfortable in the poor neighborhoods of Cairo now that they have become used to the comforts of life in Kambos, will Maria have to have the operation (i.e., female circumcision), she would ask the neighbors again and again.

Thus for Anthi there was no option but to assume a new role at the age of fifty-nine, that of a transnational protector who would regularly visit the family in Cairo. During Ramadan Anthi would bring presents to Maria and Makis and give money to Souzana (whom she trusted more than Adonis) that had been raised by the whole neighborhood, which had also come to love the family and miss Makis's obscene warnings that his surname, Hamisi, should

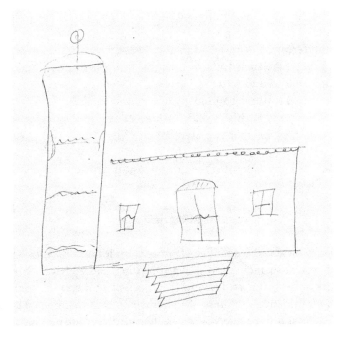

Figure 16. "Isn't it like this?"

be pronounced correctly since it has nothing to do with *ghamisi*, a less elegant way of referring to sexual intercourse. As Anthi had firsthand experience of Muslim life both in her house and in Cairo, I was very curious not only to discuss my research with her, but also to ask her to draw the mosque of Kambos.

To do this I didn't even have to walk to her house, since Anthi would come by ours almost daily. During one of these visits, the pretext for which was the offering of *tsighara*, Arvanitic spinach pies that had just come out of the oven, I presented her with a blank page and practically ordered her to sketch. With Anthi I felt there was no need for introductions—our relationship was at another level.

Responding to my request, Anthi drew a stairway, a room with an entrance door that did not reach the floor, two windows, a tile roof, and a minaret attached to it. After completing each of the above elements, she would seek affirmation and ask, "*Etsi dhen ine?*" (Isn't it like this?)

After a short break for spinach pies, I asked her what she thought about Muslims and the mosque in Kambos, thinking that she would emphasize the

112   Chapter 4

constant difficulties in an immigrant's life and her special bond with Souzana's family.

As if the term "Muslims" had caused some sort of reflex reaction and
triggered a very particular train of thought, Anthi responded that Muslims
should not be allowed to settle in Greece, and went on to refer to terrorism
and our country's historical animosity toward the Turks.

How can you say such things, I interrupted in astonishment, when you
told me some days ago that you are planning to go to Cairo to visit Suzana
and the kids?

"My dear *manari*, is it the same thing?" Anthi replied.

Babis and His Father

Babis was the owner of a small electronics shop located on Kambos's commercial strip whose reputation as hardworking and reliable far exceeded
the confines of his business. Previously Babis had worked for Themis, Kambos's most prominent accountant. This actually meant that he met on a daily
basis with at least fifty people, had access to sensitive information, and, most
important, personally knew every single tax official in the broader area. Babis
was a key public figure with a shop close to the *platia*, where many would stop
by for a short chat, and it was highly possible that he might have heard stories
and gossip about the mosque.

He was a good friend and a fellow classmate of Konstantinos, and over the
years I too had come to know him and appreciate his lively personality and
the fact that he always seemed to be in very good spirits. Our familiarity, built
on cigarettes and espressos, beer and whiskey, gossip and obscene comments,
was enough to ensure his participation in my project. I walked to his shop on
a Monday morning and without saying much I gave him a blank page and
repeated the usual instructions: there is no right or wrong, whatever comes
first to mind, and the like. Babis appeared truly excited by the unexpected
invitation to sketch, saying, "I'm going to draw tons of mosques for you,"
while drawing the minarets.

In the sketch that he gave me there is clearly a fortress idea at work. The
mosque's entrance door is divided into two parts and has six dots on each side.
These probably represent metal nails and bring to mind the doors of medieval
castles often depicted in games such as *World of Warcraft* or in Babis's favorite
film saga, *Lord of the Rings*. The drawing also depicts a figure wearing a hat

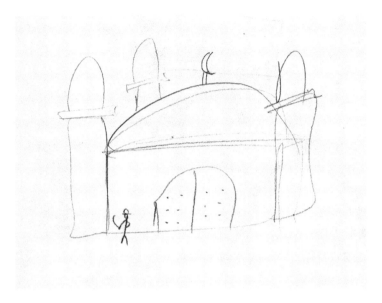

Figure 17. "I'm going to draw tons of mosques for you."

and holding a curved blade. It is as if Muslims have no conception of modern weaponry, I thought, or that history itself froze when the armies of the Mongols captured Baghdad in the thirteenth century.

"Do you want to discuss this now?" Babis said, having been informed of my fieldwork techniques by Konstantinos and Rambo's brother.

"If you have the time I wouldn't mind—but we can meet at Ora later today," I proposed as an alternative.

"I'm not conservative like people here. I really don't mind the mosque and honestly, I don't care. Don't you know that we're going to make *metagrafares* (transfers of soccer players)?" he asked me, and as proof I was shown a sports newspaper speculating about the transfer of the "great" Luciano Galeti from Atlético Madrid to Olimbiakos.

My friend's enthusiasm and loud voice caught the attention of his father, a retired mechanical engineer, who had been observing our interaction from the back of the shop. "*Ela kopse tis aïdhies!*" (Come on, cut the crap!), he said to Babis and looked at me. "You should know that the *dopii* would never allow a mosque to be built. They are very conservative." Even though he himself wouldn't spend much time with *dopii*, he was following the news closely and

Figure 18. Unexpected resemblances—the Chapel of Paleopanayia in Kambos.

the prospects of the mosque project looked quite grim to him. Like Gökhan in the coffee shop in Gazi, he went on to remind me of how the Greek state operates. "[The locals] will protest, then the government will be scared, the TV channels will come and in the end nothing will happen."

"Yet most of the people I talked to don't oppose the project, even though they thought everyone else did," I responded. "What exactly will the government be scared of?"

He looked at me in amazement. This was obviously a question he did not expect, for the process he had just described was considered common knowledge. "Reactions," he said, "the TV channels, the journalists, the fuss (*vavura*) that will be created."

"Is this, you think, the reason why the government doesn't build the mosque?" I asked again.

At that point he became upset with my insistence at enquiring about issues that appeared rather obvious to him. "Are you kidding me?" he said. "Do I really need to explain that to you? They're going to lose votes!"

Following this condensed tutorial on government operation, the father looked at his son's drawing and asked him in a rhetorical manner, "What kind of bullshit are you drawing there?" "Give me some paper," he said, turning to me, "I'm going to show you what a mosque looks like." Within two minutes or so the father had drawn what appeared to me to be an Orthodox chapel, with a cross on the entrance door and the side window. The drawing was very reminiscent of the architecture of many chapels located in Kambos in particular.

"Dad, this looks like a dick!" said Babis all of a sudden.

"Well, this is how it looks," said the father in an authoritative tone.

Was an attention to phallic connections missing from my research? On second thought, however, this seemed to be a far-fetched idea. Babis's discourse had always been sexually charged. If I were to follow this path of analysis, I might well argue that the curved blade held by the figure in his drawing was also a symbol of the phallus. I am reading too much into this, I thought.

Phallic Metonymies

A few weeks later another "drawing incident" forced me to reconsider. My mother, who was becoming more enthusiastic about this research than I was, came up with the idea that Nitsa, her fifty-three-year-old house cleaner, should participate in the research. "You should be interviewing more *kseni*," she said to me, concerned about the representational value of my sample. "In this way you will know how people who live here relate to the town's life and what their views on the issue are."

"Mom, I know how to do this, ok?" I replied, but research had now become a family issue.

Mom was holding a blank sheet of paper in her hand, and Nitsa had already sat down at the kitchen table. "I am a progressive person," said Nitsa, who had already been informed of my research topic.

"Oh, I know that," I said, "and the fact that—"

"Let the woman continue," intervened my mother.

"In any case," said Nitsa in a loud voice and in a clear attempt to stop the squabble, "and as I was trying to say, it is the issue of the *apohetefsi* (sewage) that concerns me most."[25] She spoke for some time about the lack of basic infrastructure in Kambos, which does not seem to cause any reactions on the part of the locals. "If they react to the building of a mosque, why are they not reacting to more important issues?"

"That's a valid question," said my mother, "but this is not the issue here. You should tell us whether you agree with the building of a mosque or not."

"Of course it's relevant," I jumped in, and suggested that this lack of interest in the issue of the sewer system might indicate political apathy and nonresistance to government initiatives—a point that neither my mother nor Nitsa seemed to appreciate.

"Is Nitsa going to draw? We have things to do, too!" asked my mother in anticipation.

"Of course, isn't this why we're here?" I said.

"Oh, I'm embarrassed now," said Nitsa.

"Don't be, we all drew, there is no right or wrong in this," my mother rushed to assure her.

"Nitsa, just draw whatever comes to mind," I said.

"What can I do? I have a soft spot for you," explained Nitsa, and the drawing commenced.

Within minutes she had depicted an elongated structure and found herself in a rather awkward position. "I'm so sorry, oh mother of Jesus," Nitsa said and covered her eyes with her hands in embarrassment. "How would I know?"

"It's fine, it's fine, you haven't seen mine," said my mother. "Now get ready, I'll drive you back home, it's already three."

"What was that??" my mother asked as soon as she came back home, eager to discuss the drawing incident. I didn't know how to respond, and we

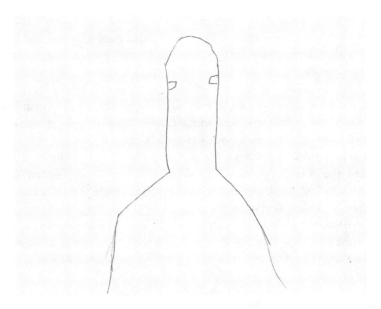

Figure 19. "I'm so sorry."

left it there. While the phallic potential of Islamic architecture is recognized in the Persian *hazl* (bawdy) tradition, the stories of Nasreddin Hoca, or psychoanalytic accounts of the interethnic conflict in Cyprus,[26] I didn't feel at all equipped to connect reactions to minarets[27] to phallic anxiety.

A week after that first encounter I had the chance to talk again with Nitsa—this time without the presence of my mother. As I was helping her move a heavy table, she told me that the building of a mosque should by no means be allowed.

"Why do you think so?" I asked.

"You know best," she answered, and reminded me of what the Greeks had suffered at the hands of Muslims. "They were stealing children from their families," she said, referring to the Ottoman child levy (*devsirme*), "they were raping girls for centuries."

"Nitsa, are you referring to the Turks?" I asked again.

"Of course," she replied without hesitation, "and now we are going to build them minarets too!"[28]

Our exchange didn't last long. Nitsa was busy and I had a meeting in the square. Yet the term "minaret" that she had used was imprinted on my mind.

Nitsa's drawing might well constitute a clear case of metonymy, I thought. A minaret that becomes the mosque, an architectural element that stands for the whole. In this way the minaret becomes a representation not only of a larger structure, but also of everything that this structure represents in popular imagination. For Nitsa, for instance, the very sight of the minaret or simply its mental image seemed to trigger a particular train of thought: Turks, the historical rivals of the Greeks, raping Christian girls, stories of oriental barbarism interconnected with notions of masculinity.

What is so troubling about minarets? Why did Nitsa react how she did to the possibility of seeing them in a familiar landscape? Psychoanalytic explanations aside, I realized that at the time Dimitris Zafiropoulos, a candidate for mayor of Athens (enjoying the support of LAOS, the nationalist party), had just launched his electoral campaign by placing huge posters in central parts of the city depicting the Parthenon with three minarets attached and asking for his fellow citizens' preference: "*Athina me dzami i Athina Elliniki?*"

Figure 20. "Athens with a mosque or Greek Athens?"

(Athens with a Mosque or Greek Athens?) With these posters, Zafiropoulos—familiar largely in ultranationalist circles as the publisher of the newspaper *Eleftheros Kosmos* (Free World)—was trying to reach out to a wider
audience by employing a strategy of polysemy. While his poster capitalized
on the widespread Islamophobia that followed 9/11, his particular depiction
of the Parthenon also intended to revive a memory of Ottoman Athens, in
which the symbol of Hellenism par excellence was turned into the Kale Cam-
isi, the Castle Mosque (see Stathi 2014:171; Fowden 2019).

Getting It Wrong

This chapter has subjected to ethnographic examination news media accounts
of local views on the mosque and in particular the widespread assumption
that Kambiots overwhelmingly opposed the structure, which they supposedly imagined as a potential center of radical Islam. In the aftermath of 9/11,
this certainty about local public opinion and imagination rendered any systematic investigation of actual local perspectives unnecessary. Soon enough,
articles appeared with titles such as "Villagers try to block the mosque of Athens," and their authors' assumptions about Kambos became accepted facts
that were endlessly reproduced by journalists, scholars, and, most important,
government officials, who eventually came to believe that building a mosque
in the former military base of Votanikos would be easier. As we read in a
Ministry of Education report that was sent to parliament in 2015, "the solution of Kambos was permanently abandoned following reactions of the local
society" (MCERA 2015).

In response to this situation, I examined local imagination by using drawings as an entry point into discussion on the mosque. I am well aware that a
drawing on its own hardly reveals anything in a straightforward way about
its creator's thoughts. As Roland Barthes (1977:39) indicates, the semiologist
always faces great uncertainty with floating signs, which initiate diverse interpretations. The anchoring of meaning has to be achieved by interlocution
and observation. A drawing may denote lack of information about Muslim
architecture or just as likely it may not. It may speak of a profound lack of
interest in the debate over the mosque or it may not. As I soon realized with
my own attempt to draw the imagined mosque of Kambos, sketches do not
constitute "language" for most people. A drawing provides creators with con-
tinual feedback, and that affects the very way they proceed. What it depicts

may be connected to images of radical Islam but also to memories of nearby chapels, photographs of world heritage monuments, and scenes from video games and films, as well as imaginations of phallic-shaped structures.

The value of these drawings to my research therefore lay less in the correlation between drawings and individual stances on the mosque debate and more in the interactions that the occasion of drawing produced. The speculative nature of these materials created a *susuro*, a certain fuss, over my research, brought about meetings with informants of different age groups and socioeconomic and educational backgrounds, facilitated reflection on local politics, and raised two interrelated questions to which I will now turn. What is the representational value of the opinions one encounters in the *platia*? And through what processes and technologies are popular resistance and potential political consequences assessed by local and national government?

Though the *platia* is by all accounts a public space, it doesn't represent everyone and surely doesn't belong to all. Those initiated to its poetics understand how factors of time (particularly the transition from day to night), gender, class, identity (*dopii* and *kseni*), and ethnicity (Greeks and Albanians) determine the range of opinions that can be encountered there, who speaks to whom, and when. "*Ela re manari mu pu ise?*" Kalomira said to me in an empty café, signaling "cultural intimacy" (Herzfeld [1996] 2005)—fellowship in origin, kinship, and the existence of a cosmos almost impenetrable to outsiders.

If you enter the *platia* as a *ksenos*, and especially as a correspondent from ABC or BBC, eliciting meaningful statements about the mosque might be rather challenging. Locals know that expressing clear-cut opinions on the issue, especially in the presence of others or on camera, might incur a cost and are better left to mayors and bishops. Konstantinos's case, in particular, demonstrates how embedded secrecy can be in public life. Because of his incisive understanding of the situation, he provides only diplomatic answers at Ora. The demands of kinship (to maintain family alliances) and finances (to protect the family's interests) impose severe constraints on what can be said in public. In this small town, asking someone about the construction of a mosque is really asking them to divulge so much more.

Yet there might be another, more straightforward reason for the reluctance to speak to the press. As my encounters with Nikos, Kalomira, and Babis suggest, opinions can be formed in the very moment they are being expressed, and prior consideration of a topic may well be limited, superficial, or altogether nonexistent. In this sense, the press creates local opinion as much as it reports on it. Out of the one hundred interviews that I conducted, forty-eight informants had not thought about the issue before and showed a lack of interest in ever doing so. Questions about betting, hunting, and soccer would certainly have initiated more lively discussions. Both journalists and scholars miss a key dynamic at play when they overlook this indifference or approach their inquiries in a way that obscures it.

But even if someone expresses clear and seemingly unqualified opposition to the mosque, what does this really tell us? Anthi, for example, reproduces a nationalist, Islamophobic discourse upon hearing the terms *dzami* and Muslims, while her daily life speaks to a deep connection to a Muslim family in Egypt. She articulates ideas that seem disconnected from her personal experiences, her love for Suzana and her kids, and her frequent travels to Cairo. My meeting with her also raises another question: to what extent does a negative stance toward the mosque translate into concrete political action and, more specifically, into a vote of support for reacting local authorities?

As we now know for certain, it doesn't. In fact, those who attempted to capitalize on the mosque's publicity at the time were not reelected, including Nikolis, the mayor. Despite his many interviews with the press, his contacts with the Church and the area's MPs, and, most important, his successful pressure on the government to change the location of the mosque and thus avoid local reactions, his political career came to a swift end. In retrospect, his assessment of the political landscape was misguided. Local concern for the mosque was not nearly as significant as the *platia* and the media might make one believe. My research indicates that some Kambiots opposed the project, just as many were openly for it, and most couldn't care less. At election time other issues were prioritized by voters, new political alliances were formed, and Nikolis's anti-Islamic stance was of little significance. Even those locals who took great interest in the issue—like Kostis, an ultra-Orthodox Christian and a protagonist of the mosque debate to whose story I now turn—didn't appreciate the mayor's efforts.

CHAPTER 5

The (Other) Church

Perceptions

It wasn't only Samir, Hassan, Dora, and Halil-Latif who, in their efforts to explain why the mosque in Kambos was never built, held the Orthodox Church responsible. These accusations were prevalent in the media, and not just in Greece. One of the most creative encapsulations of this assumption came in the form of a 2003 illustration in the Turkish newspaper *Zaman* titled "*Atina'daki cami tartışması semboller savaşına dönüştü*" (The debate on the Athenian mosque has turned into a war of symbols). The image depicts a structure reminiscent of the Parthenon, on top of which there are both a cross and a crescent. Within the structure is an inscription revealing to readers who is responsible for the project's failure: "*Atina camii'nin yolu kiliseden geçiyor*" (The way to the Athens mosque passes through the Church). The meaning of this inscription is further elaborated in the main body of the accompanying article: "[Athens] is the only capital in Europe that does not have a mosque, because the strongest institution in the country is the Church. The Orthodox Church is against the building of the mosque. Subconsciously there is the thought that one day the Turks will come back. For this reason, a very simple matter of worship is turning into a crisis" (Arslan 2003).

Similar sentiments could be found in the discourse of many international organizations including the European Commission, who sent its representative Alvaro Gil-Robles to meet with Archbishop Christodoulos to discuss the mosque. When the two men met, in June 2002, Christodoulos said in his welcoming speech:

> We, being Greeks, were subjected to the [rule of the] Turks for four hundred years. And this occupation by the Turks was paid for with

Figure 21. "The way to the Athens mosque passes through the Church." Scanned reproduction from Arslan 2003.

sacrifices in blood. We had hundreds of victims who were sacrificed for the freedom of this land. Our religion played the primary role in protecting our language, history, religion, and identity, for at that time it had no political power. In the mind of the Greeks, everything Islamic is Turkish.... Thus, there is this hatred, which, I would say, we do not cultivate. We are trying to silence it and this is also known to the government. For this reason, [the government] has chosen a place outside the city of Athens, so that [the Muslims] are not right in the middle.... We are afraid that such a mosque right in the center of Athens, with a minaret ... and a muezzin who would be heard five times a day performing the prayer, would provoke a reaction from the Greek people, the extent of which we cannot predict. (Tsatsi 2006)

Like the *Zaman* journalist, the archbishop refers to the Greek subconscious and adopts an almost psychoanalytical perspective concerning the mosque issue to explain the popular conflation of Islam with Turkey and, ultimately, local culture. The Greek population, he suggests, constitutes a homogenous body whose contemporary behaviors can be explained in terms of severe trauma brought about by imagination and collective memory rather than direct experience. In this particular case, the opposition to the establishment of a central mosque stems from the remembrance of a Turkish "occupation" that lasted for "four hundred years,"—an idea central to national education from the state's foundation to this day. For the archbishop, this national remembrance also creates a persistent aftereffect. In the case of the collective trauma that he describes, it passes from one generation to the next and unfolds in a two-stage process. First it leads collective cognition to an immediate identification of "everything Islamic" with "Turkish" (cf. Balta 2008:41). Then it causes a reflex reaction against anything that can be associated with the original trauma whose exact form and extent cannot be foreseen. To avoid the triggering of such a process, the archbishop suggests hiding the mosque from the public eye by building it in the suburbs, which, he thinks, is an inevitable prerequisite for its very materialization.

The European commissioner seemed to believe that the Church might block the initiative altogether. He had good reasons to think so. The Church traditionally identifies with a reactionary "underdog culture," the state (of which it is legally a part; Alivizatos 1999),[1] and the nation (in that it was established as an autocephalous church as a result of the same processes that led to independence and national "rebirth"), and tends to oppose anything associated with Turkey (here a mosque, but in other cases even the Ecumenical Patriarchate in Istanbul; Roudometof 2008) (Diamandouros 1994; Chrysoloras 2004; Mavrogordatos 2003; Stavrakakis 2003; Prodromou 2004). Also, from a legal point of view, the Church at the time could still draw on Metaxas's Law 1672 of 1939, according to which local Christian bishops had to issue permits for the construction of non-Christian places of worship, to oppose the mosque. Most important, however, Archbishop Christodoulos's ascension to power made it clear that the Church had entered a new era. Unlike his predecessor Serafim, he wanted a more visible and vocal church that would effectively reach out to the youth ("come to the Church even with piercings," he had said in a call to the youth) and intervene in all matters of "general public interest" (Manitakis 2000:117–118). When Christodoulos organized two massive rallies (called *laosinaksis*, "people's gatherings," by the Church) in Athens and Thessaloniki in June 2000 against PASOK's decision to remove religious affiliation from identity cards, it became abundantly clear that he was a powerful political actor capable of mobilizing voters and thus effectively putting pressure on governments.[2]

Yet, as the commissioner noted in a subsequent report to the European Committee of Ministers and the Parliamentary Assembly, the archbishop would not in principle oppose the mosque: "When this question was raised [i.e., the construction of a mosque in Athens], the Secretary General for Religious Affairs—as well as Archbishop Christodoulos—assured me that he had no objection to the building of a mosque, but invoked potential local resistance. I appeal to the solidarity, spirit of tolerance and good will of all concerned to pick out a place readily accessible to worshippers on which to build a mosque for Muslims established in Athens District" (CE/CHR 2002:6). Indeed, a careful examination of Christodoulos's speech shows that while the archbishop shares his concerns and lectures the commissioner on the country's Ottoman past, Greek collective memory and trauma, and the centrality of Orthodoxy in the formulation of a national identity, he doesn't disagree with the core proposal. In fact, in February 2002, nine months prior to their meeting, the Church's Holy Synod had voted in favor of the construction of a mosque in Athens (Kalokerinos 2002). Although overshadowed by the archbishop's statement, this decision marked a complete reorientation of the Church's policies toward the building of a Muslim space of worship and its willingness to negotiate with the government. As Metropolitan Chrysostomos of Zakinthos explained in an interview (Tsatsis 2003b), until the 1990s the Church opposed any government initiative of this kind, but now, he said with some irony, "to sizitame" (we discuss it).

Overall, the Church's message about the mosque was mixed. While there were formal decisions that didn't object to building a mosque somewhere in Athens, when it came to Kambos all sorts of concerns were raised, and not only by the archbishop. Other members of the Holy Synod, the local bishop, and frustrated Christians from around Greece spoke to the media about their opposition to the project, the mosque's proximity to the airport, Kambiots' fight against it, and the possibility that Muslims would use it against the country and its people. These mixed messages were also reflected in how scholars described the Church's stance, with some claiming that it supported the mosque project (Ziaka 2009:273) and others suggesting the opposite (Anagnostou and Gropas 2010:100; Hatziprokopiou 2019:211; Evergeti and Hatziprokopiou 2013:185; Triandafyllidou and Gropas 2009:972; Skoulariki 2010:306; Tsitselikis 2004:288). All of these takes are correct to some extent, as they point to different moments in a long and ever-shifting debate and highlight different voices, statements, and decisions. Yet they don't provide a framework for understanding the Church's institutional polyphony, nor do they explain how exactly it blocked the building of a mosque in Kambos—if it did at all.

126   Chapter 5

To fill in these gaps, I turn to Kostis, the doctor from Kambos whose appearances on television were commented on by Dora. In an attempt to map the cosmology of a man who, in the media, became the personification of local Christian resistance, I revisit his efforts to fulfill a supposed national vow and investigate the symbolism of an ultra-Orthodox publication to which he was particularly attached. Ultimately, Kostis's opposition to the mosque in Kambos leads me to examine the Church through the perspective of its ultra-Orthodox critics—as yet another political party constantly concerned with public opinion.

The Prefabricated Chapel

I first became interested in Kostis when one day in 2002 I saw him on television saying that he had erected a chapel on the site where the mosque was supposed to be built. That chapel, he explained, temporarily fulfilled an old promise that the Greek nation had made to God. As I soon discovered, he was referring to the so-called *Tama tu Ethnus* (Nation's Vow), another unrealized state project that dates back to the nineteenth century.

The term "Nation's Vow" refers to the Church of the Savior that the Fourth National Assembly voted on July 31, 1829, to construct. With this initiative, the then revolutionaries hoped to express their gratitude for the partial liberation of the Greek people from the Ottoman Empire and emulate similar initiatives in other countries meant to signify national rebirth.[3] While the state's financial resources at the time were rather limited, the Church of the Savior was conceived of as an impressive structure that would incorporate a monument dedicated to the philhellenes, who sacrificed for the Greek cause, and would dominate the landscape and show to anyone in doubt that the country was indeed Christian. One of the first visionaries of the project, the architect Ferdinand von Quast, published an article in *Museum: Blätter für bildende Kunst* in 1833 (as quoted in Russack 1991:200) in which he proposed that the new king's palace be located on the Acropolis and be connected by a bridge to "the Church of the Savior, the cathedral," built on the nearby Areopagus hill. "A majestic dome," he wrote, "should cover the sacred site, on top of which the cross, a symbol of Christian victory over Islam will shine. And this shining would reach the ships sailing around Sounio" (Russack 1991:26). The intention to build the church was once again declared by the government of King Otto in the form of two decrees published in the Official Gazette of the

Figure 22. The Nation's Vow compared to St. Sophia in Istanbul, as imagined by the jewelry designer Ilias Lalaounis. *Eleftheros Kosmos*, August 22, 1972, p. 7.

Hellenic Kingdom in 1834 and 1838 (GG 1834:5; 1838:54), but again nothing concrete happened.

Some one hundred and thirty years later, this initiative was revisited by the Greek military regime of 1967–1974 when it engaged in an imaginative reading of the historical record to present this unbuilt edifice as an unfulfilled national vow (thus the term "Nation's Vow"). It seems that the idea of fulfilling an old promise that was so intimately connected to the "rebirth" of the Greek nation was particularly appealing, and soon a fundraising committee was established, several architectural contests were launched, and extensive appropriations of private property took place to facilitate the building of a modernist megachurch on top of Turkovunia (literally the Turkish Mountains)[4]—the site that the regime had designated. Several architects (most notably Constantinos Doxiadis, an urban planner of international renown; see Antoniou 2016:149) and artists found the idea intriguing and submitted plans and models to the organizing committee.

There is undoubtedly a parallel between the mosque in Athens and the Nation's Vow; both are state initiatives that never materialized. Kostis, for his part, was upset with the government's loss of memory, its disrespect for those

128 Chapter 5

who had fought for independence, and its preference for building a mosque rather than a church. Here he employs a double strategy: on the one hand, the little chapel on the site where the mosque was supposed to be built is an effective way to block the project (what Greek, after all, would dare to demolish a chapel?).[5] On the other hand, it constitutes a concrete reminder of a battle that takes place at the level of imagination. In this context, the Nation's Vow emerges in his narratives as a counterstructure.

Neither my father nor a good number of friends could see the rationale behind a meeting with Kostis. They all agreed that, unlike me, he was very religious, and they were quick to predict a social catastrophe in the form of a big fight between us. "What do you find yourself involved in?" my dad would say.

"Watch out Dimitri! Uncle Kostis follows the Old Calendar," my friend Ghrigoris would concur.

Despite all these warnings, our first meeting was facilitated by the person who worried the most. By coincidence my father ran into Kostis and informed him of my intention to discuss my research with him and an appointment was arranged—Thursday evening at his office.

The Waiting Room

As I enter the waiting room, I immediately notice the particularity of its social geography. To put it bluntly, Kostis's patients look different from my father's, although both have their offices in Kambos. They seem economically disadvantaged and obviously religious. There are two elderly nuns, one priest, and another man waiting. The man must work in the fields—I infer from the stains of mud on his trousers and the white truck parked outside.[6] Surely I constitute a spectacle for them. It is clear to all of us that I have entered a world to which I don't belong. They see difference in my clothes, my new phone, the notebook that I carry, the very way that I say to them "*Kalispera*" (Good afternoon). I take a seat among them, thinking that it will take quite some time before I finally meet Kostis.

In the room there is a large couch, four chairs, a small television showing the evening news, and a coffee table placed right in the middle. It is fully covered with several days' worth of ultraconservative newspapers that I have never seen before, called *Athinaïki Protovulia* (Athenian Initiative) and *Ellinorthodhokso Kinima Sotirias* (Helleno-Orthodox Salvation Movement). On the walls, I see depictions of a faded world that Kostis is trying to preserve: a color picture of an elderly woman and a framed black and white picture of the church of St. Sophia in Istanbul.

This was certainly not the first time that I had come across a reference to the famous Byzantine church during my fieldwork. On the contrary, St. Sophia seemed to play a central role in the debate over the establishment of a mosque in Athens. It was a clear case of collective memory. References to its current state were easily traceable on television, radio, online debates, and articles published in the local and national press. The statements of the former minister of education Stelios Papathemelis and Bishop Anthimos of Thessaloniki were particularly telling in this regard (Antoniou 2003:170; Papakhristou 2004; *Eleftherotipia* 2004). Both figures argued that there should be a quid pro quo from Turkey and that the Greek government should allow the operation of a mosque on the condition that St. Sophia be restored to its previous status and used as a church by the Orthodox (PP 2000). In Kambos, Kosmas Karanikolas, a mayoral candidate, offered a similar approach in an interview with a local newspaper: "I belong to the 99 percent of my fellow citizens but also [those in] the surrounding areas who say no to the cultural center and the mosque in our area. Perhaps I was greatly influenced [by my visit] years ago . . . to a close friend in Constantinople, when I visited St. Sophia. I felt sorrow and shame, [seeing] its awful transformation into a tourist site and place of exhibition for Turko-Baroque art. It was then that I remembered the 'civilized' and 'multicultural' decision of the Greek government to erect a Center for Islamic Studies and a mosque in our country and more specifically in our town, Kambos" (*Attiki Yi* 2004:6).

St. Sophia emerges as a symbol of opposition to the mosque, imbued with symbolic value. Its prominence in the Greek Great Idea iconography and irredentist narratives challenges the mosque proponents to approach the issue through reciprocity: if the Turks don't have any respect for Greek symbols, why should the Greeks allow the existence of a Turkish symbol (i.e., a mosque) in their capital city? With these kinds of thoughts on my mind, I find myself waiting for almost two and a half hours. The door finally opens and Kostis, by way of welcome, says: "*Dimitraki aghori mu, ti kanis?* (Little Dimitris, my boy, how are you?)

"Oh, I'm fine, thank you. Nice meeting you," I reply. I cannot help but notice that, right from the beginning, he is very keen on attaching the diminutive suffix *-akis* to my name. I have now become *Dimitraki mu*, "my little Dimitris." That's what happens when your dad makes your fieldwork appointments!

130 Chapter 5

As I soon find out, Kostis is not a man of few words. During that first meeting, he isn't very interested in interlocution but rather in posing to himself rhetorical questions and reciting endless monologues. The meeting lasts far into the evening and a great many things are said concerning his humble origins; his mother, who instilled in him the values of religion and family and taught him to respect every sacrifice made in the name of faith and homeland; the importance of studying the lives of the Neomartyrs;[7] the activities of an Orthodox association of which he is the president; the plans of the "New Order" and the impact of globalization on Helleno-Christian tradition; Turkish aggression over the Aegean Sea; the Nation's Vow; the building of a chapel; and the "miracle" of carrying an eight-meter-high metal cross and erecting it on the hill on which the mosque was supposed to be built.

There is also a strong sense of disappointment and betrayal. On a number of occasions, I am told that people are no longer interested in the preservation of "our" faith and traditions and that present-day Greeks are in a state of "functional hibernation," incapable of understanding the detrimental effects of Islamic immigration to the country. And after all, "How can you have a dialogue with fanatics who are ready to kill themselves?" Kostis would ask.

"What about the Church? What about the local bishop? Wasn't it in 2003 that he had had a rather polemic message regarding the mosque sent out to be read at the end of a Sunday mass in all the churches of his diocese?" I asked, showing him that I too was knowledgeable about the debate.[8] I received a surprising answer.

"Who do you think wrote it?" said Kostis, pointing at himself. "I must have met with Agathonikos more than ten times," he said, and started recreating a series of dialogues with the local bishop: "'Your eminence, this is an important issue. They are planning to build a mosque in your area! You have to do something!' 'I understand your concerns,' said the metropolitan, 'but I met with the archbishop last week and he said I shouldn't take any initiatives. Let's meet sometime soon to discuss this again!' And I kept on going to his office, with books and evidence, *Dimitraki mu*, warning him of the oncoming danger. I guess at some point he had had enough of me and sent out the document that I had drafted for him. I have it right here," he said, opening one of his folders and reading:

We will not accept the establishment of a mosque in any area of our diocese, for the following reasons:

The (Other) Church 131

1. This will not be a simple mosque, but a gigantic complex in whose property of 35,000 square meters a center of Muslim studies and Balkan propaganda will also be located . . .
2. . . . From a strategic point of view, it is also improper . . . since the person in control of the hill will have full control of the airport.
3. . . . The possible establishment of such an Islamic center will alter the social fabric and image of our population. A new Mecca will be created.
4. . . . The imam of Rome's grand mosque has said, "Death to the enemies of Islam," and "Allah will bring victory to the Muslim warriors."
5. . . . Following the examples . . . of the heroes of our faith and homeland, both clergy and laity, who were slaughtered at the altar of freedom, we declare that we will fight to the end in order to stop the establishment of the aforementioned Islamic center.

"I wrote it! I wrote it," he reiterated.

Saint Aghathangelos

On the desk in front of me is a magazine that Kostis gave me on my first visit to his office—a souvenir from a meeting that lasted more than four hours. While he was reluctant to lend me his extensive collection of videotapes with recordings of his many appearances on TV, this magazine he offered without reservation. He was clearly proud of it and claimed that anyone with a sincere interest in his struggle should study it. It is titled *Ayios Aghathangelos, o Esfighmenitis*, taking the name of a minor saint whom few would know: Neomartyr Aghathangelos of Esfighmenou, a monk from the Esphighmenos Monastery in Mount Athos.[9] His biography, as reported in the *sinaksaria* of the Eastern Church (abridged listings of feast days and compilations of saints' vitae; see Dhoukakis 1962:128–123; Mattheos 1968:367–395),[10] follows an established narrative pattern: a young Christian becomes Muslim, feels remorse, confesses to a friend what has happened, prepares for martyrdom, and goes back to the place of conversion to denounce Islam, where the Turks try to dissuade him. The story's end is fairly predictable. Not succumbing to the pressures

132   Chapter 5

of his tormentors, the young man is beheaded on April 19, 1818, only three years before the outbreak of the Greek revolution.[11]

Interestingly enough, the magazine's cover doesn't feature Aghathangelos. Rather, it presents a fresco depicting the martyrdom of several monks in Mount Athos, entitled *I Ayii Ayiorite Osiomartires epi Patriarkhu Vekku tu Latinofronos Martirisandes* (The holy [fathers] of Mount Athos who became martyrs at the time of Patriarch Vekkos, the Latin-minded).[12] The fresco is thematically divided into four quadrants that narrate their own history of violence, sacrifice, and state cruelty. Byzantine soldiers are shown decapitating and hanging monks in front of the church of Protato and the Vatopedi Monastery (first and fourth quadrant), burning alive those living in the Zoghrafou Monastery (second quadrant), and drowning monks in the sea of Khalkidhiki (third quadrant). All of this takes place in the presence of the highest civil and religious authorities, the Byzantine emperor and the patriarch Ioannis Vekkos. In a way, this depiction of profound suffering and subsequent martyrdom ordered by a Latin-minded patriarch perfectly corresponds both to the subtitle of the magazine, "*Martiria Aghonizomenis Orthodhoksias Ayioriton Monakhon*" (Witness of the struggling Orthodox monks of Mount Athos), and to its content.[13]

Almost all of the magazine's articles convey a strong sense of anti-Westernism, which echoes centuries-old Orthodox resentment for the Latins who sacked Constantinople in 1204. These sentiments—a contemporary reflection of the fifteenth-century Byzantine proverb "Better to see the Turkish turban [in Constantinople] than the Latin mitre"[14]—account nowadays for the portrayal of Archbishop Christodoulos and Ecumenical Patriarch Bartholomeos as traitors. They are compared to Ioannis Vekkos, who sought union with the Church of Rome, and are believed to have tacitly accepted papal supremacy and the validity of the Latin doctrine on the procession of the Holy Ghost through their involvement with the ecumenical movement.[15] Yet these are not the only accusations launched against them. A black-and-white picture of a young officer reminds readers that Patriarch Bartholomeos is a Turkish citizen who has served in the Turkish army. This image is supplemented by supposed statements of his condemning the Greek revolution with the clear implication that the patriarch serves Turkish interests. As for Christodoulos, *Aghathangelos*'s contributors harshly criticize his frequent appearances on TV and complete embrace of popular culture—clear signs, they say, of the Church's westernization and secularization. Though articulated in a quite different manner, they seem to very much agree with scholars such as

Figure 23. "The holy [fathers] of Mount Athos who became martyrs at the time of the Patriarch Vekkos, the Latin-minded." *Ayios Aghathangelos o Esfighmenitis*, May–June 2006, cover.

Alivizatos (1999), Demertzis (2001), and Georgiadou (2009) in suggesting that under his leadership a "public church" has been turned thoroughly into a "publicity church" (Georgiadou 2009:129).

The Greek state, for its part, is described as an advocate of the "New Order," a new global reality aiming to erase the Helleno-Christian tradition. Greeks might think that they choose their representatives in elections, but in reality, claim *Aghathangelos*'s writers, they have become puppets of billionaires like Bill Gates and George Soros, who have waged war against Orthodoxy and have established regimes of mind control through mobile phone networks, vaccines, and coded messages embedded in TV commercials. They of course will be defeated—this has been prophesied by monks and saints, who know that God turns the pope's acolytes into monkey-like mummies. Yet the war will be a long and difficult one that will often appear unending if not completely lost.

134   Chapter 5

Having met people with radically different conceptions of Orthodoxy at the School of Theology in Athens, I wasn't surprised that the authors—priests, doctors, and retired judges and army officers, for the most part—could seamlessly combine their academic studies with prophecies and stories about miracle-performing icons, angels, and divine wrath, nor that this publication comes from Esfigmenos Monastery, the alma mater of Agathangelos and nowadays the spiritual center of the Old Calendarists. This is a group of Orthodox zealots who continue to follow the Julian calendar despite the Church's decision in 1924 to adopt the New Style Gregorian calendar. As Ware (2002:3) explains, "For this group, the Julian Calendar possesses a profound symbolical experience" and "is seen as the touchstone of loyalty to the Orthodox faith in its true and full integrity." Nowadays the Old Calendarists have their own bishops, parishes, and monasteries; operate totally independently from the New Calendar State Church; and maintain a strong presence in the formerly Albanian-speaking villages in the outskirts of Athens. They identify themselves as Ghnisii Orthodhoksi Khristiani, the genuine Orthodox Christians of Greece, and are profoundly anti-Western and anti-Turkish. Nevertheless, the Orthodox Church does not consider them schismatics but simply devoted Christians obsessed with the preservation of insignificant traditions and somewhat conservative in their understanding of the contemporary globalized world.[16]

As I leaf through the pages, I come across an article written by Kostis. In it he refers to his successful efforts to prevent the construction of a mosque in Kambos, his televised skirmishes with Muslim spokesmen and leftists, and, most important, the authorities' reluctance to support him. Kostis challenges the readers to ask themselves what the official position of the Church is. He seems to know all too well that, with the exception of the "genuine Christians," everybody else is a traitor. Yet, as we will see, this does not prevent him from meeting with the archbishop and asking for his help.

Second Meeting with Kostis

When I enquired further into Kostis's contact with the Church on my second visit to his office, I learned that in the summer of 2003 he had managed to meet with Archbishop Christodoulos. As if in affirmation of this fact, he put before me a ten-page text dated August 25. This was the speech that he had prepared for that meeting. I leafed through the document only to realize

The (Other) Church   135

how similar it was to the document that we had discussed in our previous meeting.

Kostis's texts are polemical in nature, aimed at awakening Orthodox Greeks and incorporating security and strategic considerations, popular religious beliefs, and didactic references to both the ancient and more recent revolutionary past. There is a repetition of specific phrases and arguments against the construction of the mosque. He suggests that the "Islamic complex" will be too big (35,000 square meters), that it will eventually be transformed into a center of propaganda, and that it will soon become "a new Mecca." His writing also aims for an academic appearance by including citations and references taken from Old Calendarist magazines and nationalist pamphlets that he collects in great numbers. Every text is personally signed by him at the end: Dr. Kostis, medical doctor, Ph.D. (University of Athens).

"Tell me more about the meeting with the archbishop," I said.

"I was in charge of the campaign committee that the mayor and I had put together, and in that capacity, I was able to arrange a meeting with Christodoulos in Ayia Filothei."[17] He continued:

I had tried really hard to organize that meeting and I had told both the mayor and the members of parliament to meet in Tsiminis [a local coffee shop] early in the morning on the day of the meeting. No one had replied to my messages, and when I went to the coffee shop I thought that it would only be myself and some other members of our association meeting with the Archbishop. Naturally everybody came, despite their initial reluctance. Who would miss that opportunity, all that publicity? I saw Nikolis [the mayor], who was originally very skeptical about that meeting, coming down the street and I shouted at him in excitement: "*Ela re Nikoli, Ela re dhimarhe! Pos tha pame khoris esena?*" [Come on Nikolis, come on mayor! How are we going to go without you?] And so we went, *Dimitraki mu*. Christodoulos kept us waiting for two and a half hours. He really did not want to meet with us. I guess he thought we would get tired and leave. Eventually he appeared. "*Evloyite Makariotate, Evloyite*" [Blessings, Your Beatitude, Blessings], I said, only to be interrupted by the local New Democracy MP, who knew nothing about our efforts. And then Nikolis started talking. Remember, this is the guy I had to convince to join us. It did not occur to him that he was the mayor, that this is what he was supposed to do.

The Archbishop replied—you know, talking and saying nothing at the same time—along these lines: "Mother Church understands your concerns and will stand by you in your attempts to empower Orthodoxy and disseminate the message of our Lord, Jesus Christ," and so on. I got so upset at one point that I interrupted him. "Your Holiness, I have prepared a text to read and with your permission I would like to do so." And then, *Dimitraki mu*, I read for thirty minutes with all of them standing. Would I let them go that easily? Whenever I think of this meeting, I get so angry that my blood pressure goes up. But you know what? It was for the best. Because the next day I was able to say that everybody supports our activities, the mayor, the MPs, the people of Kambos. But the truth is, *Dimitraki mu*, no one really cares.

Interestingly enough, the strategy employed by Kostis was extremely effective. By mobilizing reluctant local authorities, he was able to fill a representational void, to fight a battle that few people wanted to engage in, and to become the living metonym of the "rebellious" locals in the media. Some fifteen years later, when construction of a mosque in Votanikos was about to begin, his methods of resistance became a source of inspiration for a Golden Dawn group that erected a makeshift chapel in the designated site to show local opposition to the project (Verousi and Allen 2021:8). So successful was Kostis that even the archbishop himself believed that the people of Kambos and the surrounding villages were ready to actively oppose the establishment of a mosque in their area, and some days after his meeting with Kostis and the "campaign committee," he sent a letter of complaint to the minister of foreign affairs. The letter was published in *Ekklisia* (2003), the Church's official magazine, and describes the Church's ambiguous position: in principle, it supports the construction of a mosque in Athens; however, it also takes into consideration local reactions. When I showed that article to Kostis, he was not surprised. As he explained to me, he was well aware of the fact that the Church engages in double-talk.

As I now understand, what Kostis was witnessing in all of his meetings was a concrete effort on the part of the Church to navigate a complex political landscape. In particular, what caused him much distress was the realization that the Church was also a political institution.[18] The archbishop, like any other party leader, had to balance the demands of different factions within the Church (some of them progressive, like Vlakhou and Father Epifanios, some of them, like the bishop of Thessaloniki, extremely conservative with beliefs

The (Other) Church   137

closer to those of Old Calendarists), manage public opinion as expressed in media coverage and opinions polls, and act on ratings of the liturgies broadcast on TV and opinion polls measuring his popularity, which had suffered a significant blow after the clash with the government over identity cards (see Georgiadou 2009:135, 152). Several articles at the time also discussed Christodoulos's constant negotiations with the government over two primary objectives. As it turns out, the archbishop wanted to use the mosque as leverage to ensure government support for his intention to fulfill at last the Nation's Vow through the construction of a new cathedral in Athens and the continuous generous funding of Allilengii (Solidarity), the Church's aid organization, by the Ministry of Foreign Affairs (see Petropoulou and Leontopoulos 2006).

One of his most vocal opponents, Metropolitan Chrisostomos of Zakinthos, aptly described in an interview how those following the mosque controversy were likely to miss the point entirely. Church politics on the issue should not be understood in terms of theology and culture or in the context of Christian-Muslim and Greek-Arab relations, he explained, but as part of negotiations with the government aimed at securing the operation of Allilengii:[19]

> St. Nicolas Church in Cairo is next to the biggest Islamic center. There too the church bells ring in the morning and at night and no one ever disturbed us. How can we deny this [the construction of a mosque in Athens]? My recommendation is that we need to approve the construction of the mosque as soon as possible. For it is unacceptable what is happening on the Church's side. In this way, we are creating problems for the Orthodox of the Arab Islamic countries. In Antioch, it is written in Greek letters "Helleno-Orthodox Patriarchate of Antioch," even now that the Patriarch is not Greek. . . . What would a mosque do to us? Would I be able to discourage an Orthodox [Christian] if he wants to convert to Islam? . . . But this is not the issue. The issue lies in the negotiation. For what you [i.e., the state] are giving me for Allilengii is not enough because of the lack of transparency in my administration. (Tsatsis 2003b)

Sacrifice and the Institutional Production of Ambiguity

In this chapter, I have examined the politics of the Orthodox Church regarding the mosque debate through my encounters with Kostis and conflicting media and scholarly assessments of its position. In adopting the lens of an agonistic and marginal Orthodoxy, I have studied the Church as a political organization and Archbishop Christodoulos as akin to a mainstream party leader who is subjected to the pressure of various ecclesiastical factions, while engaging in delicate negotiations with the government and assessing public opinion. The question this examination raises is how Church leaders navigate the complex contemporary political landscape.

In response, I have shown that an ethnography of ecclesiastical politics will be shortsighted if it is structured around binary questions that anticipate straightforward answers and assume consistency. As my archival research and discussions with Kostis illustrate, the Church on many occasions says yes and no to the mosque at the same time. The answer depends on the interlocutor. If it is the European Commissioner for Human Rights asking in public, then it is an ornamented, heavily qualified yes. If it is Kostis asking, it might be a no. We have seen, for instance, Bishop Anthimos of Thessaloniki express his dissatisfaction with the government's decision and ask for a quid pro quo from Turkey, even though he is well aware of the Holy Synod's decision to allow the construction of a mosque in 2002.

Undoubtedly, the potential of the mosque issue for public controversy created space for political maneuvers, in which Church authorities were quick to engage. In other words, because the state's decision to construct an official place of worship for the capital's Muslims did not touch on the creed of Eastern Orthodoxy, the official Church's discourse did not have to express an absolute and nonnegotiable certainty. In fact, the Church systematically, willingly, and knowingly engaged in a politics of calculated ambiguity that was not solely exercised at the level of interlocution. As I have shown, the Church through its various publications and pronouncements also produced a written record that could be used to justify total support or complete opposition to the government's decision to construct a mosque. Archbishop Christodoulos, through his institutional position and constant media exposure, came to epitomize this approach. He agreed to the establishment of a Muslim place of worship on the condition that there would be no controversy, trying in this way to please the government after his previous clash with it damaged his popularity. Yet, when he becomes convinced by the media and Kostis's interventions that there is strong anti-Islamic sentiment in Kambos, he publicly complains to the Ministry of Foreign Affairs. This intentional mixed messaging and reluctance to directly condemn reactions, even if coming from Paleoimeroloyites, explains why so many journalists, scholars,

The (Other) Church 139

and government officials who already considered the Church and its leader naturally reactionary interpreted this calculated ambiguity as opposition to the mosque. If the Church played a significant role in blocking the initiative, it was exactly through this discursive strategy, which also capitalized on widespread perceptions of Greek Orthodox culture as being simultaneously anti-Turkish and anti-Islamic, added yet another layer of complexity to the government's assessment of possible political damage, and, ultimately, contributed to the Kambos project's abandonment and the selection of Votanikos as a new site for the construction of the mosque.

The archbishop's maneuvers, however, also enraged Kostis. The mosque debate made it amply clear to him that the Church operates as a political party with a long-established negotiating mechanism and worries about favorability ratings and the political cost of its decisions. Yet such behavior did not come to him as a complete surprise. History, after all, taught Kostis that sometimes it is the leaders of the Church who harm it the most, as in the case of Ioannis Vekkos. At these moments, it is the duty of the "true Christians" to safeguard the faith and, if necessary, fight a calculated war from within. So what then would be for Kostis the ideal way for the Church to deal with this troubling issue? The story of Aghathangelos and the cover of the Old Calendarists' magazine are particularly telling in this regard. Following the pattern of sacrifice that the Neomartyrs' stories offer, Kostis also thinks of sacrifice metaphorically and would like the Church to sacrifice its political and economic interests stemming from its relationship with the Greek state and the European Union. As in the case of Aghathangelos, whose death signifies in the collective memory and imagination of the Old Calendarists ultimate dedication to Orthodox Christianity and to the cause of the Greek nation-state, he seems to assume the necessity of political martyrdom as a prerequisite for safeguarding Orthodoxy and Greece.

His attempts to honor those who gave their lives for independence by fulfilling the Nation's Vow and the stories and analyses featured in the Old Calendarist publication point to the centrality of the concept of sacrifice in Kostis's cosmology. They also shed light on how individuals and groups draw on miracles, prophesies, and stories of divine intervention to reconcile religion with agonistic behavior and political action (e.g., Campbell 1964; Dubisch 1995; Hirschon [1989] 1998; Herzfeld 2008), while operating in a framework dominated by opinion polls, popularity ratings, and public opinion that hardly ever makes space for the supernatural. Yet, when Kostis refers in his discussion of the mosque to a martyr's sacrifice or to the maladies

140 Chapter 5

that await in the afterlife for those who don't opt for the difficult road, he tries to position himself in the present and in an Orthodox context that provides him with possibilities for political intervention. In this sense, and as a means of introducing the following chapter, it is useful to draw on the theologian S. W. Sykes (1980:63), who notes that when the concept of sacrifice is transferred from the religious sphere to other domains, "it brings the dimension of cost and suffering in the series of actions involved."

CHAPTER 6

Political Cost

Questions

Let me pose once again the question around which my ethnographic fieldwork was structured: why was the Kambos mosque never built? Understanding why a certain government initiative doesn't materialize, why certain things don't happen, entails a consideration of politics that simultaneously examines historical conjuncture, the international context, and government structures as well as key actors, their competing agendas, and their assessments of reactions as presented by the media. In a passage that captures views broadly expressed in the media, the journalist Nikos Papakhristou summarized the main reasons preventing its construction up to 2010: "In the near future tens of thousands of Muslims living in Attica (visitors too) will be able to pray in the first official place of [Muslim] worship to be erected in the capital city after almost two centuries. . . . Discussions, laws, architectural plans, bureaucratic obstacles, reactions of citizens and ecclesiastical authorities coupled with 'political cost' had inhibited every attempt to deal with a crucial social issue that tested respect for human rights and religious freedoms." Having already examined the two other main factors that were popularly believed to prevent the building of the Kambos mosque, namely the locals and the Church, I will now ask what exactly people mean when they talk of *politiko kostos*, "political cost." In what ways does the concept account for the nonmaterialization of a place of worship? The concept has come up throughout the preceding chapters. In my account of the meeting with the Foreign Ministry expert, I noted his view that "politicians always calculate political cost," having already referred to a deputy who accused PASOK's ministers of delaying discussions on the mosque until elections had taken place. Then, in my description of the interfaith meeting in the following chapter, I mentioned

142   Chapter 6

that George Papandreou himself used the concept to explain why the mosque in Kambos remained notional, while in a subsequent chapter I considered Kostis's allegations that the mayor Nikolis and the Church always calculate the possible political cost of their positions.

I will now delve deeper into these statements and consider contemporary Greek politics on the terms of its main actors in an attempt to understand the processes, technologies, and economies at work in not realizing state initiatives. While I do not myself endorse the intrinsic analytical value of political cost, I do find it necessary to examine a concept that for years now has provided a language through which Greek politics is articulated and a framework for analyzing government operation.

This particular inquiry takes me away from Athenian masjids, Muslim activists, and coffee shops in Kambos, and instead into the offices of pollsters, marketing experts, journalists, and prominent politicians. In pursuing an ethnography of political cost and of those who employ, critique, assess, and operate on its basis, my aim is to answer a few basic questions. What is political cost? How is it assessed, measured, and quantified? How does it shape the practice of politics and the production of news? Finally, to what extent does the concept account for the failure of the Kambos mosque project? What emerges through this line of inquiry is the centrality of political cost in the workings of a technoeconomic apparatus, a larger system of governance shaped by media technologies and economies created through public opinion assessment, that powerfully shapes public understandings and the practice of democracy.

Preparations

My research on political cost began in June 2008 at the parliament's press archives, where I looked for patterns of use, frequency of occurrence, and information concerning the concept's origins. Soon it became apparent that while many newspapers referred to political cost on a daily basis, the concept was noticeably absent from *Avgi* and *Rizospastis*, which were published by the parties of the left (SYRIZA and the Greek Communist Party, respectively).[1] In their case, whenever *politiko kostos* was mentioned it was either placed in quotation marks or used ironically. In an illustrative excerpt from an article in *Avgi* entitled "The Cross of Political Cost," the author alludes ironically to the New Testament and the Gospels to build a metaphor through which

Political Cost 143

to mock established politicians, their supposedly unparalleled "courage," and their frequent pronouncements about doing right despite "political cost":

> When politicians of the two major parties talk about transcending political cost, they imply that they make a choice of unparalleled courage, that they perform an act of heroism and ultimate sacrifice that could be seen as responding to a messianic call. Just as the Nazarene [Jesus] delivered his impassioned sermon and risked a rupture with the clergy, even though he knew that he would be crucified, he too ignored the political (and the bodily) cost, though from a safe standpoint since he knew that he would be resurrected. An analogous conviction concerning resurrection does not result from any prophecy for Mr. Pangalos, Mr. Papandreou, and all the more for Mr. Mitsotakis, who decide for us, without us, and against us "while being indifferent to political cost." (Kibouropoulos 2010)

For the author, the concept is telling of the political theology and moral cosmology of the two major political parties. Given *Avgi*'s political orientation, one can also read this commentary as part of a larger critique of capitalism, its binary emphasis on profit and loss, and its impact on domestic politics. But if political cost appears in the 2010s as a concept of the establishment to be mocked and disparaged by the Left, was this always the case?

In fact, as I was able to establish, political cost has had a relatively short lifespan in Greek political vocabulary. Until the early 1990s references to the term are sporadic, and the most prominent term in mainstream political analysis is *laïkismos*, "populism." The first mention of "political cost" that I was able to locate was made in the newspaper *To Vima*'s October 4, 1987, issue, in the context of an interview with the then mayor of Athens and later leader of New Democracy, Miltiadis Evert. There the mayor—nicknamed "the bulldozer" for his imposing appearance and determination to break the monopoly of state media and create a municipal radio station—reacts to the way in which certain journalists jump to conclusions about the reception of his initiatives by saying, "Let me announce anti-municipal measures, even if these carry a political cost" (*Afiste me na eksangilo andidhimokratika metra esto ke an ekhun politiko kostos*).

In addition to its use by politicians and journalists, I also encountered the term in several instances during fieldwork in Kambos. In particular, my informants of a higher socioeconomic status used "political cost" to comment on both local and national politics and to account for a wide range of failed government initiatives. In all those instances, the term described a calculated consideration of the possible negative consequences on voting behavior that a government initiative may have.

While those of lower socioeconomic status would hardly ever use the term, their explanations for *praghmata pu dhen yinonde*, "things that don't happen," emphasized the same themes that dominated the accounts of the more well-off. Their descriptions of contemporary Greek politics, too, conveyed a widespread cynicism (cf. Kafetzis 1994, 1997; Navaro-Yashin 2002:174–179) primarily directed toward "corrupt" politicians through cliché expressions like "politicians only care about votes" and "when the time of the elections comes they'll see." When asked about the mosque in Kambos, the initiative's failure was for the most part explained with a single word: *fovunde*, "they're scared." But how do governments and elected officials get scared? Here is the mechanism of fear as presented by Kannelos's father: "They (i.e., the locals) will protest, then the TV channels will come, the government will be scared, and in the end nothing will happen." Gökhan in Gazi had also predicted the mosque enterprise's failure in a strikingly similar manner some years earlier: "Nothing will happen. There will be some *fasaria* (fuss), the TV networks will gather, and the politicians will get scared."

All of these references and allusions to the idea of political cost implied a prevailing belief that politics as currently practiced involves the daily assessment of "public opinion," that TV networks play a crucial role in this process, that public expressions of criticism can effectively stop any kind of government initiative, and that a government ultimately operates much like the people who constitute it; it can experience fear, lack courage, and, most of all, care about what people say. In all these instances, particular emphasis is placed on the operation of memory, which compensates for the lack of political action and a weak civil society (much discussed by sociologists and political scientists of Greece; e.g., Mavrogordatos 1988, 1993; Tsoucalas 1993; Mouzelis and Pagoulatos 2002; Sotiropoulos and Karamagioli 2006; Huliaras 2015). Even though Kambos's locals were reluctant to pursue their rights actively and demand a sewage disposal system, as Nitsa indicated, they did make it explicit that they were capable of remembering and punishing politicians and political parties when election time came.

As far as when the term first appears and gains prominence in the English-speaking world, Aaron Wildavsky's 1966 article "The Political Economy of Efficiency: Cost–Benefit Analysis, System Analysis, and Program Budgeting" offers a rare mapping of its genealogy. It commences with a passage that could be understood as the author's criticism of his own discipline and its failure to provide decision-makers with comprehensible analytic tools:

> The encroachment of economics upon politics is not difficult to understand. Being political in perspective is viewed as bad; having the perspective of the economist is acclaimed as good. As a discipline, economics has done more with its theory, however inadequate, than has political science. Under some conditions economists can give you some idea of what efficiency requires. It is a rare political rationality. Economists claim to know and work to defend their interests in efficiency: political scientists do not even define their sphere of competence. Thus, the market place of ideas is rigged at the start. (Wildavsky 1966:292)

In the first part of the article Wildavsky discusses cost-benefit analysis and moves on to lay out his criticisms. He critiques the unquestioned adoption of economic rationality in political domains, where quantification becomes extremely difficult or even unethical (as in the case of health care economics):

> Although cost-benefit analysis presumably results in efficiency by adding the most to national income, it is shot through with political and social value choices and surrounded by uncertainties and difficulties of computation. . . . Economic analysts usually agree that all relevant factors (especially nonmarket factors) cannot be squeezed into a single formula. They therefore suggest that the policy maker, in being given the market costs and benefit of alternatives, is, in effect, presented with the market value he is placing on nonmarket factors. The contribution of the analyst is only one input into the decision, but the analyst may find this limited conception of his role unacceptable to others. Policy makers may not want this kind of input; they may want *the* answer, or at least an answer they can defend on the basis of the analyst's legitimized expertise. (Wildavsky 1966:297)

To my mind, Wildavsky's article explained the concept's popularity among Greek politicians: in contrast to other analytic tools, a market approach to politics offers a comprehensible binary assessment of political situations (e.g.,

146   Chapter 6

high cost, low cost), while at the same time enabling political personnel to justify decisions by citing numbers and statistical data. I decided to discuss this idea with academics with firsthand experience of government operation, pollsters, politicians, and journalists whose analyses have shaped understandings of the mosque controversy. I started, in the summer of 2008, with Phaidon, a journalist who referred to political cost regularly in his articles and was widely considered an expert on American politics. Would he connect the emergence of political cost in Greece to trends in economic analysis that first became noticeable in the United States decades earlier?

The Future in the Past

As far as Greek journalism is concerned, Phaidon was surely an upper-class rarity, almost destined to succeed. His Ivy League credentials and extensive contacts with American journalists, government officials, and businesspeople resulted in access to the White House, a deep understanding of media operation in the United States, and a couple of very popular books on Greece's more recent political history. In many ways, it seemed, Phaidon had seen the future of Greek media in the United States, and he contributed to its rapid modernization upon his return to Athens. As a columnist of one of the country's most prominent newspapers of the center-right, he was advocating that the government adopt a reform agenda and become more integrated into EU structures. He always seemed to ask politicians the same questions: Why don't you take action? Why are you so afraid of political cost? This position was very much in line with the views of the media corporation controlling a TV station and various radio stations in addition to his newspaper—which strongly supported market liberalization and a less bureaucratic state.

When our meeting at his newspaper's headquarters was finally arranged, I tried not to lose time in long introductions and asked him to define the concept for me. Phaidon began:

> I think political cost is basically the alibi the politicians use every
> time they want to defend the status quo and avoid taking a risk.
> Every time there's a big reform that the experts or the EU deem
> necessary, some party official will come out and say: Well, this is a
> wonderful thing to be done, but there will be tremendous "political

cost." It's usually supported by some *polling numbers*. . . . It's usually a self-fulfilling prophecy. The politician doesn't want to go against the unions, or some very small interest group, and they make it a bigger story than it actually is. I think a classic case of this was the education reforms, where the excuse for the last twenty years in which nothing happened in the Greek university system was political cost, but then once we started changing something the polling numbers showed clearly that people wanted change.[2]

Like most political scientists studying unrealized state initiatives, my interlocutor was keen on placing our discussion in the larger context of failed reforms and, surprisingly enough, he too seemed doubtful of political cost's usefulness in political analysis. For Phaidon, governments seemed to understand the concept in a rather problematic manner, political cost was a "self-fulfilling prophecy,"[3] and its assessment was based on "some polling numbers" that created the phenomena that they supposedly documented.[4] In this context reality itself is distorted to the point that even a small interest group is perceived as capable of hindering the country's development (see Featherstone 2005:740).

Phaidon's example of the interrelation between political cost and government reforms also suggested an interesting possibility: even though it was first believed that the reform of higher education undertaken by New Democracy in the early 2000s was unpopular, when the government finally decided to challenge the status quo, polling numbers showed that the public endorsed the initiative. Could it be that the building of a mosque in Kambos would not necessarily cause as much reaction as was widely believed?

During our discussion I also enquired about the moment when the concept made its appearance in Greece. Phaidon described a remaking of the political landscape at the intersection of polling, market research, and media privatization, and in his response I saw a connection between all the things that troubled Wildavsky and political cost's emergence in Greece: "I think the first time I really heard about it was in the early 1990s. I think this has to do with two matters. One was the media boom. The fact that TV was privatized. It was much more open, there wasn't a hidden debate about these things. Whereas in the past, it was a very closed media environment where you would talk to a publicist to make arrangements. You know, it wasn't so open. Also, I think, polling became very important. We didn't have any polls before the late eighties, early nineties."

148   Chapter 6

Over the days that followed our meeting I sought out information concerning the Greek "media boom," the literature on which can be read as a delicate exercise in narrating a long story of corruption, lawlessness, and continuous negotiation between major business interests and the government. The story is as follows: The first Greek TV channel, ΥΕΝΕΔ, was operated by the armed forces until it merged with the National Radio and Television Foundation (EIRT) to form the Hellenic Broadcasting Corporation (ERT)—the only channel broadcasting in the country until the late 1980s. This is why Phaidon refers to "a very closed media environment" that one could only infiltrate with the assistance of a publicist, perhaps insinuating that TV and radio stations at the time were capable of censoring any news critiquing the ruling party. This changed in 1989, when the coalition government of New Democracy and Sinaspismos passed Law 1866, which allowed licenses to be granted to the private sector for ownership and operation of TV channels (Papathanasopoulos 1993:250). Within months two broad business coalitions were formed to establish Mega Channel and Antenna TV, and subsequently there was "a steady increase in the number of private TV channels with at least eight reaching a nationwide audience and many more transmitting to local audiences" (Yannas 2002:72).

While Phaidon was right to point out that the attempts of New Democracy and Sinaspismos to challenge PASOK's exclusive access to the media resulted in the "opening up" of a "closed media environment," I couldn't help but wonder whether plurality in information was indeed possible at the time of our interview. In fact, what I was reading was pointing in the opposite direction. Scholars of the media landscape in Greece usually arrive at the same conclusions. All major Greek TV and radio stations are owned by tycoons heavily involved in the country's banking, business, construction, and shipping sectors and deeply interconnected among themselves (Nevradakis 2014b). The stations operate in a rather anarchic manner, broadcasting any programming that they desire on the basis of temporary licenses (Nevradakis 2014a); run at a significant deficit and receive most of their revenue from state advertising (Nevradakis 2014b); and consequently have a symbiotic relationship with political parties and members of parliament.[5] If anything, the deregulation of Greek TV and radio created a new space for the exchange of favors between the business and political establishments and completely restructured Greek politics. In fact, any attempt to examine Greek politics in the last quarter century is grossly misguided if it overlooks the economies and technologies of news production. As Yannas (2002:72) notes:

With no controls or enforcement mechanisms in place, the commercialization process of the Greek TV scene has proceeded in an unregulated manner, producing a manifold increase in political media outlets and placing no restrictions on the content of political advertising or political broadcasts in general. Ascribing to commercial criteria of TV viewership and profit making, the owners of these private TV channels do not openly identify or support certain political parties. Under these conditions the two major parties position themselves in the media environment in such a way as to appeal to the average TV viewer in non-ideological terms.

Nowadays there is no doubt that private TV stations constitute the most powerful link between the politician and the voter (Papathanasopoulos 2000a:17–19), and clearly those "who appear regularly on television programs have an edge over their competitors, old and new, to get reelected" (Papathanasopoulos 2000b:54; see also Yannas 2002:74). Indeed, some of the country's most prominent politicians today were once journalists or television hosts themselves.

The great impact that TV has had on the reconfiguration of the Greek political landscape was insightfully depicted in an episode of the SKAI TV's show *Fakeli* entitled "In the Biggest Electoral Constituency of the Country" (*Sti meghaliteri ekloyiki periferia tis khoras*). The journalists follow the campaign of Katerina Adhamopoulou, a candidate with the New Democracy ticket in the vast Athens B electoral district, which encompasses 15 percent of Greece's electorate (forty-seven municipalities and more than 1,300,000 people) and elects forty-two members of parliament. Overcoming anonymity in this constituency is nearly impossible for any candidate who lacks significant financial resources and preferential treatment by TV stations. Candidates like Adhamopoulou who do not yet have access to channels broadcasting nationally thus try to seize every possible opportunity for a TV appearance. As *Fakeli* shows, the candidate is so eager for publicity that she even participates in a show called "Byzantine Empire" presented by supporters of the AEK soccer club and broadcasted by High Channel, a local TV station. There Adhamopoulou tries to appeal to an AEK electorate by saying: "I am not just a fan [of AEK], I am an *opadhos*," a term denoting fanatical, almost blind support of a club (*Fakeli* 2009).

While the political power of TV broadcasts is commonplace in Greece, it has only rarely become the subject of systematic research. But if

150   Chapter 6

Papathanasopoulos and Yannas are right, if most Greeks primarily relied by the early 2000s on TV for information on politics, then certain questions need to be addressed. What is the nature of the information that the prime-time evening news provides to its viewers? How do viewers form opinions about, let's say, the construction of a mosque in Kambos?

Evening News

In the early 2000s, most evening news broadcasts in Greece would start at eight o'clock sharp with a number of private stations, including Mega, Antenna, Star, Alpha, and Alter, competing for the highest ratings. Yet it was Mega's evening news that maintained first position in the ratings for ten years. Similar to its counterparts, Mega's evening news lasted for fifty-five minutes (with a four-minute break for commercials), commencing with a twenty-five-minute discussion of domestic affairs followed by short reports on international news. Then the "cultural agenda" was presented, often focusing on the activities of a philanthropist and member of the family controlling a significant share of Mega's stocks. Sports, the weather, the stock market, and currency exchange rates were presented in the final ten minutes. In sum, it was usually within a time slot of twenty-five minutes that the country's sociopolitical and economic situation could be discussed by the presenter, two commentators, and a rotating cast of guests. It was a standard feature of all evening news programs that MPs would engage in a spirited discussion while the presenter would try to impose order. This was, of course, a difficult task, as the guests were usually numerous and each wanted to dominate the airtime. Producers came up with a particular arrangement to ensure that the presenter, commentators, and guests appear on screen at the same time: the so-called *parathira*, "windows." A single frame is divided into many boxes so that every participant can face the camera and look viewers in the eyes. What in the United States would be considered a parody of discussion is in Greece a standard feature of the news.

In an evening broadcast during a peak in the mosque debate, Mega commenced with a presentation of British concerns over Greek efforts to organize a successful Olympic Games. The British, it was reported, doubted that the venues would be ready in time and questioned the police's ability to guarantee the safety of thousands of visitors from Islamic terrorism. "Meanwhile," reported the anchor, "reactions persist in Kambos, where the *temenos* will be built. But let us discuss this issue with tonight's guests." At that moment six *parathira*

Political Cost 151

appeared on the screen. "In the studio with us we have Dr. Kostis from Kambos, Mr. Halil-Latif, and Imam Hassan. Dr. Kostis, could you explain to our viewers why people in the area react to the government's initiative?"

"We will never allow the construction of a *dzami*! Our grandparents did not sacrifice their lives for us to build mosques and shelter terrorists," shouted Kostis.

"But Islam is a religion of peace," intervened Hassan.

"Go and tell that to the New Yorkers," replied Kostis, who went on to explain that it is the *Tama* that should be built instead (see Chapter 5).

"Let us have Halil-Latif's opinion," suggested one of the commentators.

"I come from Western Thrace," said Solidarity's president, "and I am very used to having others speaking on my behalf."

This kind of ironic introduction might have made some sense had Halil-Latif had the time to narrate his personal history and the predicament of Western Thrace's minority population. But already almost three minutes had passed, and the news presenter was informed that a government minister was ready to join the broadcast live from his office to discuss current affairs.

"Gentlemen, thank you very much for your participation. This is an important issue that we will be discussing in greater detail over the coming days. Now we should welcome the minister, with whom we will discuss the findings of Mega Channel's latest opinion poll on the Olympic Games. Minister, 46 percent of the population expresses doubts over the government's ability to organize a successful Olympic Games. How do you respond?"

As I continued my research on the structure of the evening news, I kept thinking of Phaidon's remark that "polling became very important," which I took to mean that political cost is usually assessed through polls. However, networks would also use polls as a means of manufacturing news; that is, to structure a whole news segment around public opinion research that they themselves had commissioned. In these instances, the presentation of poll results was usually followed by commentary by government officials, journalists, and pollsters, who were usually given under a minute to decipher the numbers' meaning. While percentages in this context have an unclear semantic content, they are clearly capable of initiating infinite inconclusive discussions, the goal of which is not necessarily to shed light on the complexity of Greek politics, but rather to fill airtime and keep viewers engaged.

In the context of the evening news, where statements tend to be short and sharp and information is mediated through camera angles, infographics, panels of "experts," and live interruptions, the mosque issue was never

152   Chapter 6

discussed for more than five consecutive minutes and always by several people at once. In fact, the average time that a guest was given to present his views was forty-two seconds. Kostis appeared to have been aware of this and was very keen on using short and provocative phrases. Halil-Latif, Samir, Hassan, and Dora, on the other hand, were more reserved and their contributions must have made little sense to those unfamiliar with the situation of the capital's immigrant population. If scholars like Yannas and Papathanasopoulos were indeed right about the importance of TV as the medium par excellence of information, then the public's understanding of the mosque issue must have been rather limited.

Out of curiosity, a few weeks later I visited AGB Nielsen's website to look at the viewership for Mega's evening news on the day of the panel in question.[6] This broadcast might have been the most popular in comparison to other networks' news, but in reality few Greeks watched the news that day. The most popular TV broadcast that day was instead a soap opera called *Kalimera Zoi* (Good Morning, Life), watched by 709,000 viewers, constituting a share of 38.6 percent.

Election Mechanisms

Iosif is a *meghalodhimosioghrafos* (celebrity journalist), a former leftist now liberal to the core, whom I felt I already knew, even though we had never met. Every day I would listen to his radio show in the morning, read his newspaper article in the afternoon, and watch him commenting on current affairs on the evening news. When I realized that Nana, a neighbor in Kambos, knew him and could put us in touch, I seized the opportunity and arranged a meeting.

For Iosif, the mosque became a real issue when Greece won the Olympic Games bid in 1996 and Archbishop Christodoulos began negotiating with the government. Like Phaidon, Iosif traced political cost's emergence to the early 1990s, but he placed his analysis in the context of the two major parties' ideological convergence toward the center (much anticipated by scholars of democratization and the consolidation of democratic regimes; e.g., Burton, Gunther, and Higley 1992; Katsoulis 1990:40). Yet, for Iosif, there was something particular in the way the concept is used and understood in Greece:

> This is not a general conception of political cost, that no politician
> will do things that opinion polls designate as unpopular. That's a

conception of political cost that can be found in every parliamentary democracy. . . . In this [Greek] case we are talking about something else, which is not political cost in general, but a particular category of political cost that results in an endangerment of the politician's relationship with the mechanism that secures his comfortable election. You cannot go against the priest or the bishop of your area, the mayors or those municipal parties that themselves operate a whole network of small interests that are intertwined with the interests of contractors who build roads . . . and this expands and makes a vast network which is a spider's web; the kind of web that if you find yourself in it you're eternally its captive. . . . It's a special category; it's the cost of endangering your relations with the mechanisms without which you cannot be elected.

As I asked him to elaborate on "election mechanisms," it became apparent that for Iosif the centrality of political cost in Greek public discourse is the direct result of the manipulation of the capital's electoral district boundaries, which (in 1958) created the massive electoral constituency of Athens B to prevent the Left from securing a majority in parliament. In particular, he explained how crucial access to TV was to the success of candidates' campaigns. Iosif claimed that any candidate elected in these vast constituencies depended on a whole army of brokers: prefecture officers, mayors, priests, and presidents of local sport and cultural clubs, who could effectively block any candidate's wish to engage in principled politics. To use his words, these election mechanisms practically translated into a condition of "enslavement," which severely constrained politicians in decision-making. Yet, if Adhamopoulou's campaign was successful, to use her case again as an example, this whole effort would really be worth the trouble.

Iosif repeatedly stressed that those elected in Athens B, by virtue of representing so many voters, usually become ministers and occupy key positions in political parties. If they want to—and this has happened on a number of occasions in the country's recent history—they can effectively pressure their own party leader to the point of making him step down. Political cost in this sense is distinctly urban in nature and refers to a political actor's attempts to always keep content a rather diverse body of potential supporters. It is important to understand at this point what Iosif clearly implies and Samir (in Chapter 2) openly discussed: those not partaking in such election mechanisms are by definition excluded from any consideration of political cost. In

154 Chapter 6

other words, only voters and those who claim to control them factor into political considerations over a range of government initiatives. Cynical as it may be, those who don't vote or are not capable of "bringing votes" to a candidate are irrelevant.

The Prime Minister's Cell Phone

At the time of these interviews, a close friend had just begun to work under Phaidon and was eager to help with my research in any way that he could. Petros was a political scientist who, as he would say, was not "wholly convinced" about the usefulness of an ethnographic exploration of political cost—a concept that his newspaper used frequently, he nonetheless acknowledged. Yet, for Petros, its usage was logical and to be expected from a media corporation that had clearly adopted a market-oriented agenda. As he described to me over dinner:

> This term [political cost] is mainly used by liberal newspapers. Liberal in the European sense of the word, meaning right-wing, people who are libertarian. My newspaper is libertarian, in favor of the privatization of everything. Keep in mind that 40 percent of the Greek GDP is produced by the state. It's basically a mixed economic system. So, privatization is still an issue in Greece. It's not like the U.S., where there is nothing public to privatize. My newspaper uses the term in every single issue of the newspaper, I think. The question is always the same: Why don't you do that? Why do you pay so much attention to the political cost, when you know that you have to modernize the country?

To Petros's mind, research on political cost only seemed exciting to me because of my lack of familiarity with basic political science and theories of populism. "These phenomena have been studied, there are no surprises there," he said. A couple of years later, however, Petros had reconsidered. As he became more familiar with the media establishment and started calling senior journalists, ministers, and high-ranking officials by their first names, he noticed practices that departed from textbook understandings of politics—attitudes and strategies, as he would later say, that are better captured in TV series such as *Borgen* and *House of Cards* than in most scholarly works. Despite his academic background, Petros soon became critical of scholars' ability to describe political phenomena in ways that bear any resemblance to reality. For him, current research in political science or sociology—or anthropology, for that matter—mostly reflected power struggles within academia to secure disciplinary boundaries rather than any political actuality. By the time he left the newspaper to work abroad, he had direct access to Greek prime ministers and had formed a solid understanding of what local politics meant and, most important for me, how political cost was assessed.

In 2014, the two of us met again. Having worked as a journalist for seven years, Petros explained to me how the system works, that is, how key political actors assess public opinion, calculate potential costs, and arrive at decisions. Every single political party assesses public opinion in two ways, he said, through opinion polls and by monitoring news broadcasts. Regardless of their political orientation, every party works closely with one or two polling companies, which conduct daily research on their behalf. Usually these companies run polls structured around the same questions regarding the popularity of the prime minister and the government. Before a government pursues any new policy, these companies will conduct ad hoc polls and focus groups in which the possible reactions of the average Greek are assessed. At the same time, there will be a group of advisors responsible for following radio and TV broadcasts and preparing the MPs chosen by the party's leader to participate in the evening news broadcasts. Usually their number is small and often the same people will participate in two or three evening broadcasts from their office. This group of advisors starts preparations for the evening broadcasts early on, when they have "morning coffee" with the party leader, and they will be on the phone with journalists for the rest of day scheduling appearances and figuring out the details of their representatives' participation.

An hour before the evening news there is frantic preparation and nothing else can take priority. The party's representative has to be well informed, well groomed, in good spirits, and sharp, able to seem natural and focus on the camera, and, crucially, has to remember the slogans that the polling company has designated as important. The preparations of a whole day lead to this moment. In other words, the evening is the pinnacle of daily politics, and this is why journalists, pollsters, and party officials so frequently refer to what will happen *to vradhi*, "in the evening." At 10 p.m., unless there is a current affairs emergency, a hard day's work comes to an end and it's time for leisure. Journalists, party representatives, and their advisors will go to one of a handful of usual hangouts for dinner and drinks. For young reporters, participation in these daily rituals signifies a bright professional future. But what does all this mean for political cost and the way that the concept is assessed?

156   Chapter 6

For Petros, this routine points to the existence of a closed circuit consisting of a small group of people. This closed circuit is the microcosm that key political actors inhabit, and it is through the technologies that this group uses to assess public opinion and the information that it exchanges that "public opinion" is constituted, assessed, and understood, becoming a conceptual entity.[7] Practically speaking, this means that Petros can call every single minister and the prime minister on his cell phone and is expected to answer any calls that he might receive from them at any time. While the prime minister negotiates the Greek debt with EU and International Monetary Fund officials behind closed doors, Petros texts him, "How are we doing?"

The prime minister responds, "Good for the time being, I will tell you more, what are people saying out there?"

The Two Agendas

I met with Stratos, the founder and director of a major polling company, in early April 2010. As he spoke, Stratos was very attentive to his language and very precise in his answers, and it took considerable effort to extract extended responses from him. As was the case with most interviews, I introduced my research on the Kambos mosque, and in response I was told that it was mainly the Orthodox Church that should be held accountable for the project's non-materialization: "The former government [i.e., that of New Democracy] had secured its domination through an alliance with the Church." Stratos then went on to define political cost for me: "This is the loss of social and electoral support due to particular political positionings and initiatives. That is, to lose social and electoral support (*erismata*) because you took one or another stance or initiative when in the country's government. . . . This concept is anything but new. It is actually intertwined with bourgeois democracy." He assured me, "There is substance to [the concept of] political cost." The concept, I was told, incorporates notions of endangerment, it refers to a risk that a politician or a government incurs (or not) in the attempt to follow a particular plan of governance.

"So how do you, as a professional, assess political cost?" I asked him.
He responded:

A well-structured monitoring of the political climate presupposes both permanent questions—"index questions" about electoral influence, popularity, and political acceptance—and "ad hoc" questions concerning issues of conjuncture every time. I think if you forget one of the two, and especially if you forget to place the ad hoc question within a framework of index questions, then you're risking serious interpretative mistakes, for it might well be that a particular stance is formed within a greater framework that might have been created for other reasons. For this reason, we always try to have our projects—and this is something one has to keep in mind [when conducting] research for the media—include permanent questions, even when an issue is very hot and they want to present it tomorrow and they are just interested in asking two questions. . . . There are many who want to conduct a "pre-test." They don't say "I want to assess political cost." It doesn't matter really if they use the term, but in essence many want to conduct a "pre-test" for one public position or another. Practically speaking, this translates into what influence or effectiveness one stance or another may have. From a reverse point of view, what political cost you can incur by one choice or another.

Stratos quickly realized that I was very skeptical of polls and "public opinion," the very premise of his profession. Having recently read classical works on the subject (e.g., Bishop 2005; Bourdieu 1979; Osborne and Rose 1999), I thought that pollsters operated on the assumption that "public opinion" was an aggregation of individual opinions, which disregarded how people form opinions "as a function of a society in operation" (Blumer 1948:543), and that the very question "What do you think about x?" presupposed a belief on the part of the pollster that the respondent had enough knowledge on the topic and indeed was interested in it. "Let me make something clear," said Stratos.

I myself admit that there are limits to what can be achieved with this research method, and also that the number of opinion polls in Greece has grown to an inordinate degree. Yet there are two reasons for this. First, opinion polls have replaced the articulation of a coherent political discourse. Their proliferation also suggests the inability of political parties to talk about politics in clear terms. In this way, political parties look for a third party that will speak on their behalf, and this is clearly public opinion. At the same time, you have to accept that political research in Greece has been extremely successful and that the reliability of opinion polls remains particularly high.

158   Chapter 6

Like the founding fathers of polling, George Gallup and Elmo Roper, who claimed, "Elections come only every two years, but we need to know the will of the people at all times," and described public opinion surveys as "the greatest contribution to democracy since the introduction of the secret ballot," Stratos strongly believed that his profession was essential to democracy. In fact, that it was a form of direct democracy capable of combating unresponsive legislatures and lobbying groups, which Gallup described as "minorities representing themselves as the majority" (Igo 2007:121). He continued:

> I would challenge you to consider for a second the countries in which no opinion polls take place, and then you'll see that political marketing is a feature of democracy. The problems you allude to are very real, and actually I do agree with you. You ask, for example, whether Karamanlis's previous cabinet relied solely on opinion polls. But there is a contradiction in the schema that you propose here. What does it mean, "He [Karamanlis] took opinion polls seriously?" Here lies the big problem. If taking opinion polls seriously means to have a policy like a rod that easily bends to one direction or the other, then I would say that this is a grossly mistaken approach to the study of public opinion. You are making a strategic mistake that touches on the very essence of politics, what politics means and what your responsibilities are. Serious management of public opinion is not the political system bowing to opinion polls. It is [a politician] understanding what the trends of society are and how to adjust his quests and declarations to these trends, so that his opinions dominate at the end of the day.

"What happens if a politician does not have the money to run opinion polls?" I asked rhetorically. "He relies on the press and the broadcast media for the assessment of public opinion," I continued, and told him the story of the BBC reporter looking for enraged locals in midsummer, and then went on to explain that few people in Kambos seemed to really care about the mosque.

With a smile, Stratos responded: "There is a public and a social agenda. . . . The public agenda is usually formed by the media . . . and the social one [is what in reality concerns the public]. I have often found them to be completely mismatched. What you describe is a classic example of a public agenda, as it was expressed at that time, mismatched with a social agenda that could have been [expressed as] 'Let's go for a swim.'"

At that, we laughed together!

Becoming Darth Vader

At the time of my fieldwork research, Jason, the son of a prominent businessman, owned an up-and-coming communications firm in Athens offering services to politicians, the public sector, philanthropic associations, and multinational corporations. We had previously collaborated on an American university's project in Greece, during which it had become abundantly clear to me that his family contacts granted him access to an extensive network of businesspeople and government officials. To my eyes, Jason had an insider's understanding of the market, the world of the media and advertising, and the daily operations and aspirations of politicians and political parties—and that made him an ideal interlocutor on political cost.

Jason took interest in my investigations on the mosque and political cost for professional reasons. As I learned, he had been offering his services to a number of private companies trying, without much success, to establish wind turbines in different parts of Greece. Such initiatives were usually met with opposition from local communities, and when these reactions attracted the media's attention it was almost guaranteed that the initiative would be blocked. Local MPs would be convinced that there was insurmountable political cost attached to the project, and everything would stop. As Jason put it, political cost is an overly simple concept that lacks precision. In his view, it should be called electoral cost.

Like me, Jason was never convinced that local reactions were as important and widespread as the central government believed. Moreover, the whole system of assessing public opinion as a prerequisite for measuring political cost was anything but transparent. "You ask me how I assess public opinion," said Jason:

> You can never assess public opinion. . . . What we do assess is the public opinion polls. And equally, that can appeal to the media. The media influences the public. It is something that in principle is false, or not absolutely true. Technically, the best way to go out and find public opinion is to have an opinion poll. Having worked two and a half years with one of the biggest European companies in public opinion polls, I can tell you there's nothing more funny, silly, whatever, than designing a public opinion poll. I can have a group of 1,200 or 1,300 households saying you, Dimitris, would be the ideal new Darth Vader. Is that their opinion? I'm sure they don't

160   Chapter 6

> even know who Darth Vader is, but in designing the questions, and this is where the whole issue is important, you can actually guide the answer. And if you also examine the fact that no matter how large a place or country is, the relevant sample for a national sample or a local sample is the same. . . . Whether you are in the States or you are here, we are always between 700 to 1,400 max, because then there is this great science of statistics that works.

"And then of course there are all these practical issues that you guys don't get but are so important for understanding polls, public opinion, the mosque debate," continued Jason; he went on to explain that if scholars were serious about their research then they would draw on some "practical knowledge." That would entail working for a polling company to grasp what it means to spend hours on end on the phone trying to find people with enough time to answer a questionnaire that may take ten to twenty minutes, and to know that you have to reach your daily quota if you want to keep your job. This, he continued, wasn't too difficult in the past (in the early 2000s). Some people were excited to think that someone was interested in them, and the whole thing felt sincere and genuine. But things are no longer the same. The profile of those using landlines has become very specific: primarily women over fifty years old with a lot of time to spare and eager to get in a fight. Polling is increasingly viewed as a research method of the establishment, what corrupt politicians and international business corporations use to pursue their interests. As Jason hears from former colleagues, frequently after fifteen minutes of answering questions, interviewees will say something completely out of left field ("I vote for the soldiers of the light"), insulting, or obviously false, or stop answering questions altogether. Meanwhile, a conspicuous absence marks these research practices—large parts of the voting population do not figure in the sample at all, particularly those who no longer use landlines (Stratos mentioned in a later interview that his company is the only one in Greece that calls cell phones).

"If political cost is that problematic and its assessment is so unscientific," I asked Jason, "why do marketers and communication strategists, like yourself, use it?"

Jason looked at me as if the answer was already obvious: "People think or the leaders think or the decision makers think that there's a political cost. Great. Let's use it for ourselves. I will create the perception that the political cost of not having the minister of foreign affairs coming out and saying we need this project is larger than [that of him] staying in his office. I will create the perception that the political cost of meeting you is larger than not meeting you. This is basically the way we work."

Time-Framed Democracy

At the time of our meeting, Thanos, a professor of political history, had completed his tenure as president of the Higher Educational Council—a new state body created to support a much-advertised educational reform by the government of Kostas Karamanlis that, like so many others, was stalled. The course of events was fairly predictable and quite similar to what had previously happened with the Kambos mosque. Marietta Giannakou, the minister of education and religious affairs, attempted to implement new legislation introducing significant changes to university administration; reactions followed that became the subject of extensive media coverage; and eventually Giannakou was replaced and the initiative put on hold. Apparently, Karamanlis became convinced that the political cost of this initiative would be enormous, even though he himself frequently spoke about the necessity of reforming higher education.

Thanos knew about my research on the mosque and he, like Stratos, believed that I should focus on the Church. As he said, it "would be a perfect example of how you are confronting traditional Orthodox society, which looks at Islam as the enemy from the past coming back." He also warned me against arriving at any generalizations regarding political cost's use and popularity, saying, "The public doesn't speak of a political cost unless they're speaking of what they would like the government to do and it does not do. It's mostly the government, or politicians, who invoke political cost. They think, 'We can't do that because the cost is too high.'"

So, what does political cost mean to you? I asked.

It means, he responded, "being obsessed with public sentiment, whatever that may be." He continued: "Now public sentiment can be genuine or manufactured. I mean, the late Andreas Papandreou was a great manipulator of public sentiment, so what he did was he created a public, and a public opinion, and then he proceeded to fall in line with that public opinion, which was his creation in a way. But it takes a confident artist to do that kind of thing. Most other politicians just fall in line with what they find, what is there, and it is endless. The recent sport of politicians is a stream of polls on every possible issue. What do people think about practically any issue." He went on: "All the parties are running opinion polls every day, on every subject. I mean, political parties are big clients. . . . So there is an explosion of seeking out the sentiments of the public on different issues. But it's counterproductive because the public on most occasions doesn't know day from night and will respond according to the whim of the moment, and then the next day [their answer] may be entirely different." Thanos considered political cost the epiphenomenon of a new kind of populism that was imported to Greece from the United States in the early 1980s, when Andreas Papandreou became prime minister. Papandreou believed in the value of the average Greek.[8] Despite the fact that he himself was a member of the elite, he refashioned Greek politics to have space for the common citizen, a person of no spectacular achievements. In this context, the predominance of polling in Greek contemporary politics can be easily explained. It's mainly the result of Papandreou's populist legacy and his calculated attempt to introduce to Greece American political traditions that seek to understand the "simple man."

At first sight, the kind of politics that Andreas Papandreou pursued might seem modern in nature. However, for many political scientists and historians of Greece, a shift of political emphasis from meritocracy to mediocracy is a clear manifestation of "cultural dualism." This is a theory ventured by Nikiforos Diamandouros to which Thanos also subscribed. In a 1994 paper Diamandouros identified two competing political cultures that have shaped Greek political life from the foundation of the Greek state to this very day: the underdog culture and the reformist culture. Especially since the restoration of democracy in 1974, the former is believed to have the following characteristics: "a) a leveling egalitarianism especially salient in the world view of the petit-bourgeois, agrarian, and working class strata; b) a distinct preference for the unmediated exercise of power and hence, towards charismatic leadership; c) an indifference for intermediary institutions; d) a powerful and pervasive populist ideology; e) diffidence towards capitalism and the market operation; and f) an obsessive preoccupation with short-term perspectives to the detriment of long-term considerations."

The experience that Thanos acquired during New Democracy's tenure confirmed for him the binary schema that Diamandouros proposed. Trying to convince so many ministers, MPs, and their advisors of the necessity of educational reforms indeed reinforced his faith in the analytic power of "culture." "You see," he would say, "'culture' accounts for failure in a way that resists conventional analysis of the right-left divide." To put it in Diamandouros's

Political Cost   163

terms, both the underdog and reformist culture have the tendency to cut across institutions, strata, classes, or political parties in Greek society. In this sense, anthropologists, Thanos believed, were well equipped to understand why similar views might be expressed by those supporting different parties, and also how adherence to certain systems of beliefs results in diverse negotiations of time: "You see, most party members don't care about true change. I mean, they don't care because their time frame is limited. They don't think in terms of ten years or twenty years or even five years. I think they think in terms of the next election, whatever that may be, municipal, Euro election, or national election, and I think that's what they're really aiming at. . . . And I think this is actually the worst feature of our present democracy. It's time-framed, limited, *short-term democracy*."[9]

The Blockage of Reforms

In addition to interviewing "as many politicians as possible," Thanos also suggested that I get in touch with Elias, a professor of electoral sociology, whom I would often see on TV commenting on public opinion and voting outcomes. As I later realized, he was also the person who introduced Greek TV to exit polls and was capable of recalling the most incredible information on past elections.

When we met at his office, I presented him with an overview of the project and summarized what others had told me about the failure of the Kambos mosque due to calculations of political cost. My interlocutor contested Iosif's idea that political cost made its appearance in the 1990s at a time when party allegiance became more blurred. The problem with that kind of analysis, he explained, is that party allegiance was blurred already from the 1970s. In particular, some sort of voter movement from PASOK to New Democracy and from New Democracy to PASOK had taken place in the past. Elias offered me the following example: "The victory of PASOK in 1981 was the outcome of a very important direct swing from New Democracy," though political cost was never mentioned at the time. Rather, he found it more likely that the concept entered Greek political discourse in the mid-1980s, more specifically, when Andreas Papandreou's government was forced to adopt severe economic measures to avoid a default. In this vein, he was also hesitant to examine the emergence of the concept in the context of the "media and polling boom" described by Phaidon. Nevertheless, he did agree that political cost must be

164 Chapter 6

understood as a concept describing the blockage of reforms, arguing that important reforms became very rare from the early 1990s onward:

> Konstantinos Karamanlis's government in 1974 and the first Papandreou government in 1981 implemented reforms that, if one thinks about them today, taking into account the situation at the time, were extremely important. Legalization of KKE, the establishment of demotic Greek as the official language of the state, negotiations for accession to the EU . . . and then during the period 1981–1985 recognition of national resistance,[10] decentralization, redistribution of national wealth [cf. Clogg 1992:180–181]. . . . Since then the only real reform that we have is the Economic and Monetary Union . . . and the removal of information on religious affiliation from identity cards.

At that point, I thought of my discussion with Thanos, and more specifically his reference to "a new national sport," and I asked Elias if the assessment of political cost through opinion polls was as extensive as I had heard. He assured me that it was so and referred to Kostas Karamanlis's government losing the 2009 elections by a staggering margin of 10 percent. New Democracy, he said, largely operated on the basis of political cost, and he went on to connect the concept to opinion poll surveys: "Every reform, whether suggested, realized, or postponed, was the result of opinion polls. No minister could operate without being watched by the eye of the *Maximu* [the prime minister's office], and the particular team that subjected everything to opinion polls. They conducted opinion polls constantly. Almost every day."

In the case of the reforms in higher education that Giannakou and Thanos had tried to implement, he claimed that they were primarily opposed by their own party. In a manner very much reminiscent of the work of Nancy and Lacoue-Labarthe (1997), Elias suggested that the political had completely retreated and had been replaced by the spectacle. There were no principles guiding New Democracy's politics, no visions of a better economic future, no consideration of what it means to be democratic and European in the twenty-first century. Only a day-to-day assessment and management of public opinion that for the most part excluded immigrants, refugees, poor people with no landlines—anyone, in other words, who would not fit into the new apparatus that was being created at the intersection of polling, marketing economies, and the media. Under the guidance of a small communications team led by a former journalist, New Democracy ordered polls on everything from educational reforms and the mosque to attitudes about anarchists and identified key words to which the public was believed to react well.

"But isn't that a deepening of democracy," I asked, "if you consult the public every day in a scientific manner?"

"Absolutely not!" said Elias: "This is the conjuncture of public opinion. These are not established opinions. What you calculate in those instances is the way things appear, and then you try to take advantage of it. This impedes you. . . . There is no government that operated in this way that made real breakthroughs. If I don't do this because there is a cost, if I don't do that because there is a cost, then I end up doing nothing. . . . There is a lack of proper political leadership."

Policy Paralysis

Anastasis was at the time of our interview one of the most popular MPs in Athens B. Unlike Katerina Adhamopoulou, he participated regularly in TV debates and projected an image of a young and independent politician not afraid to speak the truth and in so doing disappoint some of his supporters. This attitude occasionally caused him problems, since he openly identified with certain ideas expressed by other parties. Could it be that Anastasis was one of those rare cases of a politician who did not care about the possible political cost of his public statements? Maybe he did care but had a different way of calculating political cost? Or maybe opinions were not that important after all, and all that mattered was access to the media?

When I went to his office I was warmly greeted by his secretary, who was almost out of breath from having to answer the office's constantly ringing phones, and shown to his office, which combined modern technology and minimal design. Our discussion began with an overview of my research on the Kambos mosque and a definition. Political cost, according to Anastasis, "is the tangible, negative implication in terms of voter behavior of a significant policy initiative." Like many others, he too was unsure as to when exactly the term made its appearance, but he hastened to emphasize, "The notion that in a democracy certain actions will incur political cost that is measurable has always been part of the democratic process." Perhaps, he continued, the concept gained its current popularity from the moment it became possible to measure political cost.

"So how do you measure it?"

166   Chapter 6

"I am mainly referring to opinion polls and focus groups," replied Anasta-sis, "that can give you quite a detailed understanding of how the electorate or specific groups within the electorate will react to any given policy initiative."

My interlocutor was very careful to avoid the impression that he himself was running opinion polls and focus groups, and he made it immediately clear that he had neither the resources nor the interest to test his policy ini-tiatives. After all, he explained, "this over-reliance on polls is potentially quite damaging, because any given reform initiative will be met with some reac-tion. If you focus only on the reaction, chances are you are not going to move in that direction." He continued: "Being a politician also involves short-term sacrifices to achieve long-term objectives."

We agreed that there was something deeply worrying about the current state of political affairs. Political cost appeared to be causing "a policy paral-ysis," as he put it, capable of creating unprecedented social tension and even leading to economic disaster. It was in this context that Anastasis suggested the institutional restructuring of Greek parliamentary politics that would prevent the kind of shortsightedness that Thanos had described:

The problem is, how can you implement institutional changes
that would make politicians less exposed to what we have termed
political cost. Term limits would be an example. If you are elected
only for one term, for example, you have no particular reason to
worry about political cost, because you're not going to run again. If,
for example—I'm just going to share some ideas—if the executive
branch, which makes most of the policy decisions, is completely
separated from the legislative branch, for example. . . . If ministers
cannot run for election again they will be much less susceptible to
political cost. If, for example, you change the electoral law and MPs
are appointed by the party on nationwide lists rather than elected in
specific districts, again, you reduce the exposure of the politician to
the electorate. Now the counterargument to that would be that all
these measures are in a way undemocratic, because they hold politicians less accountable for their direct actions. And it also presupposes that you have some type of benevolent politician [who] always
[acts] in the public's interest and would not need to be checked very
aggressively by exposing himself to election every x years. Or you
could even extend terms, [rather] than having elections every four
years, having elections every five or every six years. That would give

Political Cost 167

you more time to create this sort of virtuous cycle by which you can afford to absorb the pain or the political cost early on, but hope that your policies have created a positive impact by the time you get reelected. So, all these are interesting ideas related to how you can overcome what I believe is causing a lot of policy paralysis today in Greece. And also, one should not confuse what is termed by many political cost with what, in a way, is quite frequently happening when you initiate certain specific policies, which is less related to political cost and much more related to sectorial cost or to the fact that you are causing pain to a specific group. That group may be quite vocal; they may protest, but that does not mean that they have significant impact in shaping public opinion or that the actual cost is as diffused as we may want to believe.

As in the case of Phaidon, Anastasis alluded to a problematic calculation of political cost that through the broadcast media and in a metonymic fashion attributed far greater significance to smaller yet more robust and visible groups. In the absence of polls on a given issue, political parties heavily relied on news to assess the public's mood and possible reactions to government policies. Usually politicians were so immersed in that system of assessing the public and its opinions and moods that the validity and representational value of news was almost never questioned. In this context, questions such as "What is this public that is being created through polls and news coverage?" and "How is it averaged so that it expresses a majority view for or against the mosque?" are hardly ever posed. "Sometimes I wonder," continued Anastasis, "how the public responds to complicated policy initiatives about economic reform that I myself struggle to understand." He went on to offer the golden rule of news production: "Negative stories play much better in the media than positive ones. Simple stories are by nature preferred. Complex policy initiatives are not. . . . [They are] almost never properly explained by the media."

The Handler

In October 2014 I finally got a chance to meet with Marietta Giannakou, the New Democracy minister of education and religious affairs from 2004 to 2007, who had openly supported the construction of a *temenos* in Athens and had passed Law 3512 of 2006 regarding the building of a mosque in Votanikos. She was one of the most progressive members of her party and in many ways an exception within New Democracy. A former member of the European Parliament, she was a firm supporter of greater European integration with a deep knowledge of EU politics. Her relationship to other high-profile members of her party was that of an occasional pariah. She had strong ideas about reforms that many deemed unpopular and occasionally even supported initiatives taken by PASOK—the perfect recipe for political suicide in the mind of her fellow MPs.

In my long research on the mosque, this was perhaps the interview that I enjoyed the most. Having spent a good forty years in politics, Giannakou had a deep understanding of what it takes for "things to happen." Talking to her made me realize how out of touch scholars can be with the reality of Greek politics. In particular, research on the mosque tended to analyze parliamentary debates and focus on the most extreme opinions expressed in that context to suggest that the mosque was being blocked by Greek society's nationalistic sentiments.

This kind of approach—very much in line with the international press—created a rather rigid framework of enquiry that didn't take into account the difficulties that politicians encounter in implementing legislation, and the very operation of the Greek justice system. Indeed, since the restoration of democracy in 1974, every significant piece of legislation has been appealed to the highest court by different interest groups. For Giannakou, this practice could also be explained on the basis of a microeconomy. In the case of the Votanikos Mosque, some lawyers tapped into nationalist groups, convincing their members to make €50–200 contributions in order to appeal the state's decision to construct the *temenos* (e.g., CS 2013). When supporters of the National Front, for example, gathered in Votanikos in 2013 to oppose building a mosque there, waving flags and chanting, "We don't want Sharia, we want Greece and Orthodoxy," there was some talk of "local resistance" but never of the finances of nationalism.

Going against the grain of most scholarly analyses, Giannakou also claimed that establishing a mosque in Athens was a rare instance in which most political parties agreed on something. "And of course there were disagreements and of course some MPs and priests expressed outrageous opinions about the issue, but this is democracy," said the former minister. "Why focus on these statements and the way that the media represents them and not on the fact that most of us agreed that there are Muslims in Athens who deserve an official place of worship and that the state has a constitutional obligation to protect their right to practice their religion?" she asked.

Giannakou clearly understood that it was one thing to pass legislation for the construction of a mosque in Athens and a whole different story to follow up on it. "I always start with a phone call to a supreme court judge," she said. "You need to have a sense of what is most likely to happen with an appeal and what the timeline is. You cannot rely on gossip! You see, I respect institutions." As she went on to explain, this meant that she wouldn't have drinks with reporters, pollsters, and other marketing experts after the evening news, and that she would be reluctant to answer journalists' phone calls. "They would always try to oblige me," said Giannakou, and then described how journalists would tell ministers what the prime minister and his advisors thought of them and constantly would negotiate the making and presentation of news. If I understood Giannakou correctly, a good journalist could make sure that something was mentioned in the evening news in the way that a government official wanted, but this meant that sooner or later the favor would have to be reciprocated.

For Giannakou—and in affirmation of what Petros had told me—even some of her smartest colleagues became so lost in this short circuit that they came to consider whatever was presented to them and their advisors as concrete reality. Over the course of our discussion I was told that she took seriously the secret services' fears over the activities of the "illegal" mosques that I had visited and believed that once a central mosque was established the state would have every excuse to close down all other Muslim places of worship. Giannakou had also been following opinion polls on the issue, but her reading of them was different from others. As it had happened with her proposed reform of higher education, which though considered unpopular was embraced by the public, she believed that opinions toward the mosque might be less adversarial than what was widely believed to be reported by the polls. "After all, these polls usually contain so many questions that can be interpreted in radically different terms. The Public Issue poll (2010) on the issue is a telling example," she continued and pointed to a poll whose results were open to radically different interpretations (51 percent believe in the correlation of Islam and violence, 70 percent believe that the "Islamic threat" is not much of a threat for Greece, 41 percent agree with building a mosque, while 46 percent completely disagree).[11]

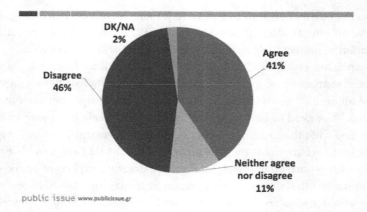

Figure 24. Public Issue's 2010 poll on the construction of a mosque in Athens.

Trajectories of a Local Concept

What happens when anthropologists "study up" to engage the conceptual toolkit of political actors on its own terms and view their analytic frameworks as local concepts? By being attentive to the various conceptualizations of political cost and its place in contemporary Greek politics, I have tried to show how the concept, as assessed through technologies of citizenship inclusion and exclusion (i.e., polling through landlines, conducting focus groups, observing TV panels with native speakers), occupies a central place in the workings of a technoeconomic apparatus whose imagination of the public powerfully impacts decision-making and the very praxis of democracy.

Let me support this assertion with a review of political cost's history, semantic content, and use. The concept established its presence in the Greek political vocabulary in the early 1990s. So what were the important developments at that time? At a global level, cost-benefit analysis had become a powerful paradigm due to its capacity to quantify politics, reduce complexity to binary schemata, and effectively move accountability concerns from the domain of decision-making to that of expertise. As Wildavsky (1966:297) noted some sixty years ago, "Policy makers... may want *the* answer, or at least an answer they can defend on the basis of the analyst's legitimized expertise." At a local level, private broadcasting corporations were being established, the communications sector was rapidly expanding, the ideological differences between PASOK and New Democracy were becoming blurred, standards of living were reaching those of Western Europe (or even surpassing them in the case of Kambos), and, as we have seen in Chapter 2 in relation to the administration of European research schemes, the country was becoming more integrated into the European Union and exposed to the auditing cultures of neoliberal governance (Herzfeld 1992:142; Gefou-Madianou 2000). Subsequently, a series of government initiatives in higher education, social benefits and insurance, public administration, and privatization were blocked, and their failure was accounted for on the basis of the public's actual or potential reaction.

This attention to the people's will on the part of successive governments seems to link populism and political cost, and one may well suggest that the two concepts speak to the very same phenomena. Both of them, for example, prioritize political survival (thus Jason's equation of political cost to electoral cost) over the needs of the wider community, as well as the "here and now" over long-term planning. In that sense they both describe the replacement of principled politics with political maneuvering and a strict adherence to the temporality of a narrowly conceived electoral cycle. Despite the significant consequences of such a decision, a minister of economy would allow excessive spending or a party leader would postpone educational reform. It is such an attitude that Thanos criticizes when he speaks of "short-term democracy" as characteristic of present-day politics. "I don't think they [politicians] care," he says. "They don't care because the time frame is limited. . . . I think they think in terms of the next election."

Yet there are also important differences between populism and political cost to be taken into consideration. The former is invoked to explain why something happens (e.g., tax cuts), whereas the latter is used to describe why something does not (i.e., why a reform fails and/or an initiative remains unrealized). Furthermore, populism posits *a direct link* between the leader and the people. Political cost, on the other hand, introduces a third term that stands *between* the leader and the people. It is connected to notions of political legitimacy and accountability (to return again to Wildavsky) and plays a mediating role by translating the people's will into an abstraction. It is this abstraction rather than the unmediated will of the people that is taken into account by politicians, journalists, and political marketing experts. There is indeed a difference between the sentence "The mosque in Kambos was not built because *the people* were against it" and the sentence "The mosque was not built because the *political cost* was too high."

Unlike populism, political cost is not a freestanding concept. It presupposes a structural belief in the analytic value of "public opinion" (much criticized by Bourdieu 1979) on the part of politicians, statisticians, pollsters, marketing experts, and the media, who constantly try to decipher its desires. "And how could it be any different?" a more cynical commentator would note. Through the lens of these concepts, the unrealized mosque in Kambos appears as a vehicle of potentially significant gains for a great many actors. Not only is there serious money involved in these interdependent notions (Jason describes how they "sell" political cost and "capitalize on it"), sustaining a marketing industry catering to political parties, the media, and multinational corporations using the very same research techniques, but also a set of technologies in place (*parathira*, live coverage, split screens, breaking news, graphics software, sound effects, Skype connections) dedicated to their effective translation into news, cheap airtime, and endless discussion. It is the combination of these two factors—the economy that political cost's assessment creates and its capacity to create and structure news—that accounts for its prominent place in Greek politics and that I consider a key technoeconomic apparatus powerfully shaping understandings of the public and, ultimately, the nature of democracy as practiced in contemporary Greece.

Of course, the ubiquity of political cost as a tool for governing at various levels (local, national, and international) and among different actors (mayors, ministers, prime ministers, the church, etc.) does not necessarily imply its effectiveness. Its widespread use as a concept that condenses complex processes of public opinion assessment is by no means telling of an intrinsic analytical value, but often points to an inability and/or calculated reluctance to envision, plan, and implement meaningful policies. The spectacular failure of administrations that viewed polling as the primary mode of government was clearly conveyed by all of my interlocutors. I described, for instance, the belief that Karamanlis's cabinet (2004–2009) relied heavily on cost-benefit analysis and opinion polls for the country's governance. This point was also implied by Stratos, who referred to "pre-tests," policy trials that political parties run before introducing initiatives. In this manner, an uninformed "public opinion," as assessed through statistics, becomes the determining factor in decision-making, and important policies are tested through adherence to the notion of an average TV viewer qua voter. This assessment, in turn, prevents an alternative reading of the political landscape. Most notably, New Democracy's loss in the 2009 elections by a margin of almost 10 percent revealed a widespread distrust of the party's ability to govern in a decisive manner. By adopting the rationale of political cost, the party had managed to create disappointment even among those whose perceived resistance to government initiatives blocked their materialization. Would Kostis ever vote for New Democracy in the future simply because the party had in the past held back from building a mosque that he vehemently opposed? In other words, the nonmaterialization of a government enterprise by no means ensures political support in future elections among those who apparently resist the enterprise. Disappointment in this regard stems from a memory of political intention that is not necessarily reversed by putting an initiative on hold. In sum, those who govern solely on the basis of political cost, while momentarily benefiting from its economy, can hardly escape the heavy political consequences of inactivity. As far as political praxis is concerned, this is perhaps the greatest lesson to be learned: from a long-term perspective there is great political cost to political cost.

CONCLUSION

The Productivity of the Unrealized

As my research on the mosque of Kambos continued, the sociopolitical and economic environment also changed, much faster than I could have ever imagined. The onset of the economic crisis in early 2010 radically altered the political and media landscapes, and questions regarding state operation, reform capacity, and popular resistance came to dominate public discourse. At a time of unimaginable financial catastrophe and widespread introspection concerning its causes, it also became easier to see how a debate about a mosque, identity, and belonging was connected to a much larger consideration of what it takes for government projects to succeed or fail in a contemporary democracy. Closing this book by looking at what transpired with the mosque and the country after my research concluded allows us to think in much broader terms about what it takes for things to happen in Greece.

So how did the crisis start? As an ethnographer of the crisis put it, "With a number, or rather a revision" (Kim 2017:5). In October 2009, George Papandreou's recently inaugurated government announced that the estimated national deficit figure for the current year was revised from −6.7 to −12.7. Soon after, the three major credit ratings agencies lowered their ratings of Greek bonds, indicating in this way their assessment of an increased risk of Greece defaulting on its debt. This eventually led to a series of loan agreements with the European Commission, the European Central Bank, and the International Monetary Fund, which became known as "the Troika," and harsh austerity measures that brought the two main political parties to the brink of collapse, fomented an "indignados" movement, and led to two short-lived coalition governments. While a few economists, including the former prime minister Simitis, had openly talked about a severe financial crisis looming, both the local media and most Greeks were taken by complete surprise. An acute sense of anger and frustration was palpable in everyday life, which, within a few weeks, felt dystopic and completely different from anything that the country had experienced since the restoration of democracy in the mid-1970s. An era of rising living standards had clearly come to an end, many claimed.

In this context of unprecedented transformation of Greek politics and society, the previously small left-wing Sinaspismos party, now under the name SYRIZA, emerged as a viable political option and won the January 2015 elections. For all its initial proclamations about an alternative approach to the debt crisis,[1] SYRIZA and its coalition partner, the right-wing, anti-systemic Independent Greeks (Anexartiti Ellines), soon capitulated to the demands of the Troika and executed austerity policies that its predecessors had never dared to implement for fear of political cost. Yet SYRIZA wasn't the only party that rose to prominence through the crisis. The ultranationalist and until then fairly marginal party Golden Dawn (Khrisi Avyi) also became a mainstream political force.[2] Especially in small suburban towns with a traditionally conservative population, such as Kambos, Golden Dawn made unprecedented advances by capitalizing on the fact that most locals had lost their wealth as a result of their investments in real estate, which was severely devalued and now heavily taxed. This support didn't necessarily mean that locals now believed in the inherent superiority of a Greek race, but just as likely indicated a desire to "punish" the political establishment for the country's sudden drop in living standards (and didn't mind doing so by aligning themselves with politicians who expressed xenophobic views).

While both SYRIZA and Golden Dawn benefited from the widespread disappointment with PASOK and New Democracy, who until then had dominated Greek politics, and some of their members shared concerns over the country's future in the eurozone and the interests of the Troika, the similarities ended there, as became quite obvious right after the 2015 elections. On top of everything happening with the economy, the main refugee route had shifted from the crossing from Libya to Italy to an even more dangerous one from Turkey to the Greek islands. The economic crisis had now coincided with a refugee crisis that both the Greek and other European governments were unprepared to address. As refugees started to arrive in the thousands on the shores of small islands like Lesbos, Chios, and Samos; international media sent correspondents to report from the European front; and NGOs from around the world flew in teams to help with rescue missions in the

The Productivity of the Unrealized   177

Aegean and with the ad hoc camps that had been created, it became apparent that the situation far exceeded the country's financial and administrative capacities.[3] Golden Dawn construed the arrival of refugees as evidence of the dangers of a leftist ideology that insisted on the unconditional support of "foreigners." Especially on Facebook and YouTube, where the party's views could circulate freely and widely (Kompatsiaris and Mylonas 2015), the idea that the settlement of Muslims from Pakistan, Afghanistan, Syria, Egypt, Libya, and Sudan was depriving Greeks of vital resources and would eventually alter the country's demographic profile not only gained prominence but also shifted existing Islamophobic sentiments and public discussions on identity and belonging away from the mosque and firmly onto the refugees. That is not to say that the party leadership did not oppose the mosque that was now planned in Votanikos. To the contrary, they organized an occupation of the construction site; erected, à la Kostis, a makeshift church; and met with bishops who were sympathetic to their calls (Verousi and Allen 2021:8; Delidaki 2022:802). Yet, for all their efforts, the media were on to other things, and when a member of the Golden Dawn squad assassinated the musician Pavlos Fissas, causing public outrage, whatever access they had to the mainstream media disappeared.

At this time of radical change in all aspects of life in the country, the media industry was no exception—surely not a surprising development given its deep interconnection with politicians, parties, and domestic financial interests. When state advertising campaigns practically disappeared, revenue from commercial advertising and newspaper sales plummeted (Leandros 2013; Papathanasopoulos 2014), and many owners proved unwilling to continue to support their companies, flagship media companies such as the ones controlling Mega Channel and *Eleftherotipia* closed and their vast archives became unavailable to researchers. Other media companies survived through the adoption of a harsh austerity regime. The positions of foreign correspondents were abolished, subscriptions to international broadcasting programs weren't renewed, collaborations with polling companies were limited to the most basic packages or altogether terminated, and any costly investigative journalism programs simply disappeared. During the crisis, existing media economies and technologies for assessing and analyzing public sentiment also adapted to the new conditions to produce news in the most affordable way possible and make space for a new powerful actor that could no longer be ignored: social media (Panagopoulos and Panagiotou 2018).

178   Conclusion

As Facebook's popularity increased and Greek journalists and politicians discovered Twitter, it quickly became the case that what constituted news in traditional media outlets often originated as a social media post. In this sense, Facebook and Twitter users became the correspondents of Greek politics, economy, and society that media corporations could no longer afford. Political parties, pollsters, and marketing experts also turned their attention to social media debates, trying to shape and capitalize on them. The significant political gains that parties like SYRIZA and Golden Dawn made during the crisis, for example, were also attributed to their strong social media presence and ability to mobilize people who followed news only on the internet and rejected "systemic" traditional media.[4]

Like private television channels in the 1990s, Facebook and Twitter emerged in the 2010s as crucial sites for the creation of political discourse. And yet there has been persistent doubt about their representational value. As many communication strategists, politicians, and pollsters told me, in this new media landscape the assessment of public opinion became even more complex. While it is now clearly understood that calling people on landlines and having them answer long lists of questions isn't an effective means of assessing public opinion (especially now that response rates have dropped precipitously), it remains unclear how the kind of sentiment expressed on social media should figure in public opinion measurements (Seriatos 2021). Facebook, for example, isn't used by significant parts of the population (especially younger people, who tend to opt for Instagram and TikTok, and many senior citizens whose connection to the digital world remains limited); its algorithm tends to create "echo chambers" that reinforce a user's already formed opinion; and posts are susceptible to becoming popular as a result of bot activity.[5]

One thing is for certain, my interlocutors would admit. The last years were marked not only by the emergence of social media but also by the disappearance of previously popular items from the mainstream news agenda that could be counted on to attract attention and create controversy—the mosque being one of them. As Greeks started to discuss financial terms such as "spreads," GDP, and "haircuts," the making of a mosque was pushed definitively into the background. Times had clearly changed, and crisis as a topic and as an analytic framework came to dominate everything, explaining not only why social scientists of Greece moved to other sites of opportunity but also why people like Samir, Hassan, Gökhan, Halil Latif, Dora, and Kostis disappeared from TV panels and radio broadcasts. Simply put, there was now other news, equally cheap, if not cheaper, to create and broadcast, that

The Productivity of the Unrealized   179

felt more urgent, and other individuals were ready to take their turn in front of the camera to comment on the economy and give their takes on Greece's predicament.

The Bunker Mosque

In late 2020, amid the COVID-19 pandemic, the first photographs of the now-finished mosque of Votanikos appeared in the press. How ironic, foreign correspondents would remark time and again in their accompanying texts. After a century of failed attempts, there is finally a mosque in Athens, but because of the lockdowns no one can use it. A public health crisis aside, these photographs of the empty mosque brought more clearly into focus the new structure's peculiarities. Clearly this mosque was quite different from the one that the government had intended to erect in Kambos. It was not seen as an opportunity for cross-cultural exchange but rather as an obligation to be fulfilled, largely to put an end to domestic and international criticism. By no means was it intended to encourage interaction between Muslims and Christians. Far from being the centerpiece of a major park as envisioned in the 1930s, or a learning center as envisioned in the early 2000s, it was hidden behind a metal door regulating access to the former military base—a bunker mosque. It was also quite small, with space for only 350 worshippers—a number that was limited to 10 right after the pandemic lockdowns. From the outside, the nondescript structure could easily be mistaken for a warehouse if one didn't notice the few metal shelves for shoes and the nearby water fountain for ablutions. Its interior featured only the most basic decorative elements—a mihrab (made by a local Egyptian carpenter) featuring a Koranic verse, and a carpet (brought from Iran). Even before its opening there were repeated complaints from community members over the structure's lack of character, which made the minister of education and religious affairs state on a visit that a chandelier would also be installed. As time went by, with the structure remaining unchanged, some community members made more pointed remarks: it "resembles the toilets in the freeway or a kiosk," said Naim Elghandour, who had established one of the biggest masjids in the capital (Verousi and Allen 2021:9).

Despite the structure's simplicity, its construction was nevertheless delayed, leading me to wonder about the role of (actual or perceived) reactions and political cost as possible hindrances to the project's implementation. In the midst of all of this, a meeting with the general secretary of religious affairs

Figure 25. The Votanikos Mosque. Author's photograph.

at the Ministry of Education helped me see how my study of the unrealized mosque of Kambos had up to that point failed to fully appreciate how the workings of Greek bureaucracy could enable the subtle undermining of any initiative and systematic passing of the buck (e.g., Herzfeld 1992:142–149). Moreover, like other scholars and journalists writing on the debate, I hadn't realized how much the state employees overseeing the initiative held beliefs that overlapped with the beliefs of those who publicly critiqued them. They too thought that it was a human right for Muslims to have a place to worship and that the existence of a mosque in the capital would be a necessary sign of the Greek state's commitment to the protection of religious pluralism.

The general secretary of religious affairs, a sociologist who had written a dissertation on the Muslim minority of Western Thrace and who had managed to stay on through the change of five different governments, had been handling the issue for many years and was willing to take the time to explain the bureaucratic work that had to take place before breaking ground. Out of frustration with the inability of journalists and scholars to understand Greek state operation, he shared with me a list of all the things that had to be done

The Productivity of the Unrealized   181

before the most recent law on building the mosque could be implemented. These included a series of agreements with the Greek navy, extensive revisions to planning regulations, preparing several presidential decrees, approving the initiative budget and building plans, launching competitions for the construction contract (which failed three times), and, most important, forming a legal defense team that would support the state's decision to build a mosque against numerous lawsuits that were eventually argued in the highest administrative court. The ministry even worked with the state's Legal Council for several years to produce documents to prove beyond a reasonable doubt in court that the mosque was not part of a greater Muslim plan to take over the epicenter of Hellenism and that the use of the term *temenos* (etymologically linked to the verb *temno*, "intersect") did not indicate a hidden plan to "piece apart" the Greek state (MERA/GSRA 2014).[6] At the same time, the general secretary was working on revising the laws (mentioned by Virginia Tsoudherou in Chapter 1) that allowed Christian bishops to be involved in issuing permits for the establishment of non-Christian spaces of worship, and on simplifying the application process—something that he managed to do in 2006 (GG 2006b:1404) and 2014 (MERRA 2016), respectively. To speed up the project and avoid unwelcome publicity, he and his team asked a ministry engineer usually responsible for designing secondary schools to produce plans for a mosque without domes and minarets. So much for those older plans for a Greek Institut du monde arabe.

Yet even all that work was not enough to bring the project to completion. Much fine-tuning and countless legal adjustments had to take place before the first imam, the Moroccan-born Mohammed Zaki, was able to lead the first prayer in November 2020 and thank the Greek people, who accepted "us as Greek citizens and Muslims" (Verousi and Allen 2021:9). As an examination of the relevant laws and presidential decrees published in the Government Gazette shows, the general secretary had to strike an almost impossible balance. He had to create a flexible, independent legal entity that would still be under the state's full control; regulate the operation of the capital's numerous Muslim spaces of worship; take into account existing legislation about the practice of Islamic family law in Western Thrace; and also address security concerns over foreign involvement and international terrorism.

Going through the hundreds of pages of public documents related to the new mosque allowed me to sketch the profile of the Governing Committee of the Islamic Place of Worship of Athens, the legal entity in charge of the mosque, and to trace the evolution of the state's thinking about the project.

While technically a not-for-profit "legal person of private law" (not "public law" as is the case with most state entities), the central mosque is under the direct control of the Ministry of Education, which is also responsible for appointing a seven-member Governing Committee consisting of representatives of the Ministries of Education and Finance, two representatives of the Municipality of Athens, a lawyer "with a minimum of fifteen years of experience in areas of the Secretariat of Religious Affairs," and, finally, two representatives of the local Muslim community (GG 2017:1130–1131). In the absence of a central Muslim body, who gets to represent the "Muslim community" is decided by the state and depends on a community's ability to follow new legislation regarding the operation of existing spaces of worship (MERRA 2016). As Hassan had predicted (see Chapter 2), the new mosque cannot possibly cover the needs of the capital's diverse Muslim populations, and its existence cannot be an excuse for the closing down of the capital's masjids.

The mosque's Governing Committee is also responsible, through its subcommittee on "Religious Affairs," for issuing official documents that in Western Thrace are the responsibility of the muftis (e.g., marriage, religious affiliation, and name-giving act certificates), hiring an imam, and appointing four volunteer assistant imams (GG 2019b:2151). Most important, the Governing Committee's members oversee the production of the necessary reports that will in turn ensure uninterrupted state funding of the mosque and its personnel. If a foreign government offers a donation to the new mosque, as it was anticipated that Saudi Arabia would do in the case of the Islamic cultural center in Kambos, its acceptance must be the outcome of a joint decision of the Ministers of Education, Finance, and Foreign Affairs (GG 2019a:193–194). As the general secretary mentioned in letters sent to ecclesiastical fora to remind them of the presence of Orthodox patriarchates in Arab countries, "Whoever pays is in charge," and in this way "no national sovereignty and territory is being ceded to a foreign power or individual." After all, he continued, "for a country like ours, the protection of human rights and in particular of religious freedom coincides with the protection of national interests" (Kalantzis 2013).

Making Things Happen

"What does this mean for your research?" friends and colleagues would ask me upon reading the news. While the notional mosque in Kambos was quite distinct from the mosque that materialized in Votanikos, for more than 130

The Productivity of the Unrealized   183

years Athens had lacked a purpose-built mosque, and suddenly it had one. Thus the inevitable question: Why was the Votanikos Mosque the one that was built, and what does such a development tell us about Greek politics?

As we have seen, the concept of political cost alone cannot offer a complete answer to the project's failure in Kambos. While calculations of risk and concerns over the possible negative effects on voting behavior were very noticeable at both the local and national levels, the Church's ambivalent position and perceptions of local resistance, together with significant bureaucratic and legal obstacles, also hindered the project's realization. But rather than simply pointing to such a multiplicity of factors, as well as to the history of Greek nationalism and contemporary Islamophobia, to answer the question, this book has traced the emergence of a more fundamental theme running across diverse sites. Namely, this is the productivity of the unrealized in a largely democratic country. To state, then, the answer to my research's overarching question as directly as possible, not building a mosque made diplomatic, financial, and political sense. A structure that for decades on end had existed only in people's imagination facilitated much-needed connections with the Sublime Porte and the Arab world; became the subject of generously funded research in the aftermath of 9/11; allowed activists, local officials, and Church figures to negotiate with the central government; and generated endless, inexpensive news content. Moreover, the project became the vehicle for significant personal gain. One could enter into the debate as an undergraduate student, a neighborhood imam, a member of a repressed minority, or a follower of a marginal Christian sect, and exit it as an expert on Islam, a renowned activist, a nationally recognized community leader, and even a potential political leader. The *temenos* of Kambos, it turns out, was not merely some failed project but a key discursive topos that acquired its prominence by bringing together distinct communities to examine the nation's past and place in today's world. Debating the making of a mosque, then, was profitable because it became a way of asking and articulating answers to the question "Who belongs in Greece?"

If this analysis holds any value, and if indeed the story of the mosque in Kambos reveals the productivity of the unrealized, then how might we account for the making of a mosque in Votanikos? Apparently, the shifting factors on the ground made delaying the project no longer productive. But what exactly shifted? Each of the factors popularly believed to account for the Kambos mosque's failure was also present in the project's latest incarnation. In this case, too, there was some reaction to contend with; the general secretary had to continuously appease different Church factions and the new archbishop, who, like his predecessor, had the same ambivalent position on the subject (Lakasas 2016); and government officials and political parties continued to see some political cost to the endeavor. SYRIZA, the party that was in power when construction began, had relatively progressive ideas about the accommodation of religious alterity yet was just as sensitive to public opinion as its predecessors and relied on the same technologies and methodologies for its assessment. In fact, some years later a high-ranking party official confessed to me that it would have been "a complete disaster if the media were to say that the government was spending the people's money to build a mosque." Most important, the key person handling the matter, the general secretary of religious affairs, predated the leftist SYRIZA government. As for the larger geopolitical environment, it remains difficult to point to a crucial factor that would make the building of a mosque urgent, especially amid an unprecedented economic crisis. The country was still subject to some international criticism for the lack of a central mosque in Athens, but this criticism was by no means comparable to the one articulated on the eve of the 2004 Olympics. The refugees (whom the Far Right tried hard to present as overwhelmingly Muslim), were mostly considered transitory by Greek officials and, in the squalid camps where many of them ended up, they had far more pressing needs than a mosque. Many of those "Muslim immigrants" who possessed "papers" arrived at the same logical decision as thousands of Greeks: to leave the country as soon as possible. Furthermore, the fear of Islamic radicalism wasn't any more real in 2017 than in the immediate aftermath of 9/11. Turkey, which Erdoğan had clearly tried to establish as a regional Muslim power, continued to be left out of all discussions about the Votanikos Mosque, as per the established policy.

So again, what changed? The most consequential shift concerned the project's place in the hierarchy of Greek news, and in particular television broadcasts, whose viewership was susceptible to measurement and quantification. The onset of the economic crisis, the continuous coverage of the desperate attempts of thousands of refugees to cross Greek borders, and then the COVID-19 pandemic formed, in the words of a former minister of foreign affairs who had also handled the issue, a "dark horizon" that left little space for discussing anything else in the following decade.[7] If in the early 2000s public discussions about who counts as Greek often took place through debates about the making of a mosque in Kambos, after 2010 this question became part of a consideration of the economic and refugee crises as both an inevitable present condition and probable future prospect. This change in the way belonging was publicly discussed and socially processed in turn made possible the gradual advance of the mundane administrative work that eventually allowed a series of laws and presidential decrees to materialize and a mosque to be built. It was this very same framework that, much to the surprise of many Greeks, facilitated the realization at that time of two other emblematic initiatives that for decades were believed to be highly sensitive and carry a high political cost: legalization of the production and use of medical marijuana, and permission for the operation of the first crematory.

This story of long failure and eventual fulfillment can also tell us something about much larger processes and structures or, simply put, what it takes for things to happen in Greece. Not only does it reveal that a seemingly failed initiative can be a site of significant gain, but it also points to the fact that understanding politics requires placing its praxis within the context of the production, circulation, and consumption of news. For a complex, sensitive project like the mosque to materialize, it's necessary, but not sufficient, to resolve bureaucratic complications and appease relevant parties. Constant attention to public opinion has become a dominant mode of governing, and principled politics easily succumb to assumptions about the people's will. Therefore, the news agenda must be arrayed at a given time so that the project is kept out of the public eye, viewed as just another public infrastructure project, and consequently not turned into a point of controversy and a barometer of public opinion. When it comes to hospitality, belonging, and the making of space for participation in the polity and nation, sometimes concrete progress can only happen when no one is looking.

NOTES

Chapter 1

1. Apostolos brought to my attention that an explanatory plaque at the Turkish cemetery in Piraeus mentions that the plot "was transferred to [the] Ottoman Empire by an official certificate of the Piraeus municipality dated 24 March 1890." For more information about the cemetery, now property of the Turkish state and administered by the Turkish embassy in Athens, see "To Turkiko Nekrotafio" (2014). I am grateful to historians Eleni Kyramargiou and Nikos Belavilas for confirming that the current Turkish cemetery is the same as the one created in the 1850s and also for bringing to my attention the plans during Metaxas's dictatorship (1936–1940) to turn the cemetery into a kindergarten or a park, and the local reactions to its presence after Turkey's 1974 invasion of Cyprus.

2. At the time of the establishment of the Greek kingdom in 1832, the number of Muslims living in the country was particularly low. Alexandros Mansolas, head of the Department of Public Finance at the Ministry of the Interior, who published information on the socioeconomic and geographical distribution of the country's population (1867:19), estimated the number of all those belonging to non-Christian faiths at 552 out of 1,096,810 residents. More recently, Baltsiotis (2017) estimated the number of Muslims residing in the kingdom's realm in 1832 at 2,500 (with 1,500 of them living in Khalkidha). In any case, these figures represent a remarkable decline of the country's Muslim population, which, two years earlier, was calculated at 11,450 (Kostopoulos 2003:56). As far as the Muslim presence in Piraeus was concerned (the Muslim population was estimated at 34,569 in the 1889 census; see MI/DPFS 1890:6), historian Dimitrios Kambouroglou (1896:92) mentions that Ethiopian Muslims formerly enslaved by the Ottomans who continued living in Athens after it became capital of the new kingdom were known for spending the summer months in the area of Faliro. However, the reference to "Mohammedans" in Law 1851 suggests a substantial and diverse Muslim presence in the area, which at the time was emerging as Greece's main port and an important hub in Mediterranean commerce.

3. For an overview of Greek atrocities against Turkish populations, see Katsikas (2022:27–34).

4. Contrary to what Evergeti, Hatziprokopiou, and Prevelakis (2014:351) claim, the Convention of Constantinople of 1881 (not a "treaty" [sinthiki] as they translate it) did

188 Notes to Pages 19–31

not include "provisions for the building of a central mosque in Athens." The authors reproduce information from Triandafyllidou and Gropas (2009:963) that misdates the Greek parliament's decision to construct a Turkish *temenos* in Piraeus to 1880. For the convention's text, see GG 1882:59–62. For a discussion of its consequences and the state's attempts and eventual failure to integrate the Muslim populations of Thessaly and Epirus, see Immig (2009).

5. Katsikas (2021:85) mentions that the Ottoman Empire "was willing to pay the cost of the mosque's construction and, in exchange, offer land to the Greek Orthodox Patriarchate of Constantinople free of charge for the erection of Greek Orthodox churches in the Ottoman Empire."

6. To better understand the Trikoupis government's decision to erect a mosque in Piraeus, one might also take into consideration the impact on Greek politics of Ottomanism (*Othomanismos*), an ideology that supported the integrity of the Ottoman Empire and promoted cooperation between its Greek Orthodox and Muslim subjects. Stamatopoulos (2019:23) briefly discusses the case of the Greek banker Georgios Zarifis, who believed in the unification of the Greek kingdom with the Ottoman Empire. For a concise history of Greek Ottomanism, see Skopetea (1988:309–324).

7. As Tsitselikis (2012:56) explains, "preventing Muslims from fleeing" at the time "became a major foreign policy consideration and was described by some as a matter of 'national interest' or necessary to 'avert an economical disaster.'"

8. Dalachanis (2017:16) shows that concerns were voiced already from 1911 over the Greek presence in Egypt if capitulations were to come to an end.

9. Kekridhis (2005) discusses how the erection of Muhammad Ali's statue was meant to symbolize hospitality toward foreign merchants and connects the initiative to Greek foreign policy's objectives in Egypt.

10. Crinson (2002:88) clarifies this remark by saying that the Regent's Park Mosque "was seen at the time as a building that represented the 'gold rush' of British and other Western architects and construction companies working for Middle Eastern clients."

11. The Regent's Park Mosque was not the first purpose-built mosque in Britain's history. The first was the mosque at Woking, Surrey, founded in 1889 by Shah Jehan Begum and inspired by the Taj Mahal (Holod and Hasan-Uddin 1997:227).

12. I owe this reference to Panagiotis Poulos.

13. The Ottoman conquest of Athens in 1456 resulted in the conversion of several existing churches into mosques and the construction of some new ones. Among them was the Fethiye (Conquest) Mosque, erected to commemorate this event. After independence it was used for a time as a military bake oven, and then as an archaeological workshop (Mackenzie 1992:13). It was only a few years ago that the mosque was restored to its original architecture and became accessible to the public.

14. There is evidence to suggest that Prince Fahd and Arab ambassadors had asked for the establishment of a mosque in Athens in 1978 (Tsitselikis 2004:286; *Monitor* 2003; PP 2006:896). Allievi (2009:41) discusses Saudi Arabia's increased role in European Muslim affairs following the oil crisis of 1973.

Notes to Pages 33–39   189

15. As amended by Law 1672 of 1939.

16. The Supreme Administrative Court clarified in 1991 that the opinion of the local Orthodox bishop was not binding. The decisive word lay with the minister, who had to assess whether all legal requirements were met, namely that the religion was "known," that its worship was not against public order or morals, that there was no exercise of proselytism, and that there was a real need for the establishment of a church or other place of worship (see, in particular, Council of State Decisions 721/1969 and 1444/1991). If such a permit were issued, those responsible for the establishment of a Muslim place of worship would still have to secure additional permits from the *poleodhomia* (the local planning agency, one of the most corrupt institutions in Greece), the fire brigade, and municipal authorities.

17. Apparently this was necessary not so much in terms of legislation (as per the Council of State's decisions) but in terms of maintaining good relations with the Church (an issue that I explore in Chapter 5). Zoumboulakis (2002:103) discusses politicians' references to the Church posing legal obstacles to building a mosque in Athens after 1969 as instances of "political opportunism."

18. A former mayor of Kambos mentions in a letter to the editor of a local newspaper that on November 16, 1998, he received a communication from Theodore Pangalos concerning the government's decision to build a mosque in the area (*Politis ton Mesoyion* 2000).

19. See, for example, the U.S. Department of State's 1999 Greek report (U.S. Department of State 2000) and the European Commissioner for Human Rights' 2002 report (CE/CHR 2002), which a Ministry of Education letter (MCERA 2015) to the parliament identifies as the most worrisome for Greek officials.

20. Saudi Arabia in particular has been actively promoting the establishment of mosques throughout the world for many decades. As Holod and Hasan-Uddin (1997:272) note, King Faisal was "an active architectural patron, just as King Abdul Aziz al-Saud had been before him; he personally financed a number of important international projects, e.g. the State Mosque in Islamabad and the Islamic Centre in Rome."

21. This particular suggestion was anything but new, since Maria Damanaki, then a Sinaspismos MP, revealed that she had brought the issue to the municipal council of Athens some years before, only to be ridiculed by the newspapers (she was presented in a cartoon as wearing a hijab).

22. Prince Fahd provided financial resources for the establishment of several Islamic Centers around the globe, including those in Rome, Geneva, London, Madrid, Edinburgh, and Gibraltar.

23. A section of the minority population of Western Thrace strongly opposed the system of officially appointed muftis and proceeded to elect rival muftis themselves. The latter are termed "pseudo-muftis" by the state. For more information, see Alexandris (2003).

24. Similar views were also expressed by Panagiotis Dimitras, of the human rights organization Greek Helsinki Monitor, who warned against leaving one quarter of the capital's immigrants at the mercy of a network of illegal mosques. "Research has

190   Notes to Pages 39–56

continually shown the link between unregulated places of worship and the rise of religious extremists. The government has to take the initiative in giving legal recognition" (Howden 2003).

Chapter 2

1. For a discussion of the role of religion in postcommunist Albania and the religious identity of Albanian immigrants in Greece, see Kaplani (2002), de Rapper (2002), and Hart (1999).

2. For more information, see Fakiolas (2003).

3. Even though the Greek state (following the French example of concentration and surveillance) had tried to regulate prostitution since the end of the nineteenth century (Lazos 2002), the "houses" of Filis are technically illegal. Law 2734 of 1999 (GG 1999:3571–3574) stipulates that the operation of *iki anokhis* (literally "houses of tolerance," houses of prostitution) is not permitted within a range of two hundred meters from churches, hospitals, schools, kindergartens, youth and recreation centers, gyms, libraries, public squares, children's playgrounds, and cultural centers of any kind, and that this distance can be extended by the municipal authorities (Ios 2003). As I was told by the madams of the area, no place outside such a range can be found in central Athens, and as a consequence they are subjected to continuous blackmail by policemen, whom they try to bribe by offering money or free access to their services. For a brief overview of the geographies of prostitution in Athens, see Andriopoulos (2017).

4. For an overview of Pakistani immigration to Greece, see Leghari (2009).

5. I wasn't quite sure how the establishment of a central mosque was connected to the preparation of the deceased. After all, according to Muslim custom no coffin is supposed to enter a place of worship.

6. Pavlou and Christopoulou (2008:5) refers to the 2001 census, which "shows that while 47.26 per cent of the immigrant population live in Athens, they hold only 37.36 per cent of the valid residence permits." For an insightful ethnographic analysis of asylum seekers' fears of not having *khartia*, see Cabot (2014:41–70). Cabot's work also explores issues at the core of this book, such as the impact of European Union administrative structures on NGO operation in Greece; the legal, bureaucratic, and narrative construction of classifications (Muslim vs. non-Muslim immigrants in my case, immigrants vs. asylum seekers in hers); and the performance of identities.

7. In a previous publication (Antoniou 2003:165) I drew on interviews with the Caravel Hotel's staff members, who informed me that the prefabricated mosque on its rooftop was established in the early 1990s to serve businessmen from the Middle East who had moved to the capital right before the first Gulf War. However, Faubion's *Modern Greek Lessons*, which draws on fieldwork conducted in 1987, notes the existence of "a single mosque" in Athens "located on the roof of Caravel Hotel" (1993:45).

8. Gropas and Triandafyllidou (2005) provide a complementary insight regarding the issue raised by Samir. They show that political parties and trade unions have extremely limited immigrant membership and that the main reasons behind this lack of

Notes to Pages 56–63

participation are the immigrants' uncertain legal status, mistrust for the Greek state and its institutions, and limited financial means to participate in activities other than paid work. The literature on Islam in Europe shows how differently Muslim communities are treated according to their voting status. See, for example, Manço and Kanmaz (2005); McLoughlin (2005).

9. I myself engaged in this practice in a 2003 article, "Muslim Immigrants in Greece: Religious Organization and Local Responses," in which I present demographic data on "immigrants from Egypt, Syria, Iran, Morocco, Lebanon, Bangladesh, Algeria, Sudan, Jordan, Iraq, Palestine, Pakistan" from the 2001 population census (Antoniou 2003:58).

10. Anagnostou and Gropas (2010:92) cite the 2001 census to claim that 29.5 percent of the country's immigrant population was Muslim at the time. As Evergeti, Hatziprokopiou, and Prevelakis (2014:364) note, it is unclear how they arrived at this number, given that "no official statistics on religious beliefs are recorded in Greece."

11. The presence of this logic in discussions on Muslims in Greece is also highlighted by Skoulariki (2010:305); Evergeti, Hatziprokopiou, and Prevelakis (2014:364); and Hatziprokopiou (2019:202). Nielsen ([1992] 1995:170–171) was among the first to bring up the issue in the literature on Muslims in Europe.

12. As noted in the Open Society report *Muslims in the EU*, "This report describes the situation of 'Muslims' in the Netherlands, although in fact there are very few (if any) statistics on the 'Muslim Population.' Official statistics and census data of the population of the Netherlands do not include separate sections on religious groups. Therefore, there are no data on the situation of 'Muslims' in the housing market or on the levels of unemployment among 'Muslims'" (Demant, Maussen, and Rath 2007:9).

13. Gogonas (2011:125) includes the following telling excerpt from an interview: "We rent small houses and there are curtains all around so that people won't see us from outside. It's as if we are doing something bad. If there were a proper mosque Greek people would also learn about Islam. Because they don't know anything about Islam, only that it means Turkey, that they have tortured people, and stuff like that."

14. For an analysis of *efthinofovia*, see Herzfeld (1992).

15. At the time, the children born in Greece to parents who had immigrated to the country had no direct path to citizenship and had to find an employer and a work contract to avoid deportation (Pavlou and Christopoulou 2008:37). The situation changed with the introduction of Law 4332 of 2015, which gave these children access to Greek citizenship if they were able to meet specific school enrolment requirements and their parents were able to meet residence requirements. For more information, see GG 2015:709–725.

16. To place the establishment of masjids in Athens in a larger Western framework, see, for example, Allievi (2009); Cesari (2004); Dunn (2004); Maussen (2007); Nielsen (1992) 1995; Shadid and van Koningsveld (1995).

17. On the establishment of masjids in Athens by international organizations, see Leghari (2009); Kassimeris and Samouris (2012).

18. For a thorough analysis of the contextual productivity of religious classifications, see Sen (2006:60).

192 Notes to Pages 64–75

19. In contrast to Protestant and Catholic practices, Greek Orthodox do not typically hold meetings, concerts, and performances in churches. For most of them the church's space could only host the divine liturgy.

20. Papandreou's participation in this event is very much in line with his portrayal as a "historical constructivist" engaging in a poetics of both cultural reproduction and reform (Faubion 1993:3–8, 242); Faubion also makes specific mention of him in his exploration of the "Greek modern."

21. The term "Islamophobia," originally introduced by the Runnymede Trust report (1997), was very much in use by many European projects at the time, including ours, thus further promoting the use of the category "Muslim immigrant."

Chapter 3

1. For a fuller picture of the Muslim presence in Greece in the aftermath of the Lausanne Treaty, see Baltsiotis (2011); see Tsitselikis (2012:72–79) on the *chams* of Epirus, who were exempted from the exchange of populations between Greece and Turkey, as they were categorized as "Muslims of Albanian origin" and not as Muslim Turks. After the Second World War they were expelled from Greece, having been accused of collaborating with the occupying German forces—an accusation that, as Baltsiotis shows, served older state policies aimed at creating a religiously and linguistically homogenous Greek nation-state. As for the Muslims of Rhodes and Kos, after these islands' incorporation into Greece in 1947, they were granted citizenship, which many of them subsequently lost when relations with Turkey deteriorated and many emigrated to cities on the Asia Minor coast. Today 3,000–3,500 remain in Rhodes and 1,500–2,000 in Kos. For more on these communities, see Chiotakis (1997) and Kaurinkoski (2012).

2. For more information on the geography of immigration in Athens, see Maloutas and Karadimitriou (2001); Maloutas (2004); Psimmenos (2004).

3. The work of the anthropologist Foteini Tsibiridou (2000) on the Pomaks constitutes an exception.

4. There is a particular government decree that captures the state's inordinate fear of communism, which greatly surprised me when I first read it. On December 27, 1954, Yiorghos Fessopoulos, a staunch anticommunist and then governor of Thrace, ordered the immediate replacement of the term "Muslim" in the names of schools, clubs, and associations with the term "Turkish" (Aarbakke 2001:110, 135; Whitman 1990:51). Fessopoulos was so keen to see his orders implemented that he sent out to all "Mayors and Presidents of the Communes of the Prefecture of Rhodope" the following letter a year later, on February 5, 1955: "In spite of the strict orders of the government to replace the term 'Muslim' and use from now on the terms 'Turk/Turkish,' in the village Aratos on the public road connecting Komotini and Alexandhroupoli there exists a very prominent sign with the words 'Muslim School.' This, as well as any other such sign that might exist in the area of the Prefecture of Rhodope, should be replaced immediately" (Human Rights Watch 1999).

Notes to Pages 75–79 193

5. İlay Romain Örs's (2018) ethnography of cosmopolitanism in Greece and Turkey follows the story of Rum who left "the City" (Istanbul) and settled in Athens.

6. In this context, *laoghrafia* (folklore studies, the deeply political work of which is analyzed by Herzfeld [1981] 1986) and physical anthropology became useful disciplines in the hands of the state. Thus the "traditions of cutting the round bread into four pieces and of putting cross-shaped iron bars to windows were [found to be] . . . reminiscent of the Pomaks' Christian times" (Oran 1994:313). Even racial arguments were put forward. N. I. Xirotiris, a professor at the Democritus University of Thrace, attempted to show in his Ph.D. dissertation that the distribution of blood types among Pomaks was much more similar to that of Greeks than to that of Turks (Xirotiris 1971).

7. To be precise, these fears were not new but rather resurfaced with the Cyprus conflict. Yannis Bonos, for example, describes the rumors that became popular among members of the minority population in the 1920s concerning the area's imminent liberation by Mustafa Kemal.

8. Tsibiridou (2003:194–195) discusses the ethnographic focus on minority populations and fluid border identities as part of a third wave in Greek ethnography that emerged in the 1990s, emphasizing cultural identity. In this regard the ethnographies that I am citing in the text are very much in dialogue with the earlier works of Angelopoulos (1993), Danforth (1995), Karakasidou (1997), and Nitsiakos and Kasimis (2000).

9. I am here referring to the declaration of a policy of *isonomia ke isopolitia* (equality before the law and equal civil rights) in the early 1990s (which very much echoed Venizelos's policy for the equal treatment of Crete's Muslim population a century earlier), the lifting of the restriction of movement in the area, the implementation of new educational programs, the abrogation of Article 19 of the Greek Citizenship Law, and the implementation of new educational programs targeting at the integration of minority students into Greek education. For more information, see Dragonas (2013).

10. The work of Tozun Bahçeli (1990:177) shows that emigration to Turkey was not a new phenomenon. In 1913, 48,600 Muslims emigrated to the neighboring country under the treaties of Bucharest and Constantinople, followed by approximately 20,000 people during the years 1939 to 1951, and 20,000 in the 1950s.

11. In October 1998 the alternate foreign minister Yiannos Kranidiotis estimated the number of stateless persons at five hundred.

12. The abrogation of Article 19 did not have retroactive force, and it required substantial legal battles for anyone who had lost their Greek citizenship to regain it. For more information on Article 19 and its continuous impact, see Sitaropoulos (2004).

13. Despite my efforts to further investigate these particular claims, Halil-Latif always appeared reluctant to familiarize me with Solidarity's activities as described in the press releases.

14. This program was mostly funded by the European Social Fund and was connected to a much larger program led by Thalia Dragonas and Anna Frangoudaki aimed at reforming Muslim education in Western Thrace. For an overview of the latter

194 Notes to Pages 79–94

program and a description of the politics surrounding it, see Frangoudaki and Dragonas (2006).

15. Bournova and Stoyannidis (2018) chart the history of Gazokhori (literally the village of Gazi), the ad hoc settlement that was created upon the establishment of the Athens gasworks in 1857. As they show, Gazokhori, originally outside the city, had a long history of social marginality before its more recent gentrification.

16. Demetriou (2004:14) also touches on the identity of Gazi residents: "By the time I actually arrived in Komotini, I had met with Gümülcinelis [Turkish-speaking natives of Komotini/Gümülcine] who had migrated to London and Turkey, and had been informed that the migrants in Athens are Gypsies and not Turks."

17. Tseloni (1984:40) observes that the women of the community spent most of their time at home in the company of family members, marry at the age of twelve to thirteen, and dress in "colorful long skirts" and "sandals throughout the year." This marked difference in appearance coupled with their low socioeconomic status and perceived Turkish identity has subjected their families to racist behavior by locals (Trimis 1986; *Rizospastis* 1998). As far as religion is concerned, it is worth noting that up until the early 2000s, the literature described Gazi's Muslims as having a rather relaxed attitude toward Islam. In Tseloni (1984:40) we read that "they don't appear to have any significant religious education, which would manifest outside the family's boundaries," while Avramopoulou and Karakatsanis (2002) incorporate the words of a local informant who seems to challenge his very categorization as Muslim and unabashedly tells his interviewers, "We drink and eat pork here."

18. For an overview of the Greek Left's engagement with Islam, see Shabana (2019). For a broader analysis of the Greek Left, see Panourgiá (2009).

19. The *Mevlid* is a panegyric poem in honor of the Prophet that is chanted as part of the celebrations for the birthday of Muhammad or in religious meetings held in memory of a deceased person. It was composed by Suleyman Celebi (d. 825/1421). See Pekolcay (1960).

20. Read the treaty's text and reference to the Sheikh ul-Islam in GG 1913:810.

Chapter 4

1. Attica is the vast plain surrounding Athens.

2. I here offer a rather different version of local history than that of Gefou-Madianou (2010), who, using her research in Koropi, generalizes about the condition of all these local communities.

3. The period that I describe coincides with the rapid growth of the Greek tourism industry, the rationalization of vine cultivation, and the promotion of retsina wine as an "authentic" Greek product.

4. The coup took place on April 21, 1967. It was engineered by a group of relatively junior officers—the colonels Georgios Papadopoulos and Nikolaos Makarezos and brigadier Stylianos Pattakos—whose stated purpose was to stop an imminent communist seizure of power. For more information, see Clogg (1992:162–163).

Notes to Pages 94–98

5. This commission (*Epitropia ton toponimion tis Elladhos*) sought to systematically replace the foreign toponyms with unquestionably Greek names as a means of promoting a sense of national belonging among diverse populations. For the legislation regarding the use of the ancient Greek toponym by the people of Kambos, see Priftis (1980) and GG 1915.

6. Arvanites settled in many regions of the Greek mainland and on the islands. For ethnographic analyses of their communities, see Alexakis (1988, 1993); Oikonomou (1993); Tsitsipis (1992); Velioti-Georgopoulos (1996).

7. My grandfather's sensitivity to the public use of Arvanitika also echoes the outrage caused in Greece by the publication of Jacob Philipp Fallmerayer's book *Das albanesische Element in Griechenland* (1857), in which the author expressed doubts concerning the ancient heritage of modern Greeks. This sensitivity was also connected to widespread rumors among Arvanites that the Albanian ambassador in Athens would attempt to present them as members of an Albanian minority.

8. Katsikas (2022:111) discusses the legal complications that emerged concerning the administration and inheritance of Muslim properties in postrevolutionary Greece and, in that context, also the case of the Karelas "çiftlik, a large estate under hereditary land management," in Kambos, the history of which remains completely unknown to locals.

9. In a speech that Agathonikos gave in 1999, he warned his diocese that the Muslim complex would be constructed "on top of a hill" and thus would make a very distinct visual claim over public space. The bishop also warned locals that the enterprise might have an impact not only on the area's architectural landscape but also on its sociocultural landscape: "I owe [it] to you, my beloved flock, to include in my annual report an issue of great importance and interest. I would like to inform you of an issue that will result in numerous problems and realignments. I am referring to the Athenian Central Mosque and Islamic Cultural Center, which is to be built on a top of a hill in [Kambos]. Our holy metropolis in cooperation with the local authorities and the local population will strongly react to [this] effort to adulterate the religious, cultural, social and traditional structure and life of the citizens of Mesoyia" (Mantas 2000; translation mine).

10. Novel as the idea seemed to me at the time, drawings and other visual methods of inquiry have been commonly used in the social sciences (e.g., Collier and Collier 1986; Johnson 1985; Harper 1998) and anthropology in particular. Stefania Pandolfo (1989), for instance, published an article on spatial imagination, movement, and the body in a Moroccan village, the starting point of which was a map drawn by a local informant; Meira Weiss (1997) collected drawings from Israeli students of the human body in health and in illness; and Michael Taussig (2011) took as a point of departure a drawing that he made during fieldwork in Colombia to think about ethnographic notes as modernist literature and reflect on the interaction of memory and reverie. As far as the anthropology of Greece is concerned, Charles Stewart (1991) has used drawings that he collected during fieldwork in Naxos to analyze moral imagination in Greek culture.

Notes to Pages 98–116

11. In this respect, my research is very much in dialogue with the works of Kearney and Hyle (2004) and Nossiter and Biberman (1990) on the use of visual methods of enquiry in qualitative research.

12. For an analysis of "deep play," see Geertz (1972). To explore the performance of social status in a Greek context, see Campbell (1964:284); Herzfeld (1985:59–62); Papataxiarchis (1992).

13. *Tsipuro* is a type of pomace brandy similar to grappa.

14. *Prefa* is a card game very similar to bridge.

15. *Manari* literally means a newborn lamb. In areas inhabited by Arvanites it is used extensively as a term of affection.

16. A possible translation for *moi* could be "my dear." *Dialoth* literally means "devil." "Moi dialoth" or simply "dialoth" is a customary expression for Arvanites, used in many different contexts to convey surprise, exclamation, or moderate disapproval.

17. Kevin Dunn has written extensively on what he terms the "discourse of absence," the claim that there are no Muslims in a specific locality. As he demonstrates in the case of Sydney, such a claim is usually unsubstantiated. However, "it is a device to undermine citizenship. The form of citizenship that is being denied includes the right to claim space, to influence the cultural direction of space" (Dunn 2004:334). Similar concerns to those expressed by Kalomira were quite widespread among mosque opponents in Toronto (Isin and Siemiatycki 2002:196, 205); in Tilburg, Netherlands (Beck 2002:55); and in England and Wales (Naylor and Ryan 2002).

18. The behavior of patrilineal voting blocs has been analyzed (in opposite ways) most notably by Campbell (1964) and Herzfeld (1985).

19. It is interesting to note how the signature of this drawing dates the author. Voltron—a giant robot first featured in the animated television series *Voltron: Defender of the Universe*—would only be decipherable to those familiar with 1980s American or Japanese cartoons.

20. The issue of sound pollution is also discussed in Maussen (2005b:27).

21. Adrianoupolis is the name used by Greeks when referring to Edirne, Turkey.

22. In his essay "Landscapes of Memory," Laurence Kirmayer (1996:193) suggests that "the moral function of memory depends on the constraints of social and cultural worlds to provide a limited range of narrative forms with which to construct the coherent stories of ourselves."

23. That is, acting as an unofficial real estate agent who makes a profit when an agreement is reached. In contrast to professional and officially registered real estate agents (also called *mesites*) who receive a prearranged commission on the value of property, the remuneration of unofficial *mesites* largely depends on the goodwill of the parties involved to give some money to the intermediary upon the signing of the *simvolea* (contracts).

24. I also came across this practice of using two names in Gazi and mentioned it in an article on Western Thracian migrants. See Antoniou (2005:89).

25. Even though Kambos and the nearby suburban towns were the fastest growing areas in the capital city, they lacked basic infrastructure such as sewage treatment. As

Nitsa pointed out, this was an issue of obvious significance with grave consequences for the environment, which nonetheless had caused no protest on the part of the locals for the last forty years.

26. Already from the thirteenth century, and in the context of the Persian *hazl* tradition, verses attributed to Pur Baha Jami (d. ca. 1300) transformed urban topographies into imaginary sexual landscapes: "Before the dome of the cunt-madrasa. . . .Verily like a minaret, its head soars into the air" (Sprachman 1995:xxix). The semi-mythical figure of Nasreddin Hoca was also keen on narrating obscene jokes involving minarets: "*Minareyi görmüş. Şuna ne derler, demiş. Sordukları da: Şehrin siki demişler. Hoca da demiş ki: Ona uygun götünüz var mı?*" ("He saw the minaret. He asked, 'What do they call this?' They replied, 'the city's dick.' Hoca then said, 'Do you have a corresponding butt for it?'", Burrill 1970:50). From a psychoanalytic perspective, Vamik Volkan (1988:128) has discussed the phallic connotations of minarets in his analysis of the Cyprus conflict: "When the interethnic conflict erupted, Greek Cypriots surrounded Bayraktar [flag bearer, the name of an area in Nicosia], and twice during the mid-1960s they exploded dynamite on the minaret. The damage was inescapably suggestive of castration; with the top gone the minaret looked like a big phallus with the top removed. It made a symbolic focal point for the narcissistic hurts of the Turks, who largely unconsciously felt their phallic aggression and drive for success had been circumvented." I owe these references to Holy Davidson, Norman Itzkowitz, and Heath Lowry.

27. For an analysis of reactions to the building of mosques and, more specifically, the incorporation of minarets into their architecture, see Cesari (2005:1020).

28. Pesmazoglou (2007) examines the European roots of anti-Turkish sentiments and how they have been incorporated into the construction of modern Greek identity.

Chapter 5

Chapter 5 excerpted by permission of the publishers from: Antoniou, Dimitris. 2010. "The Mosque That Was Not There: Ethnographic Elaborations on Orthodox Conceptions of Sacrifice." In *Orthodox Christianity in 21st Century Greece*. Victor Roudometof and Vasilios N. Makrides, eds. Pp.155–174. Aldershot: Ashgate.

1. To this day there is no legal separation between church and state in Greece. Article 3 of the Greek Constitution, which recognizes the Eastern Orthodox Church as the prevailing religion in Greece, sets the overarching legal framework defining relations between church and state. The Church is considered a legal person of public law not subject to taxation, and priests are civil servants paid by the state with the right to issue a number of certificates. At the same time, the Church maintains a degree of autonomy and is allowed to construct churches and monasteries at will, without any prior authorization by the central government.

2. According to Roudometof and Makrides (2010:4), "The images of Greek bishops and believers protesting against the Greek government's effort to institute new ID cards that would exclude an entry for religious affiliation were widely circulated among the European public. . . ." [For various analyses, see Molokotos-Liederman 2003, 2007a,

198   Notes to Pages 124–132

2007b; Makrides 2005; Roudometof 2005.] Outside Greece, the ID card crisis also contributed greatly to the proliferation of a negative image of the Orthodox Church and the Greek public. The Church's image was that of an anti-modern institution set against the forces of modernization and Europeanization."

3. Similar initiatives include the Cathedral of Christ the Savior in Moscow, the Temple of Divine Providence in Warsaw, and later the Sacré-Coeur in Paris.

4. Sofos and Özkırımlı (2009:28) explain, "The urban neighborhoods where the refugees were settled were looked down upon and were stripped of their particularity and specificity through the use of the blanket term *prosfiyika* (refugee neighborhoods), or entire areas were given names that reminded of their 'Turkish' origin, such as the Athens area of Turkovunia."

5. In *A Place in History* (1991:250), Michael Herzfeld discusses how reluctant Greek authorities always are to demolish *afthereta*—structures, like Kostis's chapel, built without a permit—and how this common knowledge informs local strategies of resistance to the planning decisions of the central administration.

6. These first impressions affirm Metropolitan Chrisostomos of Florina's descriptions of Old Calendarists as belonging to the poorer and less-educated strata of society. See Ware (2002:18).

7. "'Neo-Martyrs' were those who chose to die, often in horrible circumstances, rather than compromise their Orthodox Christian faith. Most commonly they had reverted to Christianity after embracing Islam and thus were regarded by the Turks as renegades" (Clogg 1992:57).

8. This document was sent by Bishop Agathonikos on November 27, 2003, to all churches of his diocese with the note that it should be read on Sunday, November 30, 2003.

9. Mount Athos in northern Greece is home to twenty Eastern Orthodox monasteries and forms a semiautonomous monastic republic within Greece.

10. A *sinaksarion* (pl. *sinaksaria*) roughly corresponds to the martyrology of the Roman Catholic Church, and its content is arranged according to the ecclesiastical calendar.

11. Zachariadou (1990:55) describes these hagiographies as "pieces of ecclesiastical propaganda" aiming to stop conversions to Islam, which had substantially reduced the Christian populations of Asia Minor and the Balkans. Their message to the flock was simple: if one regretted his conversion to Islam, he would have to die in order to be given the possibility of eternal life.

12. Ioannis Vekkos (John Beccus to the Catholics), the patriarch of Constantinople in the second half of the thirteenth century, was in favor of reunion with the Church of Rome. It is for this reason that the Orthodox Church describes him as *Latinofron*, Latin-minded. For more information, see Schaefer (1907).

13. It is important to note that the word *martiria* has two meanings, since in an Orthodox context the term is understood both as witnessing and martyrdom. Here we are dealing with strategic ambiguity that recalls a widespread practice of the undivided

Church, that of understanding willing subjection to martyrdom as the ultimate way of paying witness to Jesus.

14. This proverb is usually attributed to the Grand Duke Loukas Notaras.

15. For Matsoukas (1999:151), most Orthodox theologians consider papal supremacy and the procession of the Holy Ghost as the main reasons behind the schism between the two churches. For a historical overview of the relations between Greek Orthodoxy and the Latin West by a public intellectual who has been against the westernization and "modernization" of Greek institutions, see Yannaras (2006).

16. The official position of the Church regarding the Old Calendarists (Paleoimeroloyites) was expressed in a memorandum sent to the Ministry of Education and Religious Affairs on March 1, 1980: "The *Paleoimeroloyite* in Greece disagree with our Church for reasons that are not doctrinal. In consequence, they are neither schismatics nor heterodox; and so they cannot claim the right to a parallel and independent existence as Orthodox Christians alongside the Church of Greece and within the limits allowed by the Constitution. . . . They have, of course, the right to leave the Church by their own free choice, in which case they would then be characterized as non-Orthodox. But they will not so much as envisage the possibility of such a course, since they consider on the contrary that they alone are genuine Orthodox" (quoted in Ware 2002:15). For an overview of Old Calendarism and the rise of religious conservatism in the Orthodox Church, see Kitsikis (1996).

17. Ayia Filothei is a mansion named after a small chapel, where the archbishop receives visitors and guests.

18. The issue of church-state relations is thoroughly discussed by historians of the nineteenth century, when the Greek autocephalous church was established and the Orthodox Patriarchate in Istanbul had to reconfigure its relation to the Ottoman Empire in the context of the *tanzimat* reforms. A good starting point for delving deeper into the matter would be Kitromilides (1994) and Stamatopoulos (2001).

19. Indeed, Allilengii ceased to operate some years later following accusations of economic mismanagement.

Chapter 6

1. SYRIZA (Coalition for the Radical Left) made its appearance in the 2004 national elections as a broad coalition embracing even more parties of the left than its predecessor, Sinaspismos.

2. Eleftheroglou ([2008] 2009) ventures similar views.

3. For a relevant discussion of Žižek's approach to self-fulfilling prophecies and Foucault's notion of the "truth effects of a discourse," see Navaro-Yashin (2002:31–36).

4. These almost magical attributions to opinion polling are also shared by the Greek state, which prohibits any poll from taking place two weeks prior to elections, out of concern that the publication of results may impact voters' behavior (see Mavris [2004] 2009:247).

200 Notes to Pages 148–176

5. According to Eleftheriadis (2006:103) there is "an extraordinary power wielded by a small number of business conglomerates controlling radio and television stations together with construction and other companies. Numbering no more than half a dozen, these business groups appear to enjoy the lion's share of public procurement contracts. There has been a widespread belief that these public contractors purchase influence over contracts in return for airtime and other favorable treatment toward a small number of politicians, members of the PASOK party and the Simitis government, whom they systematically supported through their news and current affairs programmes."

6. AGB Nielsen is a multinational corporation conducting audience measurements. Greek TV channels evaluate their appeal to the audience daily according to the statistical data released on AGB Nielsen's website.

7. The closed circuit described by Petros appears analogous to the one described by Bachner and Ginsberg (2016) in relation to bureaucrats in Washington, D.C.

8. For an exploration of populism as a lens through which to consider PASOK's governance in the 1980s, see Lyrintzis (1987, 1989).

9. Lyberaki and Tsakalotos (2002:104) also discuss the temporality of Greek governance.

10. In 1981 the government of PASOK allowed veterans of the Democratic Army of Greece (which constituted the military wing of the Greek Communist Party during the Civil War) who had taken refuge in communist countries to return to Greece. Many of them were offered pensions for their participation in the anti-Nazi resistance, and the commander Markos Vafiadis was elected a member of parliament.

11. Public Issue, a polling company that Stratos had described as credible, documented public stances toward the construction of a mosque in Athens from 2006 to 2010. The results of this poll were available on Public Issue's (2010) website, while a summary appeared on the news website *To Kerdhos Online*. The analysis is full of graphs that depict responses to the following issues: reactions to words such as "jihad," "burka," "minaret," "Arabs," and "Islam" ("neither negative nor positive opinion" is the most popular answer); knowledge about Islam and the Koran ("83 percent of Greeks have not read the Koran" and "51 percent believe in the correlation of Islam and violence"); relations between "The West" and Islam ("likely bad" say 39 percent, while 34 percent find "quite possible" the imminent clash between Christianity and Islam); relations between Greece and the "Islamic World" (70 percent believe that the "Islamic threat" is not much of a threat for Greece); and finally opinions with regard to the establishment of a mosque (41 percent of Greeks agree, while 46 percent completely disagree).

Conclusion

1. SYRIZA had promised to reverse austerity by balancing the state's budgets through an ambitious public investment program, hardline negotiations of debt relief, the restructuring of the broken tax system, and the elimination of government corruption. For an insightful critique from within the party about SYRIZA's ultimate acceptance of the Troika's terms, see Michalis Spourdalakis's interview with Gray (2017).

2. Until the elections of 2013, when Khrisi Avyi received 7 percent, the party never exceeded 0.5 percent of the popular vote. For more information about the party, its ideology, and rise to political mainstream, see Psarras (2012).

3. Papataxiarchis (2016) on the unfolding of the refugee crisis in Lesvos provides an insightful description of the situation on the ground at the time, the motivations of the different actors involved, and the larger political debates surrounding this crisis. For a broader consideration of European discourses on the refugees and shifting asylum policies, see Fassin (2016).

4. Kalogeropoulos, Panagiotou, and Dimitrakopoulou (2016) analyze research conducted by the Reuters Institute for the Study of Journalism at Oxford University according to which trust in journalists, the media, and the news in Greece appears to be among the lowest of the twenty-six countries examined (i.e., European countries as well as Australia, Brazil, Canada, Japan, Turkey, United States, and South Korea). More specifically, only 7 percent of 2,036 respondents believed that Greek media could operate independently of political influence and only 5 percent, independently from business interests.

5. According to reports on the use of social media and the internet in Greece, in 2022, when the country's population was estimated at 10.34 million, there were 5.15 million Facebook accounts. Needless to say, these accounts do not necessarily correspond to individuals. It is also worth noting that during the same year almost 2 million Greeks were still not using the internet (Kemp 2022).

6. See also MERACS/GSRA 2012, 2013a,b,c,d.

7. Even when the financial crisis ceased to constitute shocking news and turned into a sad everyday reality, there was still little room for the discussion of the mosque. With revenue reduced by almost 50 percent, TV networks began to follow the advice of marketing experts and present in their news broadcasts only the absolutely necessary "hard news" and include lighter news that a younger audience, less interested in politics, would value. In this way, it was believed that they would be able to maintain advertising revenue from companies targeting the fifteen to forty-four age groups. For an insightful analysis of agenda setting in private TV networks' news broadcasts, see Panagopoulos and Panagiotou (2018).

REFERENCES

Primary Sources

CE/CHR: Council of Europe, Commissioner for Human Rights

2002. Report by Mr. Alvaro Gil-Robles, Commissioner For Human Rights, on His Visit to the Hellenic Republic, June 2–5. http://www.unhcr.org/refworld/docid /41596fd24.html.

CS: Council of State

2013. Application for annulment. July 15. Submission number: ΕΔ 347/16.7.2013.

DHAGMFA/CS: Diplomatic and Historical Archives of the Greek Ministry of Foreign Affairs, Central Service

1933. Consulate General in Alexandria to Dimitrios Maximos, September 24, 1933, Alexandria, 1933/B/8/H/1665.
1948a. A. Papadhimos to the Greek Foreign Ministry, January 29, 1948, Athens, 1952/140/1/1, 201.
1948b. Greek Embassy in London to D. I. Pappas, February 20, 1948, London, 1952/140/1/1, 23759.
1948c. R. Rafail to D. I. Pappas, April 22, 1948, Paris, 1952/140/1/1, 34757.
1948d. A. Londos to Directorate for Greeks Abroad, May 17, 1948 Athens, 1952/140/1/1, 3430.
1948e. I. Koutsalexis to the Greek Embassy in Cairo, September 22, 1948, Athens, 1952/140/1/1, 49489.
1951. G. Triandafillidhis to the Greek Foreign Ministry, June 14, 1951, Cairo, 1952/140/1/1, 9483.

GG: Government Gazette

1834. Peri aneyerseos nau tu Sotiros is Athina [Regarding the erection of a Church of the Savior in Athens]. Nafplio: FEK 5/ A'/ January 29.
1838. Peri aneyerseos nau tu Sotiros is Athina [Regarding the erection of a Church of the Savior in Athens]. Athens: FEK 12/ A'/ April 11.
1882. Law No. 973. Peri kiroseos tis metaksi Elladhos ke Turkias simvaseos tis 20 Iuniou 1881, aforosis is ta nea oria metaksi ton dhio kraton [Regarding the ratification of

204 References

the convention signed between Greece and Turkey on June 20 (July 2), 1881, concerning the two states' new borders]. Athens: FEK 14/ A'/ March 13.

1890. Law No. 1851. Peri parakhoriseos dhorean ethniku ikopedhu pros aneyersin Turkiku temenus en Pirei [Regarding the concession of a nationally owned plot of land for the erection of a Turkish place of worship]. Athens: FEK 126/ A'/ June 1.

1913. Law No. 4213. Peri kiroseos tis metaksi Elladhos ke Turkias simvaseos peri irinis tis 1/14 Noemvriu 1913 [Regarding the ratification of the Peace Convention between Greece and Turkey of 1/14 November 1913]. Athens: FEK 229/ A'/ November 14.

1915. Ministerial Decree No. 1067. Peri onomasias tis kinotitas Liopesi is kinotita Peanias [Regarding the naming of the municipality of Liopesi to the municipality of Peania]. Athens: FEK 148/ A'/ April 20.

1934. Law No. 6244. Peri parakhoriseos yipedhu en to dhasillio Singru Kuponion dhia tin aneyersin Eyiptiaku Temenus and Institutu [Regarding the concession of a plot of land for the establishment of an Egyptian place of worship and institute]. Athens: FEK A'/ August 25.

1938. Emergency Law No. 1363. Peri katohiroseos dhiatakseon ton arthron 1 ke 2 tu en ishii sindaghmatos [Regarding the safeguarding of the provisions of articles 1 and 2 of the constitution in force]. Athens: FEK 305/ A'/ September 3.

1939. Emergency Law No. 1672. Peri tropopiiseos tu anangastiku nomu ip'arithmon 1363/1938 "peri katohiroseos dhiatakseon ton arthron 1 ke 2 tu en ishii sindaghmatos" [Regarding the amendment of the emergency law number 1363/1938 "regarding the safeguarding of the provisions of articles 1 and 2 of the constitution in force"]. Athens: FEK 123/ A'/ March 29.

1999. Law No. 2734. Ekdhidhomena me amivi prosopa ke alles dhiataksis [Sex-workers and other provisions]. Athens: FEK 161/ A'/ August 5.

2000. Law No. 2833. Themata proetimasias ton Olimbiakon Aghonon ke alles dhiataksis [Issues of preparation of the Olympic Games 2004 and other provisions]. Athens: FEK 150/ A'/ 30.06.

2006a. Law No. 3512. Islamiko temenos Athinon ke alles dhiataksis [Islamic place of worship of Athens and other provisions]. Athens: FEK 264/ A'/ 05.12.

2006b. Law No. 3467. Epiloyi stelekhon protovathmias ke defterovathmias ekpedhefsis, rithmisi thematon dhiikisis ke ekpedhefsis ke alles dhiataksis [Selection of primary and secondary education officers, regulation of issues of administration and education and other provisions]. Athens: FEK 128/ A'/ 21.06.

2015. Law No. 4332. Tropopiisi dhiatakseon Kodhika Ellinikis Ithayenias [Amendment of Greek Citizenship Code provisions]. Athens: FEK 76/ A'/ 9.07.

2017. Law No. 4473. Metra yia tin epitahinsi you kivernitiku erghu se themata ekpedhefsis [Measures for the acceleration of government work in relation to issues of education]. Athens: FEK 78/ A'/ 30.05.

2019a. Law No. 4589. Sineryies Ethniku ke Kapodhistriaku Panepistimiu Athinon, Yeoponiku Panepistimiu Athinon, Panepistimiu Thessalias me ta T.E.I Thessalias ke Stereas Elladhas, Pallimniako Tamio ke alles dhiataksis [Synergies between the National and Kapodistrian University of Athens, the Agricultural University of Athens, and the University of Thessaly and the Technical Educational Institutes of Thessaly and Central Greece, Pan-Limnian Fund and other provisions] Athens: FEK 13/ A'/ January 29.

2019b. Presidential Decree No. 42. Orghanismos of N.P.I.DH me tin eponimia "Dhiikusa Epitropi Islamiku Temenus Athinon [Articles of incorporation of the Legal Person of Private Law titled "Governing Committee of the Islamic Place of Worship of Athens"]. Athens: FEK 74/ A'/ May 20.

GPD: Gazette of Parliamentary Debates (Efimeris ton sizitiseon tis voulis)

1890a. Isiyitiki ekthesis tou nomoshedhiu peri parakhoriseos ethniku ikopedhu en Pirei pros anayersin Turkiku temenus [Preamble to the draft law regarding the concession of a national plot of land in Piraeus for the erection of a Turkish place of worship]. No. 145. May 16. Period 11, Second Special Session. Presidency of Andreas Avgerinos. Athens: Ethniko Tipoghrafio ke Lithoghrafio.

1890b. Sitting 49. May 19. Period 11, Second Special Session. Presidency of Andreas Avgerinos. Athens: Ethniko Tipoghrafio ke Lithoghrafio.

1913. Sitting 4. November 11. Period 19, Second Session. Presidency of Konstantinos Zavitsianos. Athens: Alexios Vitsikounakis Press, 1914.

HP: Hellenic Parliament

2006. Etiologhiki ekthesi sto shedhio nomu "Idhrisi Nomiku Prosopu Idhiotiku Dhikeu me tin eponimia 'Dhiahiristiki Epitropi Islamiku Temenus'" [Preamble on the draft law "Establishment of Legal Person of Private Law entitled 'Administrative Committee of Islamic Place of Worship'"]. October 2. https://www.hellenicparliament.gr /UserFiles/2f026f42-950c-4efc-b950-340c4fb76a24/i-temenos-eis.pdf.

HP/SCEA: Hellenic Parliament, Standing Committee on Educational Affairs

2006. Ekthesi sto shedhio nomu tou Ipuryiou Ethnikis Pedhias ke Thriskevmaton "Idhrisi Nomiku Prosopu Idhiotiku Dhikeu (N.P.I.DH.) me tin eponimia 'Dhiahiristiki Epitropi Islamiku Temenus'" [Report on the Ministry of National Education and Religious Affairs' draft law "Establishment of Legal Person of Private Law entitled 'Administrative Committee of Islamic Place of Worship'"]. October 25. https:// www.hellenicparliament.gr/UserFiles/7b24652e-78eb-4807-9d68-e9a5d4576eff/i -temenos-prak.pdf.

HP/SDSS: Hellenic Parliament, Second Directorate of Scientific Studies

2006. Ekthesi epi tu nomoshedhiu "Islamiko Temenos Athinon ke alles dhiataksis" [Report on the draft bill "Islamic Place of Worship of Athens and Other Provisions"]. November 6. https://www.hellenicparliament.gr/UserFiles/7b24652e-78eb -4807-9d68-e9a5d4576eff/islamikotemenos.pdf.

206 References

PP: Parliament Proceedings (Praktika tis voulis)

2000. Plenary Sitting 4, June 15. http://parliament.gr/gr/ergasies/synedriaseis/Es061500
.html.

2006. Plenary Sitting 17, November 7. https://www.hellenicparliament.gr/UserFiles
/a08fc2dd-61a9-4a83-b09a-09f4c564609d/es07112006.pdf.

HNAVA: Hellenic National Audiovisual Archive

1965. Prosefhi tu proin vasilia tis Saudhikis Aravias Ibn Saud sto dzami tou Monasti-
rakiu [The former King of Saudi Arabia, Ibn Saud prays at the Monastiraki Mosque].
Greek newsreels [ellinika epikera] D1656/ T7627/ 22/10. http://www.avarchive.gr
/portal/digitalview.jsp?get_ac_id=1656&thid=7627.

KKA: Konstantinos Karamanlis Archive, Athens

1979. Constantine Karamanlis to the Crown Prince Fahd bin Abdul Aziz, May 11, 1979,
F 59B/51.904.

MCERA: Ministry of Culture, Education, and Religious Affairs

2015. Letter to the Hellenic Parliament. Apandisi stin erotisi n. 2642/18-05-2015
[Response to question no. 2642/18-05-2015]. Athens: 122471/Φ1 ΕΞ/ 30.07.

MERA/GSRA: Ministry of Education and Religious Affairs,
General Secretariat of Religious Affairs

2014. Ekthesi apopseon epi tis etisis akirosis me arithmo E' 3343/16-7-2013 ke ton apo
3.12/2013 prostheton loghon (me arithmo katathesis 1034/6-12-2013) tis [named
removed from the original document] ke ton lipon etundon kata tu Ipuryiu Pedhias
ke Thriskevmaton anaforika me tin kataskevi tou Islamiku Temenus Athinon, i opia
ekdhikazete enopion tou D' Tmimatos S.t.E. kata ti dhikasimo tis 28/1/2013 [Presen-
tation of arguments regarding the application of annulment numbered 5 3343/16-
7-2013 and of 3/12/2013 additional reasons (submission number 1034/6-12-2013)
of (named removed from the original document) and other applicants against the
Ministry of Education and Religious Affairs regarding the construction of the Islamic
Place of Worship of Athens, which will be argued at the Third Department of the
Council of State on January 28, 2013]. January 21. Registration Number: 8258/A3.

MERACS/GSRA: Ministry of Education, Religious Affairs, Culture,
and Sports, General Secretariat of Religious Affairs

2012. Ekthesi apopseon epi tis etiseos akiroseos tu Sevasmiotatu Mitropolitu Pireos Serafim ke ton lipon etundon kata tis K.I.A khrimatodotisis tou Islamiku Temenus
Athinon [Presentation of arguments regarding His Eminence the Bishop of Piraeus
and other applicants' application of annulment against the Joint Ministerial Decision to fund the Islamic Place of Worship of Athens]. September 24. Registration
Number: 112354/A3.

References

2013a. Simbliromatiki ekthesi apopseon epi tis etiseos akiroseos tu Sevasmiotatu Mitropolitu Pireos Serafim ke ton lipon etundon kata tis K.I.A khrimatodotisis tou Islamiku Temenus Athinon [Supplementary presentation of arguments regarding His Eminence the Bishop of Piraeus and other applicants' application of annulment against the Joint Ministerial Decision to fund the Islamic Place of Worship of Athens]. February 6. Registration Number: 16089/A3.

2013b. Simbliromatiki ekthesi apopseon epi tis etiseos akiroseos tu Sevasmiotatu Mitropolitou Pireos Serafim ke ton lipon etundon kata tis K.I.A khrimatodotisis tou Islamiku Temenus Athinon ke ton apo 25-1-2013 prostheton loghon [Supplementary presentation of arguments regarding His Eminence the Bishop of Piraeus and other applicants' application of annulment against the Joint Ministerial Decision to fund the Islamic Place of Worship of Athens and the January 25, 2013, additional reasons (report registration number 67/25-1-2013)]. February 7. Registration Number: 17002/A3.

2013c. Simbliromatiki ekthesi apopseon epi tis etiseos akiroseos tu Sevasmiotatu Mitropolitu Pireos Serafim ke ton lipon etundon kata tis K.I.A khrimatodotisis tou Islamiku Temenus Athinon [Supplementary presentation of arguments regarding His Eminence the Bishop of Piraeus and other applicants' application of annulment against the Joint Ministerial Decision to fund the Islamic Place of Worship of Athens]. March 22. Registration Number: 39906/A3.

2013d. Simbliromatiki ekthesi apopseon epi tis etiseos akiroseos tu Sevasmiotatu Mitropolitu Pireos Serafim ke ton lipon etundon kata tis K.I.A khrimatodotisis tou Islamiku Temenus Athinon [Supplementary presentation of arguments regarding His Eminence the Bishop of Piraeus and other applicants' application of annulment against the Joint Ministerial Decision to fund the Islamic Place of Worship of Athens]. April 2. Registration Number: 44622/A3.

MERRA: Ministry of Education, Research, and Religious Affairs

2016. Circular order. Epikeropiisi ke simblirosi tis ar. pr. 69230/A3/6-5-2014 (AΔA: ΒΙΦΘ9-ΤΟΤ) engikliu peri khoriyisis adhias idhrisis ke lituryias kathos ke adhias metasteghasis se khorus latrias eterothriskon ke eterodhokson thriskeftikon kinotiton [Update of and addition to the circular order with registration number 69230/A3/6-5-2014 (AΔA: ΒΙΦΘ9-ΤΟΤ) regarding the issuing a permit to establish, operate, and relocate to spaces of worship to communities of people of other religions and doctrines]. July 19. Registration Number: 118939/Θ1.

MI/DPFS: Ministry of the Interior, Department of Public Finance and Statistics

1890. Statistiki tis Elladhos. Plithismos. Apoghrafi tis 15–16 Apriliu. Meros Defteron. Pinakes A´ [Statistical review of Greece. Population. Census of April 15–16. Second part. Tables I]. Athens: Ethniko Tipoghrafio ke Lithoghrafio.

208 References

Sidheris, Yeorghios and Konstantinos, Sifneos. 1934. *Pandhekte neon nomon ke dhiataghmaton* [New laws and decrees digest]. Vol. 7. Athens: Petsalis.

Svolopoulos, Konstantinos, ed.

1993. *Konstantinos Karamanlis: Arhio, yeghonota ke kimena* [Konstantinos Karamanlis: Archive, facts, and documents]. Volume 11. Athens: Ekdhotiki Athinon.

Secondary Sources

Aarbakke, Vemund. 2000. "The Muslim Minority of Greek Thrace." Ph.D. dissertation, University of Bergen.

Akgönül, Samim. 1999. *Une communauté, deux états: La minorité turco-musulmane de Thrace occidentale.* Istanbul: ISIS.

———. 2008. *Reciprocity: Greek and Turkish minorities; Law, Religion and Politics.* Istanbul: Bilgi University Press.

Alexakis, Eleftherios. 1988. "Ghamilies parohes stus alvanofonus tis NA Attikis-Lavreotikis (1850–1940)" [Marriage offerings among the Albanian-speaking Greeks of SE Attica-Lavreotiki (1850–1940)]. In *Praktika tis tritis epistimonikis sinandisis notioanatolikis Attikis* [Proceedings of the Third Scientific Meeting of South East Attica]. P. Philippou-Angelou, ed. Pp. 471–514. Kalivia, Attica: Poria.

———. 1993. "Ikoyenia ke metavivasi tis periusias stus alvanofonus tis NA Attikis-Lavreotikis (1850–1940)" [Family and property transfer among the Albanian-speaking of SE Attica-Lavreotiki (1850–1940)]. In *Praktika tis tetartis epistimonikis sinandisis notioanatolikis Attikis* [Proceedings of the Third Scientific Meeting of South East Attica]. P. Philippou-Angelou, ed. Pp. 569–642. Athens: Tekhniki Ekdhotiki-Lambrinos.

Alexandris, Alexis. (1983) 1992. *The Greek Minority of Istanbul and Greek-Turkish Relations, 1918–1974.* Athens: Center for Asia Minor Studies.

———. 2003. "Religion or Ethnicity: The Identity Issue of the Minorities in Greece and Turkey." In *Crossing the Aegean: An Appraisal of the 1923 Compulsory Population Exchange Between Greece and Turkey.* Renée Hirschon, ed. Pp. 117–132. New York: Berghahn Books.

Alivizatos, Nicos. 1999. "A New Role for the Greek Church?" *Journal of Modern Greek Studies* 17:23–40.

Allievi, Stefano. 2009. *Conflicts over Mosques in Europe: Policy Issues and Trends.* London: Alliance Publishing Trust.

Anagnostou, Dia. 1999. "Oppositional and Integrative Ethnicities: Regional Political Economy, Turkish Muslim Mobilization and Identity Transformation in Southeastern Europe." Ph.D. dissertation, Cornell University.

Anagnostou, Dia, and Ruby Gropas. 2010. "Domesticating Islam and Muslim Immigrants: Political and Church Responses to Constructing a Central Mosque in Athens." In *Orthodox Christianity in 21st Century Greece.* Victor Roudometof and Vasilios Makrides, eds. Pp. 89–110. Farnham, Surrey: Ashgate.

References

Andoniadhou, Maria. 2008. "Dzami sto Monastiraki: Mikro alla kalo yia arhi" [Mosque in Monastiraki: Small but good as a start]. *To Vima,* November 24. https://www.tovima.gr/2008/11/24/archive/mikro-alla-kalo-gia-arxi/.

Andreadis, K. 1956. *I musulmaniki mionotis tis Dhitikis Thrakis* [The Muslim community of Western Thrace]. Thessaloniki: Eteria Makedhonikon Spudhon.

Andriopoulos, Themis. 2017. "Brothels: Houses Which Stood the Test of Time." *Athens Social Atlas.* https://www.athenssocialatlas.gr/en/article/brothels/.

Angelidhis, Athanasios. 2011. "To Islam ke i musulmani sti sinkhroni Elladha ke tin Evropi mesa apo ton elliniko tipo" [Islam and Muslims in contemporary Greece through the Greek press]. Undergraduate thesis, University of the Aegean.

Angelopoulos, Yiorghos. 1993. "'Zondas anamesa': Taftotita ke politiki mias khorismenis kinotitas" ["Living in between": Identity and politics of a divided community]. *Ethnoloyia* 2:111–127.

Antoniou, Dimitris. 2003. "Muslim Immigrants in Greece: Religious Organization and Local Responses." In "Middle East and North African Immigrants in Europe." Ahmed Al Shahi and Richard Lawless, eds. Special issue, *Immigrants and Minorities* 22(2–3):155–174.

———. 2005. "Western Thracian Muslims in Athens: From Economic Migration to Religious Organization." *Balkanologie* 4(1–2):79–101.

———. 2016. "Unthinkable Histories: The Nation's Vow and the Making of the Past in Greece." *Journal of Modern Greek Studies* 34(1):131–160.

Antonopoulos, Stamatis. 1917. *I sinthiki Londhinu, Vukurestiu ke Athinon* [The treaties of London, Bucharest, and Athens]. Athens: Tipis "Avgis Athinon," T. N. Apostolopoulou.

Aretxaga, Begoña. 2005. *States of Terror: Begoña Aretxaga's Essays.* Joseba Zulaika, ed. Reno: Center for Basque Studies, University of Nevada, Reno.

Arslan, A. Yilmaz. 2003. "Atina'daki cami tartışması semboller savaşına dönüştü" [The debate over the mosque in Athens was turned into a war of symbols]. *Zaman,* March 11.

Asad, Talal. 2007. *On Suicide Bombing.* New York: Columbia University Press.

Attiki Yi. 2004. "Sinendefksi me ton ipopsifio dhimarkho Kosma Karanikola" [Interview with the candidate mayor Kosma Karanikola]. December 6.

Austin, J. L. (1956) 1975. *How to Do Things with Words.* Cambridge, MA: Harvard University Press.

Avramopoulou, Eirini, and Leonidas Karakatsanis. 2002. "Dhiadhromes tis taftotitas: Apo ti Dhitiki Thraki sto Gazi. Anastokhasmi ke singrusis sti dhiamorfosi silloyikon taftotiton: I periptosi ton turkofonon musulmanon sto Gazi" [Identity roots: From Western Thrace to Gazi. Reflections and conflicts in the making of collective identities: The case of Muslim Turkish-speakers in Gazi]. *Theseis* 79. http://www.theseis.com/index.php?option=com_content&view=article&id=774:category-774&catid=37&Itemid=113.

References

Bachner, Jennifer, and Benjamin Ginsberg. 2016. *What Washington Gets Wrong: The Unelected Officials Who Actually Run the Government and Their Misconceptions About the American People.* Amherst, NY: Prometheus Books.

Bahçeli, Tozun. 1987. "The Muslim-Turkish Community in Greece: Problems and Prospects." *Journal of the Institute of Muslim Minority Affairs* 8(1):109–120.

———. 1990. *Greek-Turkish Relations Since 1955.* Boulder, CO: Westview Press.

Balta, Evangelia. 2008. "The Perception and Use of Religious Otherness in the Ottoman Empire: Zimmi-rums and Muslim Turks." In *The Greek World Under Ottoman and Western Domination: 15th-19th Centuries.* Paschalis Kitromilides and Dimitris Arvanitakis, eds. Pp. 40–47. New York: Alexander S. Onassis Public Benefit Foundation.

Baltsiotis, Lambros. 2011. "The Muslim Chams of Northwestern Greece: The Grounds for the Expulsion of a "Non-existent" Minority Community." *European Journal of Turkish Studies* 12:1–31.

———. 2017. "O ekhthros endos ton tikhon: I musulmaniki kinotita tis Khalkidhas (1833–1881)" [The enemy within: The Muslim community of Khalkidha]. Athens: Vivliorama.

Barthes, Roland. 1977. *Image-Music-Text.* Translated by S. Heath. London: Wm. Collins Sons.

Batur, Nur. 2003. "Cami arazisine haç" [A cross for the mosque site]. *Hürriyet*, August 16.

Bauman, Richard. 1975. "Verbal Art as Performance." *American Anthropologist* 77(2):290–311.

Bayoumi, Moustafa. 2000. "Shadows and Light: Colonial Modernity and the Grand Mosquée in Paris." *Yale Journal of Criticism* 13(2):267–292.

Bekiaridhis, Yeoryios. 1973. "I muftidhes os thriskeftiki ighete ton musulmanon tis periferias ton ke os dhimosie arhi" [The Muftis as religious leaders of the Muslims of their prefecture and as public authority]. *Armenopulos* 12:886–890.

Benjamin, Roger. 2003. *Orientalist Aesthetics: Art, Colonialism and French North Africa, 1880–1930.* Berkeley: University of California Press.

Bishop, George. 2005. *The Illusion of Public Opinion: Fact and Artifact in American Public Opinion Polls.* Oxford: Rowman and Littlefield.

Bissell, William Cunningham. 2011. *Urban Design, Chaos, and Colonial Power in Zanzibar.* Bloomington: Indiana University Press.

Blumer, Herbert. 1948. "Public Opinion and Public Opinion Polling." *American Sociological Review* 13(5):542–549.

Boadway, Robin. 2006. "Principles of Cost-Benefit Analysis." *Public Policy Review* 2(1):1–44.

Bonos, Yannis. 2008. "The Turkish Spelling Mistakes Episode in Greek Thrace, June 1929: Beyond Modernists Versus Conservatives." In *Islam in Inter-war Europe.* Nathalie Clayer and Eric Germain, eds. Pp. 362–386. London: Hurst and Company.

Borneman, John. 2002. "Introduction: German Sacrifice Today." In *Sacrifice and National Belonging in Twentieth-Century Germany.* Greg Eghigian and Paul Matthew Berg, eds. Pp. 3–25. College Station: Texas A&M University Press.

References

Bourdieu, Pierre. 1979. "Public Opinion Does Not Exist." In *Communication and Class Struggle*. Armand Mattelart and Seth Siegelaub, eds. Pp. 124–130. New York: International General.

Bournova, Eugenia, and Yannis Stoyannidis. 2018. "Gazokhori: The History of a Neighborhood." *Athens Social Atlas.* https://www.athenssocialatlas.gr/en/article/gazochori/.

Brown, Mark. 2000. "Quantifying the Muslim Population in Europe: Conceptual and Data Issues." *International Journal of Social Research Methodology* 3(2):87–101.

Brunnbauer, Ulf. 2001. "The Perception of Muslims in Bulgaria and Greece: Between the 'Self' and the 'Other.'" *Journal of the Institute for Muslim Minority Affairs* 21(1):39–61.

Burrill, Kathleen. 1970. "The Nasreddin Hoca Stories: An Early Ottoman Manuscript at the University of Groningen." *Archivum Ottomanicum* 2:7–114.

Burton, Michael, Richard Gunther, and John Higley. 1992. "Introduction." In *Elites and Democratic Consolidation in Latin America and Southern Europe*. John Higley and Gunther Richard, eds. Pp. 1–37. Cambridge: Cambridge University Press.

Butler, Judith. 1990. *Gender Trouble: Feminism and the Subversion of Identity*. New York: Routledge.

Cabot, Heath. 2014. *On the Doorstep of Europe: Asylum and Citizenship in Greece*. Philadelphia: University of Pennsylvania Press.

Campbell, John. 1964. *Honour, Family and Patronage: A Study of Institutions and Moral Values in a Greek Mountain Community*. Oxford: Clarendon Press.

Çelik, Zeynep. 1992. *Displaying the Orient*. Berkeley: University of California Press.

Cesari, Joselyne. 2004. *When Islam and Democracy Meet: Muslims in Europe and in the United States*. New York: Palgrave Macmillan.

———. 2005. "Mosque Conflicts in European Cities: Introduction." *Journal of Ethnic and Migration Studies* 31(6):1015–1024.

Chiotakis, Stelios. 1997. "Skholiki ekpedhefsi ke kinoniki ensomatosi ton musulmanon tis Rodhou" [School education and social integration of the Muslims of Rhodes]. *Sinkhrona Themata* 63–64:79–83.

Christidis, Yorgos. 1996. "The Muslim Minority in Greece." In *Muslim Communities in the New Europe*. Gerd Nonneman, Tim Niblock, and Bogdan Szajkowski, eds. Pp. 153–166. Reading, Berkshire: Ithaca Press.

Chrysoloras, Nikos. 2004. "Religion and Nationalism in Greece." Paper presented at the Second Pan-European Conference, Standing Group on EU Politics, Bologna, June 24–26.

Chtouris, Sotiris, Iordanis Psimmenos, and Flora Tzelepogou. 1999. "'Muslim Voices' in the European Union: Greece." Report for the project "'Muslim Voices' in the European Union: The Stranger Within, Community, Identity and Employment." Project No: ERB-SOE2-CT96-3024. CCSR/University of Manchester.

Clogg, Richard. 2002 [1992]. *A Concise History of Greece*. Cambridge: Cambridge University Press.

References

Collier, John, and Malcom Collier. 1986. *Visual Anthropology: Photography as a Research Method*. Albuquerque: University of New Mexico Press.

Crinson, Mark. 2002. "The Mosque and the Metropolis." In *Orientalism's Interlocutors: Painting, Architecture, Photography*. J. Beaulieu and M. Roberts, eds. Pp. 79–102. Durham, NC: Duke University Press.

Dalachanis, Angelos. 2015. *Akiverniti parikia: I Ellines stin Eyipto apo tin kataryisi ton pronomion stin eksodho, 1937–1962* [Communities adrift: The Greeks in Egypt from the abolition of privileges to the exodus]. Iraklio: Panepistimiakes Ekdhosis Kritis.

———. 2017. *The Greek Exodus from Egypt: Diaspora Politics and Emigration, 1937–1962*. New York: Berghahn Books.

Danforth, Loring M. 1995. *The Macedonian Conflict: Ethnic Nationalism in a Transnational World*. Princeton, NJ: Princeton University Press.

Davis, Elizabeth. 2012. *Bad Souls: Madness and Responsibility in Modern Greece*. Durham, NC: Duke University Press.

De Rapper, Gilles. 2002. "'Culture' and the Re-invention of Myths in a Border Area of Southern Albania." In *Albanian Identities: Myth and History*. Stephanie Schwenders-Sievers and Bernd J. Fischer, eds. Pp. 190–200. London: Hurst.

Delidaki, Argyro. 2022. "The Idiosyncrasy of Greek Islam and the Mosque of Votanikos as a Reconciliation Initiative: A Critical Discourse Analysis." *Ecumenical Review* 74(5):796–806.

Demant, Froukje, Marcel Maussen, and Jan Rath. 2007. *Muslims in the EU: Cities Report; The Netherlands*. Open Society Institute, EU Monitoring and Advocacy Program. https://www.opensocietyfoundations.org/uploads/e288017b-8782-4cc5-8837-bffac0f89c8c/museucitiesnet_20080101_0.pdf.

Demertzis, Nikos. 2001. "I Ethno-thriskeftiki ke epikinoniaki ekkosmikefsi tis Orthodoxias" [The ethnoreligious and communications-based secularization of Orthodoxy]. *Epistimi ke Kinonia: Epitheorisi Politikis ke Ithikis Theorias* 5:83–101.

Demetriou, Olga. 2004. "Prioritizing 'Ethnicities': The Uncertainty of Pomak-Ness in the Urban Greek Rhodoppe." *Ethnic and Racial Studies* 27(1):95–119.

———. 2013. *Capricious Borders: Minority, Population, and Counter-Conduct Between Greece and Turkey*. New York: Berghahn Books.

Dhoukakis, Konstantinos. 1962. *O meghas sinaksaristis* [The great listing of feasts]. Athens: Orthodhoksi Khristianiki Enosis.

Diamandouros, Nikiforos. 1994. "Cultural Dualism and Political Change in Postauthoritarian Greece." Working Paper 50. Madrid: Centro de Estudios Avanzados en Ciencias Sociales. https://dialnet.unirioja.es/servlet/articulo?codigo=3702732.

Divani, Lena. 2014. *I "ipulos thopia": Elladha ke kseni, 1821–1940* [The "insidious touch": Greece and foreigners, 1821–1940]. Athens: Kastaniotis.

Dragonas, Thalia. 2013. "The Vicissitudes of Identity in a Divided Society: The Case of the Muslim Minority in Western Thrace." In *Europe in Modern Greek History*. Kevin Featherstone, ed. Pp. 135–152. London: Hurst.

References

Dragonas, Thalia, and Anna Frangoudaki. 2006. "Educating the Muslim Minority in Western Thrace." *Islam and Christian-Muslim Relations* 17(1):21–41.

Dubisch, Jill. 1995. *In a Different Place: Pilgrimage, Gender and Politics at a Greek Island Shrine.* Princeton, NJ: Princeton University Press.

Dunn, Kevin. 2004. "Islam in Sydney: Contesting the Discourse of Absence." *Australian Geographer* 35(3):333–353.

———. 2005. "Repetitive and Troubling Discourses of Nationalism in the Local Politics of Mosque Development in Sydney, Australia." *Environment and Planning D: Society and Space* 23:29–50.

Durkheim, Emile. 1995. *The Elementary Forms of Religious Life.* New York: Free Press.

Eade, John. 1996. "Nationalism, Community, and the Islamization of Space." In *Making Muslim Space in North America and Europe.* Barbara Metcalf, ed. Pp. 217–233. Berkeley: University of California Press.

Ekklisia. 2003. "To Musulmaniko singrotima tis Attikis" [The Muslim complex of Attica]. 8/9:593–594.

Eleftheria. 1965. "O Ibn Saoud prosifhithi is to temenos" [Ibn Saoud prayed at the mosque]. October 23.

Eleftheriadis, Pavlos. 2006. "The Reform Agenda: The Citizen and the State; Constitutional Reform and the Rule of Law in Greece." In *Politics and Policy in Greece: The Challenge of Modernization.* Kevin Featherstone, ed. Pp. 95–112. London: Routledge.

Eleftheroglou, Nikos. (2008) 2009. "Ikones apo tin trekhusa kendriki skini i zitimata stratiyikis tis kivernisis Karamanli" [Images from the current central scene or issues of strategy of the Karamanli's government]. In *I politiki epikinonia stin praxi: Ta seminaria tu Leyin ke prattin* [Political communication in practice: The seminars of Leyin and Prattin]. Pp. 609–613. Athens: Metamesonyikties Ekdhosis.

Eleftherotipia. 2004. "Anthimos temenomenos" [The mosque-enraged Anthimos]. July 26.

Evergeti, Venetia. 2006. "Boundary Formations and Identity Expressions in Everyday Interactions: The Case of Muslim Minorities in Greece." In *Crossing European Boundaries: Beyond Conventional Geographical Boundaries.* J. Stacul, C. Moutsou, and H. Kopnina, eds. Pp. 176–197. Oxford: Berghahn Books.

Evergeti, Venetia, and Panos Hatziprokopiou. 2013. "On Muslims, Turks, and Migrants: Perceptions of Islam in Greece and the Challenge of Migration." In *Myths of the Other in the Balkans: Representations, Social Practices, Performances.* Fotini Tsibiridou and Nikitas Palantzas, eds. Pp. 177–188. Thessaloniki. https://www.viaegnatia foundation.eu/index.php/publications/myths-of-the-other.

Evergeti, Venetia, Panos Hatziprokopiou, and Nicolas Prevelakis. 2014. "Greece." In *The Oxford Handbook of European Islam.* Jocelyne Cesari, ed. Pp. 350–390. Oxford: Oxford University Press.

Fakeli. 2009. "Sti meghaliteri ekloyiki periferia tis khoras" [In the biggest electoral constituency of the country]. Television broadcast with Alexis Papahelas and Tasos Telloglou. SKAI, September 28.

214 References

Fakiolas, Rosetos. 2003. "Regularizing Undocumented Immigrants in Greece: Procedures and Effects." *Journal of Ethnic and Migration Studies* 29(3):535–561.

Fallmerayer, Jacob Philipp. 1857. *Das albanesische Element in Griechenland.* In *Abhandlungen der Historischen Classe der Koeniglich.* Munich: Verlag der. K. Akademie.

Fassin, Didier. 2016. "From Right to Favor: The Refugee Question as Moral Crisis." *Nation*, April 5. https://www.thenation.com/article/archive/from-right-to-favor/.

Faubion, James. 1993. *Modern Greek Lessons: A Primer in Historical Constructivism.* Princeton, NJ: Princeton University Press.

Featherstone, Kevin. 2005. "'Soft' Coordination Meets 'Hard' Politics: The European Union and Pension Reform in Greece." *Journal of European Public Policy* 12(4):733–750.

Featherstone, Kevin, Dimitris Papadimitriou, Argyris Mamarelis, and Georgios Niarchos. 2011. *The Last Ottomans: The Muslim Minority of Greece, 1940–1949.* New York: Palgrave Macmillan.

Fowden, Elizabeth Key. 2019. "The Parthenon Mosque, King Solomon, and the Greek Sages." In *Ottoman Athens: Topography, Archaeology, History.* Maria Georgopoulou and Konstantinos Thanasakis, eds. Pp. 67–95. Athens: Gennadius Library.

Galpin, Richard. 2003. "Greek Mosque Plans Cause Friction." *BBC News*, July 29. http://news.bbc.co.uk/1/hi/world/europe/3104893.stm.

Geertz, Clifford. 1972. "Deep Play: Notes on the Balinese Cockfight." *Daedalus* 101(1):1–37.

Gefou-Madianou, Dimitra. 1999. "Cultural Polyphony and Identity Formation: Negotiating Tradition in Attica. *American Ethnologist* 26(2):414–439.

———. 2000. "Disciples, Discipline, and Reflection: Anthropological Encounters and Trajectories." In *Audit Cultures: Anthropological Studies in Accountability, Ethics, and the Academy.* Marilyn Strathern, ed. Pp. 256–278. London: Routledge.

———. 2010. "Ethnography in Motion: Shifting Fields on Airport Grounds." In *Ethnographic Practice in the Present.* Marit Melhuus, Jon Mitchell, and Helena Wulff, eds. Pp. 152–168. New York: Berghahn Books.

Georgiadou, Vassiliki. 2009. "Dhievrinondas tin oratotita tis ekklisias sti dhimosia sfera: shesis orthodoksis ekklisias ke ellinikis kinonias epi arhiepiskopu Khristodhulu" [Broadening the church's visibility in the public sphere: relations between the Orthodox church and Greek society during the time of Archbishop Christodoulos]. *Epistimi ke Kinonia: Epitheorisi Politikis ke Ithikis Theorias* 21: 129–156.

Georgoulis, Stamatis. 1993. *O thesmos tu mufti stin Elliniki ennomi taksi* [The institution of the mufti in Greek legal order]. Athens: Andonis Sakkulas.

Glavinas, Giannis. 2009. "I musulmaniki plithismi stin Elladha (1912–1923): Andilipsis ke praktikes tis Ellinikis dhiikisis; skhesis me khristianus, yiyenis ke prosfiyes" [Muslim population in Greece (1912–1923): Perceptions and political practices of the Greek administration; Relations with the indigenous Christians and refugees]. Ph.D. dissertation, Aristotle University of Thessaloniki.

—. 2013. "Oi protes prospathiies aneyersis dzamiu stin Athina: Apo ton Trikoupi ston Eleftherio Venizelo" [The first attempts at erecting a mosque in Athens: From Trikoupis to Eleftherios Venizelos]. *Efimeridha ton Sindakton*, June 8–9.

Gogonas, Nikos. 2011. "Religion as a Core Value in Language Maintenance: Arabic Speakers in Greece." *International Migration* 50(2):113–129.

Gray, Paul Christopher. 2017. "The Rise and Retreat of Syriza: An Interview with Michalis Spourdalakis." *Studies in Political Economy: A Socialist Review* 98(3):333–349.

Gropas, Ruby, and Anna Triandafyllidou. 2005. *Active Civic Participation of Immigrants in Greece*. Country report prepared for the European project Politis. https://www.eliamep.gr/wp-content/uploads/2007/04/Greece.pdf.

Hamilakis, Yiannis. 2007. *The Nation and Its Ruins: Antiquity, Archaeology, and National Imagination in Greece*. Oxford: Oxford University Press.

Hammoudi, Abdellah. 1993. *The Victim and Its Masks: An Essay on Sacrifice and Masquerade in the Maghreb*. Chicago: University of Chicago Press.

Harper, Douglas. 1998. "Reimagining Visual Methods: Galileo to Neuromancer." In *Handbook of Qualitative Research*. N. K. Denzin and Y. S. Lincoln, eds. Pp. 717–732. Thousand Oaks, CA: Sage.

Hatziprokopiou, Panos. 2019. "From the Margins to the Fore: Muslim Immigrants in Contemporary Greece." In *Muslims at the Margins of Europe: Finland, Greece, Ireland, and Portugal*. Tuomas Martikainen, José Mapril, and Adil Hussain Khan, eds. Pp. 198–222. Leiden: Brill.

Hatziprokopiou, Panos, and Venetia Evergeti. 2014. "Negotiating Muslim Identity and Diversity in Greek Urban Spaces." *Social and Cultural Geography* 15(6):603–626.

Hatzisotiriou, Georgios. 1971. *1821: Mesoyites ke Yiannis Davaris* [The people of Mesoyia and Yiannis Davaris]. Athens: Asklipios.

—. 1973. *Istoria tis Peanias ke ton anatolika tu Imittu* [History of Peania and the regions east of Hymettus]. Athens: Asklipios.

Herzfeld, Michael. (1981) 1986. *Ours Once More: Folklore, Ideology, and the Making of Modern Greece*. New York: Pella.

—. 1985. *The Poetics of Manhood: Contest and Identity in a Cretan Mountain Village*. Princeton, NJ: Princeton University Press.

—. 1987. *Anthropology Through the Looking-Glass: Critical Ethnography in the Margins of Europe*. Cambridge: Cambridge University Press.

—. 1991. *A Place in History: Social and Monumental Time in a Cretan Town*. Princeton, NJ: Princeton University Press.

—. 1992. *The Social Production of Indifference: Exploring the Symbolic Roots of Western Bureaucracy*. New York: Berg.

—. (1996) 2005. *Cultural Intimacy: Social Poetics in the Nation State*. New York: Routledge.

—. 2002. "The Absent Presence: Discourses of Crypto-Colonialism." *South Atlantic Quarterly* 101(4):899–926.

—. 2008. "The Ethnographer as Theorist: John Campbell and the Power of Detail." In *Networks of Power in Modern Greece: Essays in Honor of John Campbell*. Mark Mazower, ed. Pp. 147–168. London: Hurst.

Hidiroglou, Pavlos. 1990. *The Greek Pomaks and Their Relations with Turkey*. Athens: Proskinio.

Hirschon, Renée. (1989) 1998. *Heirs of the Greek Catastrophe: The Social Life of Asia Minor Refugees in Piraeus*. New York: Berghahn Books.

Holmes, Douglas. 2014. *Economy of Words: Communicative Imperatives in Central Banks*. Chicago: University of Chicago Press.

Holod, Renate, and Khan Hasan-Uddin. 1997. *The Mosque and the Modern World: Architects, Patrons, and Designers Since the 1950s*. London: Thames and Hudson.

Holston, James. 1999. "Spaces of Insurgent Citizenship." In *Cities and Citizenship*. James Holston, ed. Pp. 155–173. Durham, NC: Duke University Press.

Howden, Daniel. 2003. "Muslims in Athens: In Search of a Place to Pray." *Christian Science Monitor*, October 14.

Hubert, Henri, and Marcel Mauss. 1964. *Sacrifice: Its Nature and Function*. Chicago: University of Chicago Press.

Huliaras, Asteris. 2015. "Greek Civil Society: The Neglected Causes of Weakness." In *Austerity and the Third Sector in Greece: Civil Society at the European Frontline*. J. Clarke, A. Huliaras, and D. A. Sotiropoulos, eds. Pp. 9–27. London: Routledge.

Human Rights Watch. 1999. *Greece: The Turks of Western Thrace*. January 1, D1101. http://www.unhcr.org/refworld/docid/3ae6a8013.html.

Igo, Sarah Elizabeth. 2007. *The Averaged American: Surveys, Citizens, and the Making of a Mass Public*. Cambridge, MA: Harvard University Press.

Iliadis, Christos. 2013. "The Emergence of Administrative Harassment Regarding Greece's Muslim Minority in a New Light: Confidential Discourses and Policies of Inclusion and Exclusion." *Nationalism and Ethnic Politics* 19(4):403–423.

Imam, Mehmet, and Olga Tsakiridi. 2003. *Musulmani ke kinonikos apoklismos* [Muslims and social exclusion]. Athens: Livani.

IMEPO (Hellenic Migration Policy Institute). 2004. *Statistical Data on Immigrants in Greece: An Analytic Study of Available Data and Recommendations for Conformity with European Union Standards*. http://aei.pitt.edu/2870/1/IMEPO_Final_Report_English.pdf.

Immig, Nicole. 2009. "The 'New' Muslim Minorities in Greece: Between Emigration and Political Participation, 1881–1886." *Journal of Muslim Minority Affairs* 29(4):511–522.

Ios. 2003. "Pornia ke 2004: Iki midhenikis anohis" [Prostitution and 2004: Houses of zero tolerance]. *Eleftherotipia*, November 30.

Isin, Engin, and Myer Siemiatycki. 2002. "Making Space for Mosques: Struggles for Urban Citizenship in Diasporic Toronto." In *Race, Space and the Law: Unmapping a White Settler Society*. Serene Razack, ed. Pp. 185–209. Toronto: Between the Lines.

Johnson, Allen. 1985. *Research Methods in Social Anthropology*. London: Edward Arnold.

Kafetzis, Panagiotis.1994. "Politiki krisi ke politiki kultura" [Political crisis and political culture]. In *I elliniki politiki kultura simera* [Greek political culture today]. Nikos Demertzis, ed. Pp. 217–251. Athens: Odysseus.

———. 1997. "Politiki epikinonia, politiki simmetohi ke krisi tis politikis" [Political communication, political participation and crisis of politics]. *Greek Review of Political Science* 9:168–178.

Kalantzis, Yiorghos. 2013. "I anangeotita tu temenus: Yiati prepi na yini dzami stin Athina ke yiati prepi na to plirosi to kratos" [The necessity of the *temenos*: Why a mosque must be built in Athens and why the state must pay for it]. *Vima Orthodoxias*, April 10. https://www.vimaorthodoxias.gr/eipan/giorgos-kalantzis-i -anagkaiotita-tou-temenous/?print=print.

Kalliklis, A. Z. 1931. *To Othomanikon dhikeon en Elladhi: Istoria ke isiyisis; Neoteri othomaniki nomi. Nomoloyia Ariu Paghu* [The Ottoman law in Greece: History and suggestions; The jurisprudence of the Supreme Civil and Criminal Court of Greece]. Athens: Karayiannis.

Kalogeropoulos, Antonis, Nikos Panagiotou, and Dimitra Dimitrakopoulou. 2016. "Reuters Institute: Erevna yia tis psifiakes idhisis stin Elladha" [Reuters Institute: Research on digital news in Greece]. http://www.jour.auth.gr/wp-content/uploads /2016/12/ReutersGreekReport2016digitaledition-v1.pdf.

Kalokerinos, Grigoris. 2002. "Ekklisia: 'Ne' sto temenos" [Church: "yes" to the Mosque]. *Kathimerini*, February 6.

Kambouroglou, Dimitrios. 1896. *I istoria ton athineon: Turkokratia; Periodhos Proti 1458–1687* [History of the Athenians: Turkish rule; First period 1458–1687]. Volume 3. Athens: Spyros Kousoulinos.

Kaplani, Gazi. 2002. "Thriskia ke alvaniki ethniki taftotita: Mithi ke praghmatikotites" [Religion and Albanian national identity: Myths and realities]. *Sinkhrona Themata* 81:50–57.

———. 2006. *Mikro imeroloyio sinoron* [Small border diary]. Athens: A. A. Livani.

Karakasidou, Anastasia.1997. *Fields of Wheat, Hills of Blood: Passages into Nationhood in Greek Macedonia, 1870–1990*. Chicago: University of Chicago Press.

Kassimeris, George, and Antonis Samouris. 2012. "Examining Islamic Associations of Pakistani and Bangladeshi Immigrants in Greece." *Religion, State and Society* 40(2):174–191.

Katsikas, Stefanos. 2012. "The Muslim Minority in Greek Historiography: A Distorted Story?" *European History Quarterly* 42(3):444–467.

———. 2021. *Islam and Nationalism in Modern Greece, 1821–1940*. Oxford: Oxford University Press.

———. 2022. *Proselytes of a New Nation: Muslim Conversions to Orthodox Christianity in Modern Greece*. New York: Oxford University Press.

Katsoulis, Ilias. 1990. "To 'payiomeno' kommatiko sistima" [The fixed party system]. In *Ekloyes kai kommata sti dhekaetia tu '80: Ekseliksis ke prooptikes tu politiku sistimatos* [Elections and parties in the 1980s: Developments and prospects of the

218 References

political system]. Christos Lyrintzis and Ilias Nicolacopoulos, eds. Pp. 31–43. Athens: Themelio.

Kaurinkoski, Kira. 2012. "The Muslim Communities in Kos and Rhodes: Reflections on Social Organization and Collective Identities in Contemporary Greece." In "Balkan Encounters: Old and New Identities in South-Eastern Europe." Jouko Lindstedt and Max Wahlström, eds. Special issue, *Slavica Helsingiensia* 41:47–78.

Kearney, S. Kerri, and Adrienne E. Hyle. 2004. "Drawing Out Emotions: The Use of Participant-Produced Drawings in Qualitative Inquiry." *Qualitative Research* 4(3):361–382.

Kechriotis, Vangelis. 2008. "Ellenothomanismos" [Greek Ottomanism]. *Encyclopedia of the Hellenic World, Constantinople*. http://constantinople.ehw.gr/forms/fLemma BodyExtended.aspx?lemmaID=11012.

Kekridhis, Stathis. 2005. Dhiplomatikes shesis Elladhos-Eyiptu stis periodho tu mesopolemu ke to aghalma tu Mehmet Ali stin Kavala [Diplomatic relations between Greece and Egypt during the interwar period and the statue of Muhammad Ali in Kavala]. In *KE' panellinio istoriko sinedhrio, 21–23 Maïou 2004: Praktika*. [25th panhellenic history conference, 21–23 May 2004: Minutes]. Pp. 471–492. Thessaloniki: Elliniki Istoriki Eteria.

Kemp, Simon. 2022. "Digital 2022: Greece." Datareportal, February 15. https://datareportal.com/reports/digital-2022-greece.

Kibouropoulos, Yiannis. 2010. "O stavros tu politiku kostus" [The cross of political cost]. *Avgi*, April 4.

Kim, Soo-Young. 2017. "A Future Continuously Present: Everyday Economics in Greece." Ph.D. dissertation, Columbia University.

Kırbaki, Yorgo. 2003. "Atinada Cami" [The Mosque in Athens]. *Radikal*, September 21.

Kirmayer, Laurence J. 1996. "Landscapes of Memory: Trauma, Narrative, and Dissociation." In *Tense Past: Cultural Essays in Trauma and Memory*. Paul Antze and Michael Lambek, eds. Pp. 173–198. New York: Routledge.

Kitromilides, Paschalis. 1994. *Enlightenment, Nationalism, Orthodoxy: Studies in the Culture and Political Thought of South-Eastern Europe*. Aldershot, Hampshire: Variorum.

Kitsikis, Dimitris.1996. *The Old Calendarist Movement and the Rise of Religious Conservatism in Greece*. Novice Patrick and Bishop Chrysostomos of Etna, trans. Etna, CA: Center for Traditionalist Orthodox Studies.

Kompatsiaris, P., and Y. Mylonas. 2015. "The Rise of Nazism and the Web: Social Media as Platforms for Racist Discourses in the Context of the Greek Economic Crisis." In *Social Media, Politics and the State: Protest, Revolutions, Riots, Crime and Policing in the Age of Facebook, Twitter and YouTube*. Daniel Trottier and Christian Fuchs, eds. Pp. 109–130. London: Routledge.

Kostopoulos, Tasos. 2003. "Counting the 'Other': Official Census and Classified Statistics in Greece (1830–2001)." *Jahrbücher für Geschichte und Kultur Südosteuropas* 5:55–78.

References 219

Kozaitis, Kathryn. 2021. *Indebted: An Ethnography of Despair and Resilience in Greece's Second City*. New York: Oxford University Press.

Kymlicka, Will. 1996. *Multicultural Citizenship*. New York: Oxford University Press.

Labrianidis, Lois. 1990. "The Impact of the Greek Military Surveillance Zone on the Greek Side of the Bulgarian-Greek Borderlands." *International Boundaries Research Unit, Boundary and Security Bulletin* 7(2):82–93.

———. 1999. "'Internal Frontiers' as a Hindrance to Development." *European Planning Studies* 9(1):85–103.

Lakasas, Apostolos. 2016. "Ora alithias yia emas, tus 'allus' kai to dzami" [Time of truth for us, the "others" and the mosque]. *Kathimerini*, November 3. https://www.kathimerini.gr/opinion/881917/ora-alitheias-gia-emas-toys-alloys-kai-to-tzami/.

Lalaounis, Ilias. 1972. *Eleftheros Kosmos*. August 22, p. 7.

Landman, Nico, and Wendy Wessels. 2005. "The Visibility of Mosques in Dutch Towns." *Journal of Ethnic and Migration Studies* 31(6):1125–1140.

Lazar, Sian, ed. 2013. *The Anthropology of Citizenship: A Reader*. Hoboken, NJ: Wiley-Blackwell.

Lazos, Ghrighoris. 2002. *Pornia ke dhiethniki somatemboria sti sinkhroni Elladha: I ekdhidhomeni* [Prostitution and internationalist trafficking in contemporary Greece: The prostitute]. Athens: Kastaniotis.

Leandros, Nikos. 2013. "Ta mesa sto epikendro tis krisis: Ta ikonomika apotelesmata okto meghalon epihiriseon" [The media at the epicenter of the crisis: The economic results of eight large companies]. In *Krisi ke M.M.E* [Crisis and the mass communication media]. G. Pleios, ed. Pp. 31–57. Athens: Papazisi.

Leghari, Inam Ullah. 2009. "Pakistani Immigrants in Greece: From Changing Pattern of Migration to Diaspora Politics and Transnationalism." Paper presented at the Fourth LSE Ph.D. Symposium on Contemporary Greece, LSE Hellenic Observatory, London, June 25–26.

Lialios, Giorgos. 2006. "Ston Eleona tha ktisti to dzami" [The mosque will be built in Eleonas]. *Kathimerini*, July 26.

Llewellyn-Smith, Michael. 1998. *Ionian Vision: Greece in Asia Minor*. London: Hurst.

Lyberaki, Antigone, and Euclid Tsakalotos. 2002. "Reforming the Economy Without Society: Social and Institutional Constraints to Economic Reform in Post-1974 Greece." *New Political Economy* 7(1):93–114.

Lyrintzis, Christos. 1987. "The Power of Populism: The Greek Case." *European Journal of Political Research* 15(6):667–686.

———. 1989. "PASOK in Power: The Loss of the Third Road to Socialism." In *Southern European Socialism: Parties, Elections and the Challenge of Government*. Tom Gallagher and Allan M. Williams, eds. Pp. 34–58. Manchester: Manchester University Press.

———. 2005. "The Changing Party System: Stable Democracy, Contested 'Modernization.'" *West European Politics* 28(2):242–259.

Mackenzie, Molly. 1992. *Turkish Athens: The Forgotten Centuries, 1456–1832*. Reading, Berkshire: Ithaca Press.

MacMaster, Neil. 1997. *Colonial Migrants and Racism*. New York: St Martin's Press.

Makrides, Vasilios. 2005. "Between Normality and Tension: Assessing Church-State Relations in Greece in the Light of the Identity (Cards) Crisis." In *Religion, Staat und Konfliktkonstellationen im orthodoxen Ost- und Südosteuropa: vergleichende Perspektiven*. Vasilios Makrides, ed. Pp. 137–178. Frankfurt am Main: Peter Lang.

Malaby, Thomas. 2003. *Gambling Life: Dealing in Contingency in a Greek City*. Urbana: University of Illinois Press.

Maloutas, Thomas. 2004. "Segregation and Residential Mobility: Spatially Entrapped Social Mobility and Its Impact on Segregation in Athens." *European Urban and Regional Studies* 11(3):195–211.

Maloutas, Thomas, and Nikos Karadimitriou. 2001. "Vertical Social Differentiation in Athens: Alternative or Complement to Community Segregation?" *International Journal of Urban and Regional Studies* 11(2):171–187.

Manço, Ural, and Meryem Kanmaz. 2005. "From Conflict to Co-operation Between Muslims and Local Authorities in a Brussels Borough: Schaerbeek." *Journal of Ethnic and Migration Studies* 31(6):1105–1123.

Manitakis, Antonis. 2000. *I shesis tis Ekklisias me to kratos-ethnos: Sti skia ton taftotiton* [The relations of the church with the nation-state: In the shadow of identity cards]. Athens: Nefeli.

Mansolas, Alexandros. 1867. *Politioghrafike pliroforie peri Elladhos* [Census-related information on Greece]. Athens: Ethniko Tipoghrafio.

Mantas, Michalis. 2000. "Yia to musulmaniko temenos Peanias" [On the Muslim *temenos* of Peania]. *Politis ton Mesoyion*, March.

Marshall, Thomas H. 1983. "Citizenship and Social Class." In *States and Societies*. David Held, ed. Pp. 248–260. Oxford: Basil Blackwell.

Matsoukas, Nikos. 1999. *Dhoghmatiki ke simvoliki theoloyia* [Doctrinal and symbolic theology]. Thessaloniki: Pournaras.

Mattheos, Victor. 1968. *O meghas sinaksarististis tis Orthodhoksu Ekklisias* [The great listing of feasts of the Orthodox Church]. Athens: n.p.

Maussen, Marcel. 2005a. "Mosques and Muslims in Marseilles." *ISIM Review* 16:54–55.

——. 2005b. "Making Muslim Presence Meaningful: Studies on Islam and Mosques in Western Europe." Amsterdam School for Social Science Research. ASSR Working Paper, 05/03.

——. 2007. "The Governance of Islam in Western Europe: A State of the Art Report." IMISCOE Working Paper 16.

Mavris, Giannis. (2004) 2009. "I Dimoskopisis os enas anadhiomenos atipos thesmos tu sinkhronu politiku mas sistimatos" [Opinion poll surveys as an emerging informal institution of our contemporary political system]. In *I politiki epikinonia stin praksi: Ta seminaria tu Leyin ke Prattin* [Political communication in practice: The seminars of Leyin and Prattin]. Pp. 244–253. Athens: Metamesonikties Ekdhosis.

References

Mavrogordatos, George. 1988. *Metaksi pitiokampti ke prokrusti: I epangelamatikes orghanosis sti sinkhroni Elladha* [Between Pitiocamptis and Procrustes: The professional organizations in modern Greece]. Athens: Odysseus.

———. 1993. "Civil Society under Populism." In *Greece 1981–1989: The Populist Decade.* Richard Clogg, ed. Pp. 47–64. London: St Martin's Press.

———. 2003. "Orthodoxy and Nationalism in the Greek Case." *Western European Politics* 26(1):117–136.

McLoughlin, S. 2005. "Mosques and the Public Space: Conflict and Cooperation in Bradford." *Journal of Ethnic and Migration Studies* 31(6):1045–1066.

Mekos, Zafiris. 1991. *I armodhiotites tu mufti ke i elliniki nomothesia* [The mufti's jurisdictions and the Greek laws]. Athens: A. Sakkoulas.

Mesoyiakos Tipos. 2006. "Dzami stin Athina: 30 khronia dhialoghou" [Mosque in Athens: 30 years of discussion]. May.

Methenitis, Nikolaos. 2015. "O islamikos rizospastimos ke i sinepies tu yia tin Elliniki asfalia ke eksoteriki politiki" [Islamic radicalism and its consequences for Greek security and foreign policy]. Master's thesis, University of Macedonia.

Mikhas, Takis. 2005. "I simfonia yia to dzami" [The agreement concerning the mosque]. *Eleftherotipia,* January 13.

Minaidis, Simeon. 1990. *I thriskeftiki eleftheria ton musulmanon stin elliniki ennomi taksi* [The religious freedom of the Muslims in the Greek legal order]. Athens-Komotini: A. N. Sakkoulas.

Mitchell, Timothy.1991. *Colonizing Egypt.* Berkeley: University of California Press.

Molokotos-Liederman, Lina. 2003. "Identity Crisis: Greece, Orthodoxy, and the European Union." *Journal of Contemporary Religion* 18:291–315.

———. 2007a. "Looking at Religion and Greek Identity from the Outside: The Identity Cards Conflict Through the Eyes of Greek Minorities." *Religion, State and Society* 35:139–161.

———. 2007b. "The Greek ID Card Controversy: A Case Study of Religion and National Identity in a Changing European Union." *Journal of Contemporary Religion* 22:187–203.

Monitor. 2003. "Ieros polemos yia to temenos tis Athinas" [Holy war for the Athens mosque]. Television broadcast with Pavlos Tsimas and Tasos Telloglou, NET, July 13.

Mouriaux, René, and Catherine Wihtol de Wendent. 1997. "French Trade Unionism and Islam." *Research Papers: Muslims in Europe* 36.

Mouter, Niek. 2018. "A Critical Assessment of Discounting Policies for Transport Cost-Benefit Analysis in Five European Countries." *European Journal for Transport Infrastructure Research* 18(4):1–7.

Mouzelis, Nicos, and George Pagoulatos. 2002. "Civil Society and Citizenship in Postwar Greece." In *Citizenship and the Nation-State in Greece and Turkey.* Thalia Dragona and Faruk Birtek, eds. Pp. 87–103. London: Routledge.

Nader, Laura. 1972. *Up the Anthropologist. Perspectives Gained from Studying Up.* Microform. Washington, D.C.: Distributed by ERIC Clearinghouse.

222   References

Nancy, Jean-Luc, and Philippe Lacoue-Labarthe. 1997. *Retreating the Political*. London: Routledge.

Navaro-Yashin, Yael. 2002. *Faces of the State: Secularism and Public Life in Turkey*. Princeton, NJ: Princeton University Press.

———. 2012. *The Make-Believe Space: Affective Geography in a Postwar Polity*. Durham, NC: Duke University Press.

Naylor, Simon, and James Ryan. 2002. "The Mosque in the Suburbs: Negotiating Religion and Ethnicity in South London." *Social and Cultural Geography* 3(1):39–59.

Nevradakis, Michael. 2014a. "Savage Deregulation: Further Censorship and Crackdowns in Greek Media." *Truthout*, September 27. https://truthout.org/articles/savage-deregulation-further-censorship-and-crackdowns-in-greek-media/.

———. 2014b. "Greek Mainstream Media: Economic Interests Come Before the Law." *Truthout*, October 25. https://truthout.org/articles/greek-mainstream-media-economic-interests-come-before-the-law/.

Nielsen, S. Jørgen. (1992) 1995. *Muslims in Western Europe*. Edinburgh: Edinburgh University Press.

Nitsiakos, Vassilis, and Khristos Kasimis, eds. 2000. *O orinos ongos tis Valkanikis: Singrotisi ke metashimatismi* [The mountain range of the Balkans: Constitution and transformation]. Athens: Plethron.

Nossiter, Vivian, and Gerald Biberman. 1990. "Projective Drawings and Metaphor: Analysis of Organizational Culture." *Journal of Managerial Psychology* 5(3):13–16.

Notaras, Gerasimos. 1995. "I anomioyenia tu plithismu: Ena khronio provlima" [The population's lack of homogeneity: A chronic problem]. In *I anaptiksi tis Thrakis* [The development of Thrace]. Athens: Akadhimia Athinon.

Nyborg, Karine. 2014. "Project Evaluation with Democratic Decision-Making: What Does Cost-Benefit Analysis Really Measure?" *Ecological Economics* 106:124–131.

Oikonomou, Andromachi.1993. "Paraghoyi ke emboria tis ritinis sta Villia tis Attikis" [Production and trade of raisins in Villia-Attica]. *Ethnoloyia* 2:5–21.

Oikonomou, Marianna, dir. 2001. *To skholio* [The school]. 55 min. Athens: Greek Film Center.

Ong, Aihwa. 1999. *Flexible Citizenship: The Cultural Logics of Transnationality*. Durham, NC: Duke University Press.

Oran, Baskın. 1991. *Türk-Yunan ilişkilerinde batı Trakya sorunu* [The problem of Western Thrace in Turkish-Greek relations]. Ankara: Bilgi Yayınevi.

———. 1994. "Religious and National Identity Among the Balkan Muslims: A Comparative Study on Greece, Bulgaria, Macedonia and Kosovo." *Cahiers d'études sur la Méditerranée orientale et le monde turco-iranien* 18. https://journals.openedition.org/cemoti/249.

Örs, İlay Romain. 2018. *Diaspora of the City: Stories of Cosmopolitanism from Istanbul and Athens*. New York: Palgrave Macmillan.

Osborne, Thomas, and Nikolas Rose.1999. "Do the Social Sciences Create Phenomena? The Example of Public Opinion Research." *British Journal of Sociology* 50(3):367–396.

Panagopoulos, Andreas, and Nikos Panagiotou. 2018. "Dhiamorfonondas tin idhisi: Stratiyikes ke ierarhisis sta kendrika dheltia idhiseon ton idhiotikon tileoptikon kanalion ethnikis emvelias" [Formulating the news: Strategies and hierarchizations in the central news broadcasts of national private television channels]. In *50 khronia tileorasis: Praktika sinedhriu* [50 years of television: Conference minutes]. Dimitra Asimakopoulou, ed. Pp. 133–146. Athens: Epikentro.

Pandolfo, Stefania. 1989. "Detours of Life: Space and Bodies in a Moroccan Village." *American Ethnologist* 16:3–24.

Panourgiá, Neni. 2009. *Dangerous Citizens: The Greek Left and the Terror of the State.* New York: Fordham University Press.

Papakhristou, Nikos. 2004. Interview with Metropolitan Anthimos. *ΣΚΑΪ Radio Station,* August 1. http://www.papaxristou.gr.

Papataxiarchis, Evthymios. 1992. "O kosmos tu kafeniu: Taftotita kai andallayi ston andriko simbosiasmo" [The word of the coffee shop: Identity and exchange in the male symposium environment]. In *Taftotites kai filo sti syinkhroni Elladha: Anthropoloyikes prosengisis* [Identities and gender in contemporary Greece: Anthropological approaches]. Evthymios Papataxiarchis and Theodoros Paradellis, eds. Pp. 209–250. Athens: Kastaniotis and University of the Aegean.

———. 2016. "Being 'There': At the Front Line of the 'European Refugee Crisis,'" parts 1 and 2. *Anthropology Today* 32(2):5–9 and 32(3):3–7.

Papathanasopoulos, Stylianos. 1993. *Apeleftheronondas tin tileorasi* [Deregulating television]. Athens: Kastaniotis.

———. 2000a. "Contemporary Mass Communications and Political Communication." *Greek Political Science Review* 16:11–33.

———. 2000b. "Election Campaigning in the Television Age: The Case of Contemporary Greece." *Political Communication* 17:47–60.

———. 2014. "Greece: Press Subsidies in Turmoil." In *State Aid for Newspapers: Theories, Cases, Actions.* P. Murschetz, ed. Pp. 237–521. New York: Springer.

Pavlou, Miltos, and Nadina Christopoulou. 2008. *Living Together Programme: Migrant Cities Research; Athens.* British Council, November. http://www.i-red.eu/resources/publications-files/athens-migrantcities-britishcouncil2008.pdf.

Pearce, David. 1971. *Cost-Benefit Analysis.* London: Macmillan.

Pekolcay, Ayşe Necla. 1960. "Mevlid." *Islâm Ansiklopedisi,* vol. 8: 171–176. Istanbul.

Pesmazoglou, Stafanos. 2007. "I Evropaïki mitra tis neoellinikis aporripsis tu 'Turku'" [The European matrix of the modern Greek rejection of the "Turk"]. Symposium proceedings, "Evropi kai neos ellinismos" [Europe and modern Hellenism]. Athens: Eteria Spudhon, Moraïtis School.

Petraki, Georgia.1993. "I aghora erghasias sto Lavrio kata tin periodho 1956–87: I politikes stratologhisis tis klostoifandurghias EGHEON Lavriu" [Labor market in Lavrio during the period 1956–87: The recruitment strategies of the textile company EGHEON in Lavrio]. *Enimerotiko dheltio tu institutu erghasias tis GSEE* 30–31:58–72.

224 References

———. 1997. "Sti Ksanthi kai sto Lavrio: 'Taksikes dhiastasis tu mionotiku stin Elladha'" [In Xanthi and in Lavrio: Class dimensions of the minority issue in Greece]. *Sinkhrona Themata* 65:84–85.

Petropoulou, Marina, and Nikolas Leontopoulos. 2006. "Skhesis storyis me tin MKO tis ekklisias" [Relations of affection with the church's NGO]. *Eleftherotipia*, June. http://www.enet.gr/online/online_text/c=112,dt=04.06.2006.

Plantzos, Dimitris. 2012. "The Kouros of Keratea: Constructing Subaltern Pasts in Contemporary Greece." *Journal of Social Archaeology* 12(2):220–244.

Politis ton Mesoyion. 2000. "Dhio epistoles tu Ionna Vorre" [Two letters by Ion Vorres]. April 9.

Poulton, Hugh. 1991. *The Balkans: Minorities and States in Conflict.* London: Minority Rights Publications.

Povinelli, Elizabeth A. 2002. *The Cunning of Recognition: Indigenous Alterities and the Making of Australian Multiculturalism.* Durham, NC: Duke University Press.

Power, Michael. 1997. *The Audit Society: Rituals of Verification.* Oxford: Oxford University Press.

Priftis, Kostas.1980. "I metonomasia apo Liopesi se Peania" [The renaming from Liopesi to Peania]. *Simvoli* 11/12:31–42

Prodromou, Elizabeth H. 2004. "Negotiating Pluralism and Specifying Modernity in Greece: Reading Church-State Relations in the Christodoulos Period." *Social Compass* 51(4):471–485.

Psarras, Dimitris. 2012. *I mavri vivlos tis Khrisis Avyis* [The black bible of Golden Dawn]. Athens: Polis.

Psimmenos, Iordanis. 2004. "Metanastes ke kinonikos apoklismos sti sinkhroni poli: I periptosi tis Athinas" [Immigrants and social exclusion in the contemporary city: The case of Athens]. *Geografíes* 7:65–82.

Public Issue. 2010. "I Ellines ke to Islam: Ti ghnorizi ke ti pistevi i kini ghnomi" [Greeks and Islam: What public opinion knows and believes]. Public Issue Opinion Surveys, November. https://www.publicissue.gr/wp-content/uploads/2010/11/islam-survey-2010.pdf.

Rakopoulos, Theodoros. 2014. "Resonance of Solidarity: Meaning of a Local Concept in Anti-austerity Greece." *Dialectical Anthropology* 32 (2):313–337.

Rikou, Anthippi. 2008. "Zitimata Thriskeftikis Eleftherias Metanaston" [Issues of religious freedom of migrants]. In *Metanastefsi stin Elladha: Embiries-Politikes-Prooptikes* [Migration in Greece: Experiences, policies, prospects]. Jenny Kavounidhi, Andonis Kondis, Theodhoros Lianos, and Rossetos Fakiolas, eds. Pp. 118–131. Athens: IMEPO.

*Rizospastis.*1998. "Gazokhori: Ute na pandreftun dhe dhikeunde?" [Gazokhori: Don't they even have the right to get married?] April 29.

Rosaldo, Renato. 1994. "Cultural Citizenship in San Jose, California." *PoLAR: Political and Legal Anthropology Review* 17(2):57–64.

References   225

Roudometof, Victor. 2005. "Orthodoxy as Public Religion in Post-1989 Greece." In *Eastern Orthodoxy in a Global Age: Tradition Faces the Twenty-First Century*. Victor Roudometof, Alexander Agadjanian, and Jerry Pankhurst, eds. Pp. 84–108. Walnut Creek, CA: Alta Mira Press.

———. 2008. "Greek Orthodoxy, Territoriality, and Globality: Religious Responses and Institutional Disputes." *Sociology of Religion* 69(1):67–91.

Roudometof, Victor, and Vasilios Makrides, eds. 2010. *Orthodox Christianity in 21st Century Greece*. Farnham, Surrey: Ashgate.

Roussos, Sotiris. 2010–2011. "The Athens Mosque: From a Foreign Policy Tool to the Formation of Public Islam in Greece." *Journal of Modern Hellenism* 28:153–65.

Runnymede Trust. 1997. *Islamophobia: A Challenge for Us All*. London: Runnymede Trust Commission on British Muslims and Islamophobia. https://static1.squarespace.com/static/5ab2686bcef37284f39cbe8b/t/5cc04ca653450a97498b0263/1556106423748/Runnymede_Trust-Islamophobia-small.pdf.

Russack, Hans Hermann. 1991. *Arkhitektones tis neoklassikis Athinas* [Architects of neoclassical Athens]. K. Sarropoulos, trans. Athens: Govostis.

Sakellariou, Alexandros. 2011. "The 'Invisible' Islamic Community of Athens and the Question of the 'Invisible' Islamic Mosque." *Journal of Shi'a Islamic Studies* 4(1):71–89.

Salvanou, Emilia. 2013. "'Migrants' Nights': Subjectivity and Agency of Working-Class Pakistani Migrants in Athens, Greece." *Oral History Forum/Forum d'histoire orale* 33:1–19.

———. 2014. "Muslims in Athens: Narratives and Strategies of Belonging." *Journal of Modern Greek Studies* 32:339–336.

Schaefer, Francis. 1907. "John Beccus." In *The Catholic Encyclopedia*. http://www.newadvent.org/cathen/02380b.htm.

Self, Peter. 1975. *Econocrats and the Policy Process: The Politics and Philosophy of Cost-Benefit Analysis*. London: Macmillan.

Sen, Amartya. 2006. *Identity and Violence: The Illusions of Destiny*. London: Penguin Books.

Serageldin, Ismail, and James Steele, eds. 1996. *Architecture of the Contemporary Mosque*. London: Academy Editions.

Seriatos, Angelos. 2021. "Going Viral: Public Opinion in the Social Media." Paper presented at the online workshop "Going Viral: Public Opinion in the Social Media," Stavros Niarchos Foundation Public Humanities Initiative at Columbia University, November 26. https://snfphi.columbia.edu/events/going-viral-public-opinion-in-the-social-media.

Shabana, Ihab. 2019. "I evropaïki aristera ke to politiko Islam: Ta paradhigmata tis Elladhas ke tis Vretanias, 1979–2001" [The European left and political Islam: The case of Greece and Britain, 1979–2001]. Ph.D. dissertation, University of the Peloponnese.

226 References

Shadid, W., and S. van Koningsveld. 1995. *Religious Freedom and the Position of Islam in Western Europe*. Kampen, Netherlands: Kok Pharos.

Shore, Cris, and Susan Wright. 1999. "Audit Culture and Anthropology: Neo-liberalism in British Higher Education." *Journal of the Royal Anthropological Institute* 5(4):557–575.

———. 2015. "Audit Culture Revisited: Rankings, Ratings, and the Reassembling of Society." *Current Anthropology* 56(3):421–444.

Simon, Jacques. 1998. *Messali Hadj: La passion de l'Algérie libre*. Paris: Éditions Tirésias.

Sitaropoulos, Nicholas. 2004. "Freedom of Movement and the Right to a Nationality v. Ethnic Minorities: The Case of the ex Article 19 of the Greek Nationality Code." *European Journal of Migration and Law* 6(3):205–223.

Skiadas, Eleftherios. n.d. "I khanum apo tin Eyipto kai to zitima tu dzamiu stin Athina" [The khanum from Egypt and the issue of the mosque in Athens]. *Mikros Romios*. http://mikros-romios.gr/tzami/.

Skopetea, Elli. 1988. *To "protipo vasilio" ke i meghali idhea: Opsis tu ethniku provlimatos stin Elladha, 1830–1880* [The "model kingdom" and the great idea: Facets of the national problem in Greece, 1830–1880]. Athens: Politipo.

Skordilis, Antonis. 2002. "Gazi: Pireos ke eksathliosis ghonia" [Gazi: Pireos (Avenue) and the corner of misery]. *Eleftherotipia*. April 10.

Skoulariki, Athena. 2009. "Jihad i dhiadhilosis; I musulmani, i politia ke to dzami, pu meni sta khartia" [Jihad or protests? Muslims, the state, and the mosque that remains unrealized]. *Avgi*, June 7.

———. 2010. "Old and New Mosques in Greece: A New Debate Haunted by History." In *Mosques in Europe: Why a Solution Has Become a Problem*. Stefano Allievi and Ethnobarometer, eds. Pp. 300–317. Network of European Foundations' Initiative on Religion and Democracy in Europe. London: Alliance Publishing Trust.

Smith, Helena. 2003. "Villagers Try to Block Athens Mosque Plan." *Guardian*, September 16. http://www.guardian.co.uk/world/2003/sep/16/religion.uk.

Sofos, Spyros, and Umut Özkırımlı. 2009. "Contested Geographies: Greece, Turkey and the Territorial Imagination." In *The Long Shadow of Europe: Greeks and Turks in the Era of Postnationalism*. Othon Anastasakis, Kalypso Nicolaidis Aude, and Kerem Öktem, eds. Pp. 19–46. Leiden: Martinus Nijhoff.

Soltaridis, Simeon. 1997. *I istoria ton muftion tis Dhitikis Thrakis* [History of the mufti offices in Western Thrace]. Athens: Livanis-Nea Sinora.

Sotiropoulos, Dimitris. 2012. "The Paradox of Non-reform in a Reform-Ripe Environment: Lessons from Post-authoritarian Greece." In *From Stagnation to Forced Adjustment: Reforms in Greece, 1974–2010*. Stathis Kalyvas, George Pagoulatos, and Haridimos Tsoukas, eds. Pp. 9–30. London: Hurst.

Sotiropoulos, Dimitris, and Evika Karamagioli. 2006. *Greek Civil Society: The Long Road to Maturity*. Civicus Civil Society Index Shortened Assessment Tool Report for the Case of Greece. https://www.civicus.org/media/CSI_Greece_Executive_Summary.pdf.

References

Sprachman, Paul. 1995. *Suppressed Persian: An Anthology of Forbidden Literature*. Costa Mesa, CA: Mazda.

Stamatopoulos, Dimitris. 2001. "I ekklisia os politia: Anaparastasis tu orthodoksu millet ke to mondelo tis sindaghmatikis monarhias (deftero miso 19ou eona)" [The church as government: Representations of the orthodox millet and the model of constitutional monarchy (second half of the 19th century)]. *Mnimon* 23:183–220.

———. 2019. "Polemos kai epanastasi sta Othomanika Valkania: Isaghoyi" [War and revolution in Ottoman Balkans: Introduction]. In *Polemos kai epanastasi sta Othomanika Valkania (18os-20os eonas)* [War and revolution in Ottoman Balkans (18th–20th century)]. Dimitris Stamatopoulos, ed. Pp. 7–27. Thessaloniki: Epikendro.

Stathi, Katerina. 2014. "The Carta Incognita of Ottoman Athens." In *Frontiers of the Ottoman Imagination: Studies in Honour of Rhoads Murphey*. Marios Hadjianastasis, ed. Pp. 168–184. Leiden: Brill.

Stavrakakis, Yiannis. 2003. "Politics and Religion: On the 'Politicization' of Greek Church Discourse." *Journal of Modern Greek Studies* 21:153–181.

Stern, Nicholas. 2008. "The Economics of Climate Change." *American Economic Review* 98(2):1–37.

Stewart, Charles. 1991. *Demons and the Devil: Moral Imagination in Modern Greek Culture*. Princeton, NJ: Princeton University Press.

Strathern, Marilyn, ed. 2000. *Audit Culture: Anthropological Studies in Accountability, Ethics, and the Academy*. London: Routledge.

Sykes, Stephen W. 1980. "Sacrifice in the New Testament and Christian Theology." In *Sacrifice*. M. F. C. Bourdillon and Meyer Fortes, eds. Pp. 61–83. London: Academic Press for the Royal Anthropological Institute of Great Britain and Ireland.

Tambakis, Theologis, and Ioulia Plati (Omilos Filon Nikou Rapti). 1997. "I skholiki ekpedhefsi tis mionotitas tis Thrakis apo tin embiria ton ekpedheftikon" [The school education of the minority of Thrace according to the experience of the educators]. *Sinkhrona Themata* 63:54–60.

Taussig, Michael. 1997. *The Magic of the State*. New York: Routledge.

———. 2011. *I Swear I Saw This: Drawing in Fieldwork Notes, Namely My Own*. Chicago: University of Chicago Press.

"To Turkiko Nekrotafio stin Palea Kokkinia" [The Turkish Cemetery in Palea Kokkinia]. 2014. https://mlp-blo-g-spot.blogspot.com/2014/09/TourkikoNekrotafeio.html.

Triandafyllidou Anna. 2010. "Greece: The Challenge of Native and Immigrant Muslim Populations." In *Muslims in 21st Century Europe: Structural and Cultural Perspectives*. Anna Triandafyllidou, ed. Pp. 199–217. London: Routledge.

Triandafyllidou, Anna, and Ruby Gropas. 2009. "Constructing Difference: The Mosque Debates in Greece." *Journal of Ethnic and Migration Studies* 35(6):957–975.

Triandafyllidou, Anna, and Hara Kouki. 2013. "Muslim Immigrants and the Greek Nation: The Emergence of Nationalist Intolerance." *Ethnicities* 13(6):709–728.

Trimis, Dimitris. 1986. "I ensomatosi sto Gazi i stis piyes tu ratsismu" [The integration in Gazi or in the sources of racism]. *Skholiastis* 36:12–26.

228 References

Trubeta, Sevasti. 2001. *Kataskevazontas taftotites yia tus musulmanus tis Thrakis: To paradhighma ton Pomakon kai ton Tsinganon* [Constructing identities for the Muslims of Thrace: The case of the Pomaks and the Tziganes]. Athens: Kritiki and Minority Groups Research Centre.

Tsatsis, Thomas. 2003a. "To dzami kai i adzamidhes" [The mosque and the clumsy ones]. *Eleftherotipia*, September 17.

———. 2003b. "Epithesi Zakinthu ston Arkhiepiskopo: 'Ikonomikes' i andidhrasis Christodoulou yia to dzami" [Attack of Zakinthou to the archbishop: "Economic" Christodoulos's reactions concerning the mosque]. *Eleftherotipia*, September 18.

———. 2006. "Sti makhi tou minare ke i Dora" [Dora also enters the battle of the minaret]. *Eleftherotipia*, March 29.

Tsatsis, Thomas, and Angeliki Spiropoulou. 2000. "Temenos: I Ekklisia to evloyi, i yperpatriotes okhi" [Temenos: The Church gives its blessing, the ultra-patriots don't]. *Eleftherotipia*, June 2.

Tseloni, Andromachi. 1984. "Neoellines pisti tu Islam stin kardhia tis Athinas" [Neo-Hellenes believers of Islam in the heart of Athens]. *Prosanatolismi* 72(1–2):32–44.

Tsibiridou, Foteini. 2000. *Les Pomak dans la Thrace grecque: Discours ethnique et pratiques socioculturelles.* Paris: L'Harmattan.

———. 2003. "Anaghnosis tu 'kinoniku' apo tin anthropoloyia stin Elladha tis metapolitefsis" [Anthropology's reading of the "social" in Greece after the restoration of democracy]. *Mnimon* 25:185–202.

Tsioumis, Kostis. 1997. *I Pomaki sto elliniko kratos: Istoriki prosengisi* [The Pomaks in the Greek state: Historical approach]. Thessaloniki: Prometheus.

Tsitselikis, Konstantinos. 2004. "I thriskeftiki eleftheria ton metanaston: I periptosi ton musulmanon" [The religious freedom of immigrants: The case of Muslims]. In *I Elladha tis metanastefsis: Kinoniki simmetokhi, dhikeomata ke idhiotita tu politi* [Greece of immigration: Social participation, rights and citizenship]. Miltos Paulou and Dimitris Christopoulos, eds. Pp. 267–302. Athens: Kritiki.

———. 2012. *Old and New Islam in Greece: From Historical Minorities to Immigrant Newcomers.* Leiden: Martinus Nijhoff.

Tsitsipis, Loukas. 1992. "On Some Uses of Poetics in the Ethnographic Study of Speech: Lessons from Interaction in Language Shift Contexts." *Journal of Modern Greek Studies* 10(1):87–109.

Tsoucalas, Konstantinos. 1993. *Kinoniki anaptiksi ke kratos* [Social development and the state]. Athens: Themelio.

Tzilivakis, Kathy. 2002. "Little Room for Islam Inside Makeshift Temples." *Athens News*, October 11.

U.S. Department of State. 2000. *1999 Country Reports on Human Rights Practices: Greece.* https://1997-2001.state.gov/global/human_rights/1999_hrp_report/greece.html.

Van Wee, Bert. 2012. "How Suitable Is CBA for the Ex-ante Evaluation of Transport Projects and Policies? A Discussion from the Perspective of Ethics." *Transport Policy* 19(1):1–7.

References 229

Vasilopoulou, Sophia, and Daphne Halikiopoulou. 2020. Political Culture. In *The Oxford Handbook of Modern Greek Politics*. Kevin Featherstone and Dimitris Sotiropoulos, eds. Pp. 334–350. Oxford: Oxford University Press.

Verousi, Christina, and Chris Allen. 2021. "Problematising the Official Athens Mosque: Between Mere Place of Worship and 21st Century 'Trojan Horse.'" *Religions* 12(7):485.

Volkan, Vamik D. 1988. *The Need to Have Enemies and Allies: From Clinical Practice to International Relationships*. Northvale, NJ: Aronson.

Ware, Kallistos. 2002. "Old Calendarists." In *Minorities in Greece: Aspects of a Plural Society*. Richard Clogg, ed. Pp. 1–23. London: Hurst.

Watts, Ross, and Jerold Zimmerman. 1978. "Towards a Positive Theory of the Determination of Accounting Standards." *Accounting Review* 53:112–134.

Weiss, Meira. 1997. "War Bodies, Hedonist Bodies: Dialectics of the Collective and the Individual in Israeli Society." *American Ethnologist* 24(4):813–832.

Wildavsky, Aaron. 1966. "The Political Economy of Efficiency: Cost-Benefit Analysis, Systems Analysis, and Program Budgeting." *Public Administration Review* 26(4):292–310.

Xirotiris, Nikolaos. 1971. "Idhie paratirisis epi tis katanomis ton sikhnotiton ton omadhon tu ematos is tus Pomakus" [Personal observations on the proportional frequency of blood groups among the Pomaks]. Ph.D. dissertation, Aristotle University of Thessaloniki.

Yağcıoğlu, Demosthenes. 2004. "From Deterioration to Improvement in Western Thrace: A Political Systems Analysis of a Triadic Ethnic Conflict." Ph.D. dissertation, George Mason University.

Yannaras, Christos. 2006. *Orthodhoxia ke Dhisi sti neoteri Elladha* [Orthodoxy and the West in modern Greece]. Athens: Dhomos.

Yannas, Prodromos. 2002. "The Role of Image-Makers in the Greek Political Scene." *Journal of Political Marketing* 1(1):67–89.

Zachariadou, Elizabeth. 1990. "To dhidhaghma ton neomartiron" [The neomartyrs' moral]. *Dheltio Kendru Mikrasiatikon Meleton* 8:51–63.

Zenginis, Efstratios. 1988. *O bektasismos sti Dhitiki Thraki* [Bektashism in Western Thrace]. Thessaloniki: Idhrima Meleton Hersonisou Emou.

Ziaka, Angeliki. 2009. "Muslims and Muslim Education in Greece." In *Islamic Education in Europe*. Ednan Aslan, ed. Pp. 141–178. Vienna: Böhlau Verlag.

Zoulas, Stamos. 2006. "Ellinikos amanes yia to dzami" [Greek never-ending song about the mosque]. *Kathimerini*, May 14.

Zoumboulakis, Stavros. 2002. *O Theos stin poli: Dhokimia yia ti thriskia ke tin politiki* [God in the city: Essays on religion and politics]. Athens: Estia.

INDEX

Acropolis, 30–31, 95, 126
Adhamopoulou, Katerina, 149
Adrianoupolis, 109
AEK, 101, 149
AGB Nielsen, 152
Agora (immigrant organization), 51–54,
    60–61, 67
Al Jazeera, 39
Albania, 49
Albanian immigrants, 53, 57, 62, 67,
    100–101, 120
Alexandria, 23
Alimos, 33
Alpha, 150
Alter, 150
Amr Ibrahim, 25
Antenna, 150
Anthimos, Bishop of Thessaloniki, 129
Antonopoulos, Stamatios, 21
Arab League, 40
Archaeological Service, 30
Athenian Initiative (*Athinaïki Protovulia*),
    128
Athens Antiracist Festival, 54
Athens expressway (*Attiki Odhos*), 34, 96,
    104
Australian ABC, 34
Avgi, 142–43
Ayia Filothei, 135, 199

Balkan Wars, 6, 20–21
Bartholomeos, Ecumenical Patriarch, 132
Bayoumi, Moustafa, 27–28, 42, 47
BBC, 34
Borgen, 154
Brothels, 11, 52, 68
Bulgaria, 19, 21, 74–76

Byzantine Empire, 19, 149

Cairo, 23, 110–12, 121, 137
Center for Migrant Workers, 49–50, 60
Chios, 176
Christides, Vasilios, 25
Christodoulos, Archbishop, 87, 122, 124–25,
    132, 134–35, 137–38, 152
Chrysostomos, Metropolitan of Zakinthos,
    125
CNN Türk, 34
Coalition of the Left and Progress (*Sinaspis-
    mos*), 36, 44, 81, 148, 176
Coalition of the Radical Left (SYRIZA), 142,
    176, 178, 184
Colonial Modernity, 11, 28
Comité de l'Afrique française, 26
Convention of Constantinople, 19
Coordinative Council of Thrace, 75
Council of Arab States' Union, 33
Council of Europe, 78
COVID-19, 179, 184
Crete, 19–20
Crisis of 1929, 22
Crown Prince Fahd, 5, 31, 37

Devsirme, 117
Diamandouros, Nikiforos, 162
Dimitriadis, Konstantinos, 25
Doxiadis, Constantinos, 127

Ecumenical Patriarchate in Istanbul, 124
Egyptian Pavilion, 27
Egyptian School of Classical Studies, 23
EIRT (National Radio and Television Foun-
    dation), 148
Ekklisia, 44, 136

Index

Eleftheros Kosmos, 119

Eleftherotipia, 7, 72, 81, 85, 89, 177; "Ios," 70, 80

ELIAMEP (Hellenic Foundation for European and Foreign Policy), 3, 49

England, 21, 43, 62

Enosis, 30

Epirus, 20, 94, 188, 192

Erdoğan, Recep Tayyip, 184

ERT (Hellenic Broadcasting Corporation), 148

Esphighmenos Monastery in Mount Athos, 131

Etoile Nord-Africaine, 28

European Central Bank (ECB), 175

European Commission (EC), 66, 122, 124

European Committee of Ministers, 124

European Parliament, 78, 168

European Union, 2, 34, 50, 139, 171

Eurozone, 3, 176

Evert, Miltiadis, 143

Fakeli, 149

Fethiye Mosque, 29–30, 69

Filis Street, 52, 68

Financial Crisis of 1932, 6

Fissas, Pavlos, 177

French Communist Party, 28

General Secretariat of Tourism, 29

Genuine Orthodox Christians of Greece (*Ghnisii Orthodhoksi Khristiani*), 134

Germany, 50, 51, 77–78

Giannakou, Marietta, 41, 161, 167–69

Golden Dawn (*Khrisi Avgi*), 50, 136, 176–78

Grande Mosquée, 2, 26–28, 31, 39, 42, 46–47, 76

"Great Idea," 19, 21, 129

Greek Citizenship Law, 77, 193n9

Greek Civil War, 29, 69, 75, 77

Greek Communist Party (*KKE*), 36, 142

Greek Junta. *See* Greek Military Regime of 1967–1974

Greek military campaign in Asia Minor. *See* Greek-Turkish War of 1919–1922

Greek Military Regime of 1967–1974, 94, 127

Greek Navy, 40,181

Greek Parliament, 17

Greek-Turkish War of 1919–1922, 21,69

Greeks of Istanbul, 75

Hafiz, 62

Hayriye madrassa, 168

Hellenic Migration Policy Institute (IMEPO), 64

Helleno-Orthodox Salvation Movement (*Ellinorthodhokso Kinima* Sotirias), 128

Higher Educational Council, 161

Hijabs, 53

Holland, 77–78

Holy Synod, 44, 125, 138

Hot springs of Ipati, 22

House of Cards, 154

İbrahim Şerif, 38

Independent Greeks (*Anexartiti Ellines*), 176

"Indignados" movement, 175

Islamic Cultural Center, 2, 34–37, 42, 44, 46, 93, 182

Islamic Place of Worship of Athens and Other Provisions (*Islamiko Temenos Athinon ke alles Dhiataksis*), 40

Jihad, 4, 59

Jordan, 30, 37

Kallergis, Dimitris, 20, 22

Kapsis, Yannis, 80, 88–89

Karamanlis, Konstantinos, 31–32, 45, 164

Karamanlis, Kostas, 158, 161, 172

Karapanos, Konstantinos, 19

Kathimerini, 1

Kavala, 23–25

Khalandhri, 33

Khartia, 53, 56–57, 60, 63, 65, 68, 72

King Fahd of Saudi Arabia, 2

King Faruk, 29

King Fuad of Egypt, 2, 23–25

Koletis, Ioannis, 19

Komotini, 78, 83

Koropi, 33

Kourkoulas, Konstantinos, 30

Ksanthi, 42, 78

Kuwait, 33, 35

LAOS, 118

Libya, 30, 62, 81, 176–77

Lord of the Rings, 112

Index

Louis XV, 26
Lutraki, 29

Macedonia, 20
Mansoura, 23
Markopulo, 33
Marusi, 33
Masjids, 51–52, 55–57, 59–63, 66, 78, 82–83,
    142, 179, 182
MEGA Television Channel, 7, 148, 150–52,
    177
Metadhimotefsi, 80, 88
Metaxas Dictatorship, 33, 124, 187n1
"military surveillance zones," 76
Ministry of Foreign Affairs, 6, 29, 37–38, 41,
    69, 75, 137–38
Ministry of Labor and Social Protection, 51
Ministry of National Education and Reli-
    gious Affairs, 33, 59
Mitsotakis, Konstantinos, 33, 143
Moni Petraki, 50
Montreux Convention, 29
Moulay Ismail of Morocco, 26
Muhammad Ali, 23–25
Muhammad, Prophet, 52
Municipality of Piraeus, 18
Muslim Brotherhood, 40
Muslim Voices in European Union, 50
Muslim World League, 78

Nashat Pasha, 25, 43
Nasser, Gamal Abdel, 2, 30
Nation's Vow (Tama tu Ethnus), 126–28, 130,
    137, 139
NATO, 75
New Democracy, 36–37, 41, 44, 135, 143,
    147–49, 156, 162–64, 167–68, 171–73,
    176
1923 Exchange of Populations, 3, 8, 42,
    68–69, 74–76, 85
9th September 2001, 2, 37, 45, 50, 59, 66, 97,
    119, 183–84
Nomarhiaki Epitropi Laikis Epimorfosis
    (N.E.L.E), 80

Official Palace of Algeria, 27
Olimbiakos, 101, 113
Organization of Planning of Athens
    (*Orghanismos Rithmistiku Shedhiu
    Athinas*), 34

Organization of the Islamic Conference,
    37, 40
Orthodox Church of Greece, 49
Ottoman Empire, 2, 18–20, 56, 126

Palace of Algerian Attractions, 27
Panathinaikos, 101
Pangalos, Theodore, 33, 143
Panhellenic Socialist Movement (PASOK),
    34–35, 41–42, 56, 64, 88, 124, 141, 148,
    163, 168, 171, 176
Papadhimos, Andonios, 69
Papakhristou, Nikos, 141
Papandreou, Andreas, 81, 161–63
Papandreou, George, 33, 64–66, 90, 142–43,
    175
Papathemelis, Stelios, 129
Perivolia, 19
Piraeus, 2, 17–20, 53, 60, 101
Pomaks, 74–77, 83
Port Said, 23
Prosanatolismi, 80
Protato Monastery, 132

Qaddafi, Muamar, 81

Regent's Park Mosque (Islamic Cultural
    Centre and London Central Mosque),
    25–26, 33, 43, 46
Rendis, Theokharis, 33
Riyadh, 31–32
Rizospastis, 80, 142
Roman Agora, 29, 31
Russia, 21, 53

Samos, 19, 176
Saudi Arabia, 2, 30, 35, 37–38, 62, 182
Saudi King Saould bin Abdulaziz Al Saud
    (known as Ibn Saoud in Greece), 30
Serafim, Archbishop of Athens, 124
Service des affaires indigènes nord-africains
    (SAINA), 28
Simitis, Konstantinos, 35, 175
Skholiastis, 80
Skrip, 21–22
Society of Thracians, 72, 79, 82
Solidarity (*Allilengii*, the Church's aid orga-
    nization), 137
Solidarity (organization), 70–73, 78–80,
    83–86, 151

Index

St Aghathangelos of Esfighmenou
(*Ayios Aghathangelos, o Esfighmenitis*),
131
St. Sophia in Istanbul, 35, 109, 127, 129
Star, 150
Sublime Port, 19–21, 183
Sudan, 30, 47, 54–55, 177
Suez Canal, 30

Telloglou, Tasos, 38–39
To Vima, 143
Treaty of Athens, 20, 21, 45, 89
Treaty of Lausanne, 69, 74, 76, 85
Treaty of Sevres, 75
Trikoupis, Charilaos, 19–20
Tsoudherou, Virginia, 33, 181
Turkey, 3, 61, 63, 68, 71, 74–75, 77, 84, 86,
123–24, 129, 138, 184; Greek-Turkish
Diplomatic Relations, 23, 38, 75, 89;
Greek communities in Turkey, 19, 69, 75,
76; Turkish Invasion of Cyprus, 40, 65;
refugee route, 176
2004 Olympic Games, 3, 34, 36, 50, 86,
150–52

U.S. State Department, 2, 34

Vatopedi Monastery, 132
Vekkos, Ioannis, 132–33, 139
Venizelos, Eleftherios, 20–22, 46, 75
von Quast, Ferdinand, 126
Votanikos, 1–2, 5, 14, 40, 45, 49, 60, 67, 70,
80, 89, 97, 119, 136, 139, 168, 177, 179,
180, 182–84

Warsaw Pact, 75
Western Thrace, 4, 12, 30, 33, 36, 38–39, 42,
50, 55, 57, 70–72, 74–80, 83–84, 88, 151,
180–82; Events of 1990, 77
White House, 146
Witness of the Struggling Orthodox Monks
of Mount Athos (*Martiria Aghonizomenis
Orthodhoksias Ayioriton Monakhon*), 132

ΥΕΝΕΔ, 148

Zafiropoulos, Dimitris, 118–19
Zaman, 84, 122–23
Zoi, 30

ACKNOWLEDGMENTS

This book has been in the works for a long time. Writing it has taken me to all sorts of physical and notional sites that I would have never imagined visiting when I first began exploring the story of the unbuilt mosque of Kambos. It has also reminded me what a great mystery our own communities, cultures, and states can be. I hope that the many people whom I met along the way and who so generously shared their lives and advice with me will read the book with a smile. During fieldwork in Athens, people from all walks of life showed me unreserved hospitality and, with incredible patience, thought with me about the place of a central mosque in a contemporary democracy. I am immensely grateful to all of them. At Oxford University, my thesis supervisor Celia Kerslake and also Olga Demetriou, Renée Hirschon, Richard Clogg, Peter Mackridge, Dimitris Papanikolaou, Kostas Skordyles, and Charles Stewart gave me invaluable feedback, taught me to question every single word that I use, and helped me start putting my thoughts in order. İpek Yosmaoğlu and my fellow students at St. Antony's College—Hayden Bellenoit, Reem Abu El Fadl, Nikos Kalogerakos, Katerina Lagos, Gökhan Yücel, and Kerem Öktem—were best friends and informal tutors, always ready to come to my aid.

Early on in my graduate school days I was fortunate to meet Gregory Nagy, who treated me as a son, found my ignorance entertaining, and became a mentor and a constant source of inspiration to think and teach creatively. Along with everything else that he was doing for me at Harvard's Center for Hellenic Studies, he made sure that I had a foundation in semiotics, film, and the diachronic study of Hellenism. At Princeton, where I spent a year as a visiting student through the Oxford-Princeton Research Program on Cultures and Religions of the Eastern Mediterranean World, and another year as a Hannah Seeger Davis Postdoctoral Fellow in Hellenic Studies, I was lucky to think through my project in dialogue with Alex Balistreri, John Borneman, Charis Boutieri, Thalia Dan-Cohen, Carol Greenhouse, Elizabeth Davis, Abdellah Hammoudi, Nikos Michailidis, Leo Coleman, Dimitris Gondicas,

236   Acknowledgments

Sam Williams, Eleonora Vratskidou, Ayşe Ozil, and Amy Moran-Thomas. I reserve a very special place in my memory for my discussions with Norman Itzkowitz, who took an interest in the project and discussed for hours on end psychoanalysis, Greek-Turkish relations, and Islamic architecture. Around that time, when I was uncertain about the project's future, Neni Panourgiá sent me the most heartfelt words of encouragement and shared her very generous reading of my work.

Some years later, at a time when everything seemed to fall apart in Greece, I was offered the National Bank of Greece Postdoctoral Research Fellowship at the Hellenic Observatory at the London School of Economics. Kevin Featherstone and Vassilis Monastiriotis were always ready to discuss Greek politics and point me to political science research on reform failure. Their insights very much shaped my thinking about political cost and what it takes for things to happen in a contemporary democracy.

Karen Van Dyck brought me to Columbia and, with John Ma, gave me a home in the Classics Department, which assisted this publication through the Lodge Fund. Karen, Naor Ben-Yehoyada, and Konstantina Zanou participated in a manuscript workshop organized by the University Seminar in Modern Greek, which allowed me for the first time to see my dissertation as a potential book. At Columbia, Mark Mazower has been a constant source of support and an incredible teacher and mentor. Working with him and Marie d'Origny at Columbia's Institute for Ideas and Imagination in Paris has given me the rare privilege of doing things that one loves in the company of friends.

Michael Herzfeld believed in the project right from the start (and even pushed me to sketch out a book prospectus for Penn Press on a napkin at the Galaxy Bar in Athens). Like so many other anthropologists of Greece, I have immensely benefited from his advice and careful reading for years on end. Peter Agree, first, and then Elisabeth Maselli and Alma Gottlieb at Penn Press have worked tirelessly with me to develop and prepare the manuscript. Their advice, along with the feedback that I received from the three anonymous reviewers, has certainly produced a better book and surely made me a better anthropologist. During manuscript preparation, Nicolas Nicolaides provided much invaluable insight concerning the archival material.

I have been fortunate to have friends and family that have been a steady source of support and guidance. Stavros Davaris, Vicky Katsarou, Andreas Oikonomopoulos, Francesco Pagani, and Elina Stylianidi always grounded me in reality. Their common sense, love for architecture, and, most important, their incredible humor have been pivotal to the project. Anna and Tasos

Antoniou, Mom and Dad, keep on showing me what it means to love unconditionally, have empathy, and care for people. Finally, this book would have never materialized without Soo-Young Kim, who read the manuscript countless times and at critical moments offered encouragement, clear thinking, and much needed advice. She and little Jamie remind me daily of what really matters in life.

www.ingramcontent.com/pod-product-compliance
Lightning Source LLC
LaVergne TN
LVHW041625060925
820435LV00001B/1